My Mother Is a W
I Know to B

Frontispiece. Pendle Hill, Lancashire

My Mother Is a Witch and This I Know to Be True

The Voices of Pendle

CHARLOTTE MEREDITH

MOTTE & BAILEY
PUBLISHING

Motte & Bailey Publishing

A CIP catalogue record of this book is available from the British Library

ISBN
Hardback 978-1-7393736-0-3
Paperback 978-1-7393736-1-0

Published in the United Kingdom by Motte & Bailey Publishing

www.charlottemeredith.co.uk

For the older women who seek justice.
For Alizon, taken at such a young age.
For James, who was misunderstood.
For Jennet, who never stopped suffering.
For all of the others who experienced torment

Acknowledgements

I would like to thank my mother, Pauline Hunt (whose ability to 'chat with dead folk' has always been regarded as totally normal by her children). Her gift never fails to demonstrate and remind me that there is more to this world than physical matter. Without her input, the creation of this book would not have been possible. Likewise, it would not have been possible had it not been for the kind and patient cooperation of those who were accused of being witches at the Lancashire Witch Trials, and I want to thank them for sharing their stories with us. (I only wish it had taken less than 400 years for the truth to be told.)

I would also like to thank author and historian John A. Clayton, whose diligent research into the history of Pendle and the people who lived there during the early modern period has been an invaluable resource for me. My final acknowledgement must go to the spirit guide who has worked patiently alongside us for many years, aiding spirit communication and offering her encouragement and wisdom. Thank you, Mary Webb. I promise to write your story next.

Contents

List of Figures, Family Tree, & Map

FIGURES

FAMILY TREE

MAP

Author's Note

Original spelling has been kept for quotations. The spelling of names tended to be inconsistent during the seventeenth century, even within the same document. Therefore, when referring to the accusers and the accused, names have been standardized for consistency.

THE

WONDERFVLL DISCOVERIE OF WITCHES IN THE COVN-TIE OF LAN-CASTER.

With the Arraignement and Triall of Nineteene notorious WITCHES, at the Assizes and generall Gaole deliuerie, holden at the Castle of LANCASTER, *vpon Munday, the seuenteenth of August last,* 1612.

Before Sir IAMES ALTHAM, and Sir EDWARD BROMLEY, Knights; BARONS of his Maiesties Court of EXCHEQVER: And Iustices *of Assize*, Oyer *and* Terminor, *and generall* Gaole deliuerie in the circuit of the *North Parts.*

Together with the Arraignement and Triall of IENNET PRESTON, *at the Assizes holden at the Castle of Yorke, the seuen and twentieth day of Iulie last past,* with her Execution for the murther of Master LISTER *by Witchcraft.*

Published and set forth by commandement of his Maiesties Iustices of Assize in the North Parts.

By THOMAS POTTS *Esquier.*

LONDON,
Printed by *W. Stansby* for *Iohn Barnes*, dwelling neare Holborne Conduit. 1613.

Fig 0.1. The title page of Thomas Potts' witch trial pamphlet, The Wonderfull Discoverie of Witches in The Countie of Lancaster, printed in London in 1613

The Device Family

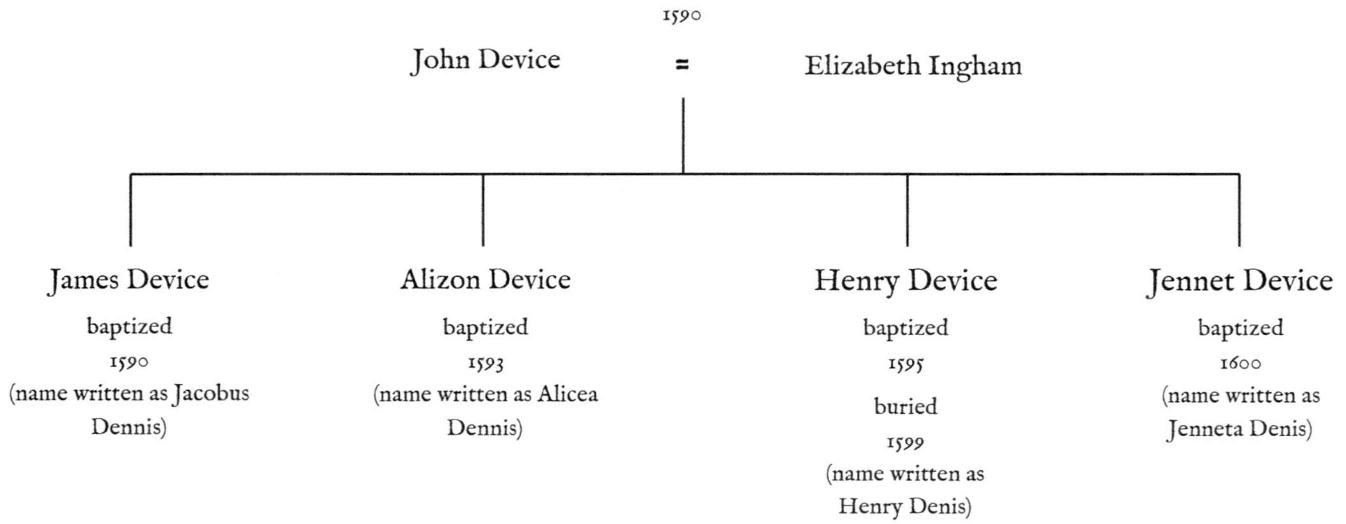

John A. Clayton first proposed this family tree in 2007 after studying the registers of St Mary's at Newchurch in Pendle. The Device family have since confirmed that it is correct. Elizabeth Sowthernes (Demdike) married twice in her lifetime. Her first husband, who bore the surname Ingham, was the father of their daughter, Elizabeth

Introduction

Many people do not believe in an afterlife. But when we are dead, we will all realize we were wrong about many things.

Witch-hunting officially died out in England during the eighteenth century; however, it is having a renaissance. In true twenty-first-century technological style, almost every single day, armed with various ghost-detecting paraphernalia, people from all around the world travel to Pendle, Lancashire, to goad witches – dead witches, that is. Specifically, *the* most famous group of witches in English history, many of whom were hung for their alleged crimes in the north of England more than 400 years ago. Footage of such escapades inevitably surfaces on the internet: 'Demdike, tell us your truth,' these wannabe celebrities whine in uncharismatic nasal tones while trespassing in a cold, wet, windy Lancashire field in the middle of the night. 'Why did you murder people? Were you a witch?' After a while, when they can no longer feel their extremities and have become annoyed because they aren't getting any response from their talky boxes and flashy light devices, these modern-day witch-hunters have a tendency to become confrontational: 'Come on, b***hes, we're not scared of you. Show us what you can do!'

Sadly, such impertinent folk are less motivated by a genuine desire to learn the truth about the Lancashire Witch Trials of 1612 than by a genuine desire to scare themselves senseless and 'go viral'. How many of them have taken the time to read Thomas Potts' contemporary witch trial pamphlet, *The Wonderfull Discoverie of Witches in the Countie of Lancaster*? Do these twenty-first-century people *really* believe in witches? Do they *really* believe the outlandish accusations levied against them? Can they *really* have such little compassion for those executed under the English Witchcraft Acts?

At this point in the introduction, it is necessary to acknowledge that many people today *choose* to identify as witches as part of their religious and spiritual vocations and distinguish those people from the subject matter of this book. Contemporary concepts of witches and witchcraft (such as Neo-Paganism and Wicca, which began in the mid-twentieth century) are not the concern of this work. This book is the truth about the Lancashire Witches: a group of people accused of and prosecuted for practising witchcraft as it was defined and understood in the early modern period. People who, more than 400 years after their executions, are still being persecuted for crimes they could not have possibly committed.

The term witch-craze is often adopted when referring to the witch trials of early modern Europe and the systematic murder of an estimated 40,000 to 60,000 people which occurred as a direct result. The term successfully captures the fact that the widespread enthusiasm for witch-hunting was relatively short-lived (beginning in the mid-fifteenth century and lasting until the middle of the eighteenth century). At the same time, it also gives the impression that the witch-hunters, or perhaps the population more generally, were wildly out of control and suffering from a form of collective insanity. Without a doubt, from our place in time, we cannot help but view this as a period when insanity reigned supreme. It was a time in which someone argued with a neighbour, months or even years later, they died, and the explanation for their death was that they had been cursed by the person they quarrelled with aeons ago. It was a time when if someone attempted to heal a sick animal, but it died, often the explanation for the death was that the very person who had come to help the creature had bewitched it. Although some dared to shout above the madding crowd that witchcraft was not a reality, most people (kings and queens included) held the opinion that there was at least some truth to the claims.

Perhaps it is most troubling that even someone as progressive as Thomas Hobbes, the founder of modern political philosophy, encouraged the prosecution of witches even though he believed they had no supernatural power.[1] His conclusion that witches had to be persecuted even though they were not real is pure madness. And yet, astonishingly, this crazy sentiment has been carried into the twenty-first century by modern-day witch-hunters. Furthermore, although the belief that people can use diabolical magic to harm and kill people was long since written out of criminal law in the UK, shamefully, most of the people executed for such make-believe crimes before the Jacobean Witchcraft Act was repealed have never been exonerated.

The family at the heart of the 1612 Lancashire Witch Trials were the Sowthernes/Device family, who lived in the Pendle Forest. According to Potts, they were a family of highly dangerous witches who met with the Devil at their home, called Malkin Tower. The family matriarch was Elizabeth Sowthernes (alias Old Demdike), an elderly widow, supposedly around eighty years old. She was the mother of Elizabeth Device, a widow who had three surviving children in 1612: James and Alizon, who were young adults, and youngest daughter Jennet, who was around nine years old. In March of that year, Alizon Device was interviewed by a local justice of the peace, Sir Roger Nowell, on suspicion of her having used witchcraft to lame a pedlar. Her brother, mother, and grandmother were subsequently arrested on suspicion of using witchcraft to murder, and some of their neighbours were also rounded up and accused of being witches. They were: Demdike's elderly sparring partner Anne Whittle (alias Old Chattox), her daughter Anne Redferne, mother and son John and Jane Bulcock, the relatively wealthy Alice Nutter, and Katherine Hewit and Alice Gray, who were both from the neighbouring market town of Colne. All were imprisoned in Lancaster Castle to await trial for their offences at the August Assizes. They were soon joined by seven alleged witches from Samlesbury, who were prosecuted by JP Robert Houlden; an alleged witch from Padiham named Margaret Pearson, who was prosecuted by JP Nicholas Bannester; and an alleged witch from Windle named Isabel Robey, who was prosecuted by JP Thomas Gerard.

Following the publication of Potts' *The Wonderfull Discoverie*, these particular witch trials became simultaneously known as the Lancashire Witch Trials and the Pendle Witch Trials (although not all of those on trial resided in the Pendle Forest). We learn from this infamous pamphlet that Demdike died in a cell in Lancaster before she could stand trial. Of the others, we learn that Alice Gray and the seven alleged witches from Samlesbury were acquitted. Margaret Pearson was found guilty of using witchcraft to harm goods and sentenced to one year in prison. John Bulcock, Jane Bulcock, and Isabel Robey were condemned for using witchcraft to cause their neighbours to become ill. Alizon Device was found guilty of using witchcraft to lame and was sentenced to death, as were Alice Nutter and Elizabeth and James Device, who had been found guilty of using witchcraft to murder. The condemned were publicly hanged at Gallows Hill on the outskirts of Lancaster on 20 August 1612.[2]

These men and women have now become part of British folklore to a large extent, but we must remember that they were real people, like you and me: wives, mothers, grandmothers, sons, daughters, sisters, and brothers whose lives were ripped apart in the name of justice. They were wrenched from their humble backwater lives and thrown onto the public stage to be baited and vilified by the whole world forevermore. The question is, why? Curiously, before the middle of the fifteenth century, virtually all trials pertaining to sorcery (generally considered to be the attempt to conjure demons for personal benefit) had been made against relatively high-ranking men. But then there was a significant shift, and European witch trials became largely concerned with lower-class peasant women. What instigated the change? To understand why Europeans made the decision to begin the systematic prosecution and execution of their wives, mothers, sisters, and neighbours, we must understand the pre-Industrial Revolution view of the universe. How did seventeenth-century people make sense of their world? How did the seventeenth-century perception of reality and the nature of existence compare to our own?

After reading *The Wonderfull Discoverie*, many authors have posed theories about the witches of Lancashire. However, we must always remember that witch trial pamphlets were not verbatim records of court proceedings and were always written with an agenda. As a result, separating fact from fiction is not an easy task. Witch trial pamphlets are also written *about* witches, not *by* them. The reality is that the alleged witches left no documentation about their lives, beliefs, and alleged crimes; their voices are missing from history. The most significant aspect of this book is that it rectifies this situation. Perhaps you are now pondering how this has been achieved. After all, they have been dead for more than 400 years, haven't they? Well, the answer to that question is no, not really. When it comes to one of the most important philosophical questions of all time: whether there is life after death, this book has been written with the belief that the answer is yes and that the best way to learn the truth about the Pendle Witches is to ask the alleged witches what happened. Thanks to the kind and patient assistance of an experienced Spiritualist medium (who also happens to be the author's mother), it is time for the Pendle Witches to be heard.

Spiritualist mediums do not 'conjure the dead'. (Despite what you might have heard.) They are simply people who are aware when spirits *choose* to draw close to us and who have developed their ability so that they can convey the messages that the spirits wish to pass on to us. Spiritualists believe that people are not just physical matter: when our physical bodies die, the non-physical part of ourselves, which is often labelled as our spiritual energy, spirit, soul, or consciousness, endures. (In this book, the non-physical part of ourselves will be referred to as spirit.) When our spirits leave our bodies, they inhabit 'the spirit world': a non-physical place which we were part of before we came to experience physical life on Earth and where we can continue to evolve spiritually (if we desire to do so). Those who have passed over to the spirit world can communicate with us here in the physical world, and they often try to. For example, when spirits first pass to the spirit world, they usually like to visit those loved ones they have recently left behind, with the intention of reassuring them that they are OK and that they live on. Sadly, for many reasons, not all of us are aware of their efforts, and often the easiest way for them to make contact is via the assistance of a medium. (Spiritualist mediums do not need technological devices to communicate with spirits.)

The spirits of those executed as witches in 1612 have messages they wish to convey to all of us. Over several years, many of those involved with the trials – made fully aware that the motivation behind this book was to educate people alive today about the reality of the Lancashire Witch Trials and to encourage a campaign for justice for the wrongly condemned – took the opportunity to come forward and share their version of events, along with other relevant details about their lives on Earth during the seventeenth century. Elizabeth Sowthernes was the first to communicate that she would like her story to be told; she wants people to know the truth about how she and the other alleged witches came to lose their lives. She still has anger about the circumstance of her death, the lies that were and are told, and the people today who constantly taunt and try to provoke her and her family. Elizabeth (like many in the spirit world) is frustrated that people alive today have not made enough intellectual and spiritual progress. She emphasizes that she does not want to be forgotten and does not mind when respectful people go to Pendle to learn about her life, for hers is an important story for us all. However, she wants the persecution to stop; the modern-day witch-hunters, who carry out their hurtful antics in and around Pendle, should desist.

During their lifetime, Elizabeth Sowthernes' family were very superstitious people who feared the supernatural. But, by the time of their trials, that fear had gone. Now, they only feared the living. What lies ahead is a true story of how cruel mankind can be.

I

The King, the Witch, & the Bible

What the Hex Is a Witch Anyway?

In the autumn of 1589, a great storm raged in the North Sea, a royal ship was wrecked, and an impatient king was denied the arrival of his new queen from a distant shore. It had been an act of witchcraft. The king, however, would have his revenge.

Although this sounds like the beginning of a fictional tale, King James VI of Scotland really did believe that as many as two hundred witches had summoned malevolent tempests in an attempt to murder him and his Danish bride. Many of the accused endured brutal torture and interrogation before being burnt at the stake in front of a baying crowd.[1] Scotland had not witnessed a witch trial on such a grand scale before. When Queen Anne of Denmark eventually set foot on Scottish soil, she brought the continental concept of witchcraft with her, and paranoid James readily adopted the European stereotype. In Continental Europe, the witch was a heretical figure and recognizably *the* most dangerous member of society. In return for diabolical favours, the witch had made a covenant with the Devil and was part of a female-led, satanic conspiracy to destroy Christendom. Even though belief in witchcraft existed in the British Isles at this time, the idea that witches were part of a secret covenant of devil-worshipers – who flew to sabbaths in the dead of night – had not yet taken hold. Instead, the British witch was primarily an anti-social figure who used demonic magic to heal or harm people and goods, foresee the future, and find lost property and treasure. While the authority figures of the day agreed that the anti-social witch achieved their ends via demonic power, it was not considered to be the case that the witch had to make a pact with the Devil to gain the use of such power.

It seems that the belief in practitioners of magic – people who use the supernatural in an attempt to achieve some particular end – is as old as humankind. As we became more aware of our environment, we had a greater desire to control it in order to stave off various forms of adversity. Our survival instinct played a part in the development of ritualistic behaviour designed to ensure good health and a good harvest, as did our unique level of self-awareness. As we began to ask the big questions such as, why are we here? How was the universe made? We first started to see supernatural explanations, causes and effects. As early human cultures became more sophisticated, such supernatural explanations became part of organized religions which both feared and worshipped supernatural deities.

Today in our 'modern, scientific world', we tend to define the supernatural as an event or force which defies our scientific understanding of the fundamental laws of nature. Arguably, the concept of the Christian miracle, such as Jesus' ability to defy the natural law by walking on water, fits this definition very well. (The science of physics informs us that the relatively weak surface tension of water cannot support the weight of a man. Any curious child at the seaside who attempts the exercise inevitably fails because the force of gravity overcomes the surface tension, and so they sink into the sand.) We will not get into the debate about whether the ability to perform miracles proved that Jesus was the son of God. Instead, taking religion out of the equation, we might simply consider that Jesus sounds a lot like a successful practitioner of magic.

In his book *Religion and the Decline of Magic* historian Keith Thomas argues that those followers of early religions, such as Christianity, usually converted because they believed doing so would give them supernatural power. This meant that the apostles *had* to perform miracles in order to attract new followers.[2] (Even though there were (according to Jewish history and lore) other Jewish men around Galilee who could perform miracles at the time of Jesus, miracles became re-branded as Christian magic.) By the twelfth century, the Roman Catholic Church had a long list of Christian magicians whom they called saints: early Christian men deemed holy for their supernatural abilities to foresee the future, change the weather, cure the sick, and various other miraculous acts.[3] Magic, it turns out, was intrinsically sewn into the fabric of the Christian faith.

By the Middle Ages, the Church faced a problem: theologians largely concluded that the age of miracles and saints was over. This meant that it was now down to the priests and bishops to attract new followers. Their promotion of the idea that the Catholic Church's magical arsenal could control the adversities of the world helped to establish a devoted network of Christian followers in medieval England. Holy relics, holy water, talismans, and Masses were tools often used by Catholic priests and bishops to try and supernaturally affect the physical world in some way. Consequently, superstition became further entwined with Catholicism during this period, for such practices reinforced the idea that particular objects and actions brought about good luck and staved off adversity.[4]

The Protestant Reformers eventually began to object to such superstitious practices because they actually went against the official Christian orthodox principles which had been laid down during the fourth century AD. According to the ancient principles, authorized Christian representatives were only allowed to use prayer, Scripture,

Fig 1.1. The Devil (or a demon) and a male and female witch fly on broomsticks while another female witch beckons them. Woodcut, 1720

or liturgy as instruments to manipulate the supernatural. This rule arose in the early days of the Christian religion as a consequence of the Roman authorities' decision to enact their laws against certain types of magicians. The Romans had begun to persecute Christians because they believed them to be ceremonial magicians: people who carried out magical rituals to bend the will of the gods for their own ends. To defend and save the Christian faith, Origen, the leading Christian theologian of the second century, assured the Roman authorities that Christians did not use the same methodology as ceremonial magicians to effect change. (Namely, rituals and oral charms.) Instead, they only used the name of Jesus and the words of the Bible. And, unlike ceremonial magicians, Christians did not claim to have any power over God; saints were merely vessels for God's will. They could not command Him to do their bidding.

When St Augustine wrote his Christian theology, almost 200 years after Origen, he specifically attributed the magic of magicians to demonic influences and the miracles of the saints to 'the one true God'.[5] Interestingly, in the second century AD, Celsus, the Greek philosopher, pagan, and opponent of early Christianity, argued that Jesus' ability to perform miracles was down to the influence of demons, not God. As Christian doctrine continued to evolve, such defamatory claims were repurposed, and it was the Catholic Church who went on to insist that witches were people who were aided by demons, or the Devil himself, not by God.

Historian Wallace Notestein argues: 'The truth seems to be that the idea of witchcraft was not very clearly defined and differentiated in the minds of ordinary Englishmen until after the beginning of legislation upon the subject.'[6] There is certainly evidence to support this argument, and it looks like the problem of deciding what witches could and could not be held accountable for was not a uniquely English one. For example, in 1080, the King of Denmark blamed witches for storms and epidemics and punished them accordingly (in a brutal manner).

At the same time, Pope Gregory VII believed storms and epidemics were forms of divine punishment, not the Devil's work, and urged him to stop.[7] The idea that the Devil was responsible for much of the adversity people faced in their lives was prevalent in the Catholic faith. But Catholics also deemed God equally capable of inflicting harm upon man. Consequently, they could never be certain which supernatural being was responsible for any form of misfortune.

We do not know why, in 1542, the first Act of Parliament which made witchcraft a statutory offence in England was passed, but perhaps it can be seen as an attempt to establish what could or could not be considered an act of witchcraft, as well as a move to suit King Henry VIII's agenda of pushing the power of justice away from the ecclesiastical courts to the secular court. Under Henry's reign, it now became a capital offence to invoke spirits in order to find lost treasure; use witchcraft (including making effigies) or sorcery to harm your neighbours' bodies or goods; use objects such as swords and rings to declare what had happened to lost or stolen goods; provoke an unlawful love; or for any other unlawful intent or purpose.[8] Henry's Witchcraft Act was repealed five years later by his son, King Edward VI, and amended in 1563 by Edward's half-sister Queen Elizabeth I. The Elizabethan Witchcraft Act was repealed in 1604 and replaced by a Witchcraft Act heavily influenced by the beliefs of King James VI of Scotland and I of England. This new Witchcraft Act was the only one to take on the continental doctrine and introduce the idea of the compact with the Devil into jurisdiction. English witchcraft had now become an act of Christian heresy.

The belief in the satanic conspiracy of witches had begun in Continental Europe at the end of the Middle Ages. The latest evidence suggests that the persecution of satanic-witches began in the Pyrenees and that networks of preaching friars from the Dominican and Franciscan orders were responsible for the propagation of the concept, as witch trials concerning the satanic-witch sprang up in the areas they visited in search of heretics. In the Alps during the 1420s, individuals confessed (under torture) to worshipping the Devil whom they met at secret meetings and conspired with to murder members of their communities. They were transported to these diabolical sabbaths on magical flying chairs in the middle of the night. The Devil appeared in the form of an animal and gave them supernatural abilities: some were turned into wolves, others were made invisible, and the rest took on the appearance of their neighbours. With the aid of Satan, they murdered, lamed and blinded, caused miscarriages and impotence, destroyed crops, stole milk, and ate the bodies of murdered children.[9]

Although there was a real drive by King James to promote the continental image of the witch in England during the seventeenth century, it is clear that many members of the English Parliament were still reluctant to subscribe to the idea, and in addition, there were some educated men who were sceptical about witchcraft altogether. As a result, the new Witchcraft Act still implied that it would be possible for witchcraft to be practised without the witch having made a covenant with the Devil, and English witch trial pamphlets show that, overall, witchcraft continued to be prosecuted as an anti-social crime rather than heresy. English witch trials were typically concerned with damage to goods or harm to people rather than allegations of devil-worship and sabbaths. But that all changed in 1612.

The Wisest Fool in Christendom

Following the death of Queen Elizabeth I in 1603, King James VI of Scotland was named as her successor. The Scottish and English crowns were thereby united under the Stuart monarch, though they remained two sovereign states. James had been born during an era of great religious turmoil. His own mother, Mary Queen of Scots, had proven to be one of the most divisive characters of the age, simultaneously revered and despised for her uncompromising Catholic faith. Baptized a Roman Catholic but brought up as a Protestant, James had thus far managed to run Scotland by steering a middle course between the opposing religions.

On his way south to accept the English throne, James soon realized that his new kingdom would require the same level of careful navigation. En route to London, Calvinists (a branch of the Puritan form of Protestantism) presented James with a petition: a document signed by 1000 Puritan ministers demanding further religious reform – specifically calling for an end to what they saw as popish superstitious practices.[1] James had officially inherited a Protestant England (although many still secretly followed the Catholic faith), but the Protestants were not united under one 'Church of England' as had been Henry VIII's desire in the sixteenth century. Following the demise of the Tudor King, religious factions in the movement moved further apart. At the time of King James's ascension to the English throne, the more radical

Puritanical ministers (driven by a desire to return to the Augustinian foundations) were demanding the dispassionate removal of virtually all ecclesiastical magic from their churches – which they likened to

THE HIGHE AND MIGHTIE PRINCE James THE SIXT BY THE
GRACE OF GOD KINGE OF SCOTLANDE R E fecit

Fig 1.2. King James VI of Scotland and I of England, as King of Scotland. Engraving after R. Elstracke, between 1800 and 1899

witchcraft. In contrast, the more conservative Anglican ministers wanted to continue to practise some superstitious Catholic rituals, such as using holy water to bless crops and cure the sick.

The English Reformation, and the break away from Rome, instigated by King Henry VIII in the 1530s, had been a catalyst for religious tension and unease. (Once opened, it was impossible for any monarch to put the lid back on Pandora's box.) In reality, the Reformation had been triggered by the tyrannical king's desperate desire to divorce and remarry rather than by any spiritual awakening. Religious reform was a tool which allowed Henry to achieve his objective. It also elevated his position of power in the country at the same time, for the Act of Supremacy of 1534 made King Henry VIII the Supreme Head on Earth of the Church of England and answerable to God alone, not the Pope. When James Stuart came to the throne, he naturally concurred with the sentiment of his predecessor. An avid scholar and writer, King James wrote his own philosophy concerning the divine right of kings (the concept of monarchical absolutism) in 1598. In his philosophical discourse, James asserted that kings were only accountable to God, not human law.[2] Like Henry before him, concerning the Act of Supremacy, he grounded his assertion in biblical stories of the Old Testament kings. But the difference between the two rulers was that James strived to be absolute in affairs of the Church *and* State. And so, although Puritans and Anglicans alike were hoping that the new monarch was going to champion their side, this god on Earth, and the new Supreme Head of the Church of England, was not intent on being the puppet of any religious faction.

After his coronation, Puritan and Anglican representatives were invited to a conference at Hampton Court to discuss their demands – chaired by the new king himself. Here a request was put forward for the revision of the English Bible. The justification for doing so was the concern that existing translations (of which there were many) were corrupt and not the true Word of God. (In other words, some versions did not carry favour with the faction who made the request, and the hope was that James would agree to take those problematic translations out of the equation.) Spying an opportunity to gain the upper hand, James agreed that the English translations were not satisfactory and that a revision was therefore necessary. He informed the audience that a universally accepted English translation would soon be created, and this new Bible was to be the only version any faction was allowed to read from in their churches. In this one move, the ministers were being reined in by the monarch. (Or at least that was the intention.) It was announced that around fifty specially selected scholars would embark upon the mighty challenge of translating God's word from the Hebrew and Greek Scripture. Bishops would then be subsequently selected to review the newly translated passages. Ultimately, however, it was King James himself who would ratify the text.[3]

In 1611, the country bore witness to the birth of one of the most important books in English culture: the King James Version of the Bible (KJV). Going on to become one of the most printed books ever, the impact of this English translation of the Holy Bible can still be felt in the way we write and speak today. Following the mass roll-out of the KJV, congregations soon became accustomed to hearing the biblical accounts delivered in the majestic style. Now, more than 400 years later, we still use KJV phrases such as, go the extra mile, the blind leading the blind, the root of the matter, and the salt of the earth.[4]

Although James had verbalized to the audience that the new text was to be formed by consideration of the original tongues, it is clear that the scholars were under orders to copy many passages from the existing English translations. In fact, the translators even state in the KJV's preface that they were instructed to make a good translation better, not to make a new one.[5] For James, the Puritan texts, with their anti-monarchical undertone, did not sit well. The Anglican Bible (Bishops' Bible) was the version he favoured, so this was to be the text which actually received the greatest amount of scholarly attention. (James's vision of the Church of England was definitely based upon Anglican doctrine.) Unfortunately for James, the new Bible did little to unite the religious factions, and over the coming years, the Puritans continued to grow further apart from their Anglican counterparts. The famous voyage of the *Mayflower* occurred in the following decade, and many dissatisfied English Puritans soon followed suit, willing to risk their own lives and travel the arduous journey to the American Colonies in search of religious freedom. (Freedom which happened to involve a fair amount of witch-hanging in a little seaport called Salem.) Little more than thirty years after the publication of the KJV, political and religious unrest built to a crescendo in the country, and the English Civil War began. Parliamentarian Puritans were pitted against the country's shiny new absolute Anglican monarch, James Stuart's son, King Charles I. (And we all know things did not work out well for him.)

The KJV is arguably King James's greatest legacy. But he is also famous for writing another earlier book, around the age of thirty: *Daemonologie.* Published in 1597, James's main aim in creating this book was to convince those who were sceptical about the reality of witchcraft to see the folly of their ways. In the preface to the work, King James begins:

> The fearefull aboundinge at this time in this countrie, of these detestable slaves of the Devill, the Witches or enchanters, hath moved me (beloved reader) to dispatch in post, this following treatise of mine, not in any way (as I protest) to serve for a shew of my learning . . . but onely (moved of conscience) to preasse thereby, so farre as I can, to resolve the doubting harts of many; both that such assaultes of Sathan are most certainly practized, and that the instruments thereof, merits most severely to be punished.[6]

Daemonologie was re-published in 1603 following James's ascension to the English throne. The new absolute English monarch also greatly desired to be regarded as the ultimate authority on witches. This book is his *divine* opinion of what witches are, what they do, how they are to be discovered, and how they ought to be punished. The publication of this text, coupled with the fact that James took an unprecedented role and interrogated many of those accused of witchcraft in Scotland and England, has earned James the reputation of being a king who was hellbent on persecuting witches. Many English magistrates had taken note; witch-hunting seemed like a sure way to impress the new king.

Thou Shalt Not Suffer a Witch to Live

When it came to justifying how and why witches ought to be punished, many early modern demonologists referred to Exodus 22:18: 'Thou shalt not suffer a witch to live.' It is often falsely claimed that this infamous phrase did not exist in the Holy Bible until the KJV was written. But the truth is that the Geneva Bible (the preferred text of the Puritans) preceded the KJV by approximately fifty years and contained the same phrase, as did the Bishops' Bible (favoured by the Anglicans and King James himself). In fact, the phrase can be found in the first authorized English translations: the Matthew Bible and Myles Coverdale's the Great Bible, which was published in 1539 by order of King Henry VIII and Lord Cromwell.

Only a few years prior, reformer William Tyndale had translated the New Testament into English. But rather than being championed for doing so by King Henry, he was instead (under the Tudor monarch's order) burnt at the stake for his heretical beliefs. (Ironically, we know that much of Tyndale's translation went on to be reproduced in Henry's newly authorized English version of the Bible.) Tyndale was a great intellect and fluent in at least seven languages.[1] The popular theory is that he initially began translating the New Testament while in Germany, under the influence of Protestant reformer Martin Luther. Nevertheless, there is no evidence that the two men ever met.[2] Tyndale was not the first man to attempt to translate Scripture into English, though. Complete bibles (in manuscript form) started to emerge in Middle English as early as the 1380s. Until fairly recently, it was widely regarded to be true that reformer John Wycliffe had personally penned this early English translation. It now seems more likely that the task was undertaken by men whom he heavily influenced: those labelled reformist 'Lollards'.[3] It is in the Wycliffe Bible that we see one of the first appearances in English of God's commandment pertaining to witches.

According to author David Daniell, Coverdale, a former Augustinian friar, did not have sufficient knowledge of Greek or Hebrew, and so when composing King Henry's Bible, he consulted secondary German, Latin, and English translations.[4] This obviously raises questions regarding exactly how accurate this Tudor-approved translation of the Word of God really was. And, having already established that the translators who created the KJV had been ordered to copy heavily from secondary translations, we can also ask the same question about this seventeenth-century Bible. But perhaps the crucial point to remember here is that these new bibles were always intended to be the reigning monarch's interpretation of the Word of God.

Those who did not like the choice of words which the King had personally ratified risked being labelled as heretics if they openly expressed their opinions. Famously, witchcraft sceptic Reginald Scot put himself at great risk when he criticized the accuracy of the existing English translations of Exodus 22:18 in 1584. Fortunately, he did not go as far as to deny the existence of witches outright, as this would have been to deny the Bible. Instead, he made the case that, rather than being women who were in league with the Devil, witches were either merely deluded individuals or semi-professional fraudsters. He also argued that the word *witch* in this particular verse was a grave mistranslation and that the word *poisoner* was a more accurate translation.[5] But was there any merit to Scot's argument? Had God commanded death to all witches, or had it all been a terrible misunderstanding?

It is in Exodus that we learn of God's commandment regarding witches. The enslaved people who Moses led out of Egypt were to

Fig 1.3. The Witch of Endor conjures the ghost of Samuel at the request of Saul, who lies petrified on the ground. Engraving by R.I. Martin after B. West, 1811

be the new followers of God. At Mount Sinai, God (via the prophet) issued a long list of commands to His new people. These were the new rules by which they were to govern themselves. Every man and woman was warned that to break a commandment was to sin against God and that sinners would receive a terrible dose of God's wrath.

(Thunder, lightning, and a smoke-filled mountain set the scene to drive His ominous point home.)

It is believed that Greek-speaking Jewish scholars first conceived the idea of putting Exodus along with various other (though not all) Hebrew and Greek scriptural passages into one scriptural book or Bible. The Septuagint Bible was probably made in Alexandria, Egypt, for the use of the Greek-speaking Jewish community there. It is believed to date back to the third century BC (although this date is approximate). The original text, written in Koine Greek, shows the word φαρμακούς in place of the English *witch*. It is usually translated today as *pharmakeia*. The beginning of the word would seem to suggest that it had something to do with people who made or sold drugs or medicine, like in the familiar word pharmacist, which we use in Britain today. However, we now know that there were categories of both magic and magician in Ancient Greece, and even though it must be stressed that there are inconsistencies within Greek texts regarding those categories, it transpires that *pharmakeia* were practitioners of magic.

There is evidence that *pharmakeis* (masculine), and *pharmakides* (feminine), were classified as a lesser form of magician who specialized in potions.[6] The exact nature of these potions is unknown, but it does not take a huge stretch of the imagination to see how a potion maker and poison maker could be viewed as one and the same, for essentially, poison is just a harmful potion (whether administered deliberately or accidentally). What we appear to have in the Septuagint, therefore, is the idea of a commandment demanding death to some sort of potion-making magicians. And yet, it is important to note that the term *pharmakeia* possibly evolved over time to encompass other types of magic and/or was considered to be a different form of magic in different areas of

Greece. In Thessaly, for example, in the north-eastern part of Greece, it was reported that there were '*pharmakides* powerful enough to drag the moon down from the sky at their command'.[7] Consequently, the precise target of the Greek interpretation of Exodus 22:18 is unclear.

The Latin Vulgate Bible was created around the fourth century AD. In this Latin translation, the term *maleficos* is used in place of *witch* in Exodus 22:18. It is composed of the Latin word *male*, which means badly or wrongly, and *ficus*, which denotes making or doing. In witch trials concerning both the anti-social and satanic-witch, we often see that the alleged witch was accused of practising *maleficium*: magic performed with the intention of causing harm. The term was originally used in the Roman Empire to describe 'deeds which caused actual harm'.[8] Although such a definition reads as though it could have been applied to many classes of wrongdoer, criminal, or sinner, not exclusively to magicians, sorcerers, or witches, historian Ronald Hutton highlights in his book *The Witch* that as far back as the second century AD, in Roman culture, magicians became equated with deeds which caused harm and *veneficium*. This imprecise word could mean both magic and poison.[9] Taking Hutton's findings into account, it seems likely that a type of amalgamation occurred over time, and by the fourth century, *maleficium* had taken on the meaning of *veneficium* as well, becoming newly defined as someone who uses magic to do harm to others. From this point on, the *maleficos* were people who practised harmful magic. (But it should be noted that *maleficos* is the masculine plural of *maleficus* which goes against the more modern satanic-witch stereotype in which witches are predominantly female.)

If we go back to our original question of whether Exodus 22:18 was truly concerned with the condemnation of witches, we must consider what was written in the original or earliest known source: Hebrew Scripture. In the Torah, we see the term *m'khashephah* in place of *witch*. Scot translated the Hebrew *chasaph* into the Latin word *veneficium* which he took to mean poisoning.[10] But because we now know that *veneficium* could also be used to describe harmful magic, we must conclude that Scot's translation was somewhat lacking. According to many Hebrew scholars, the term *m'khashephah* is a general Semitic shoresh (or root) shared between several languages such as Akkadian and Hebrew, meaning something like malevolent-magic-doer. (The specific form in the Hebrew Exodus verse is in the feminine gender, whereas in Deuteronomy, the masculine form of the word is also used.) Consequently, for argument's sake, we might conclude that the God of the Old Testament *had* condemned witches – in the broadest sense of the concept. (At least according to some of the earliest known Scripture.) But before doing so, we should also consider one final and important point: scriptural scholars have argued just as much about the Hebrew, Greek, Latin, and English translations and interpretations of the word *witch*, as they have about the whole not suffering to live part of Exodus 22:18.

In the opinion of some experts, God had not commanded that all malevolent-magic-doers be executed. Instead, He had commanded that they were not allowed to live amongst His followers. (We cannot deny that there is a great deal of difference between a Mosaic Law which demands that the righteous kill all witches, as opposed to a Mosaic Law which demands that witches be ostracized.) Therefore, as to whether God had actually commanded death to all witches, the jury is still out. All we know for certain is that the concept of the malevolent-magic-doer stretches far back into human history. In fact, the truth is that the witch is perhaps one of *the* most enduring ideas in civilization, for ideas about witches were even present in Ancient Sumer (modern-day Iran), one of the earliest known civilizations on record.

The Witch-Hunters' Bible

> There are wicked women who, turning back to Satan and seduced by the illusions and phantoms of the demons, believe and openly avow that in the hours of the night they ride on certain animals, together with Diana, the goddess of the pagans, with a numberless multitude of other women; and in the silence of the dead of night cross many great lands; and obey (Diana's) orders as though she were their mistress, and on particular nights are summoned to her service. Would that they alone perished in their perfidy, without dragging so many others with them into the ruin of infidelity! For a numberless multitude of people, deceived by this false view, believe these things to be true and, turning away from the true faith and returning to the errors of the pagans, think that there exists some divine power other than the one God.[1]
>
> *canon Episcopi*

The *canon Episcopi* is a small part of the monumental and ever-evolving body of Catholic ordinances and regulations known as canon law. It is estimated to have been written around the ninth or tenth century AD, originating in the Franco-German region. (It was possibly composed soon after the conversion of the Franks from paganism to Catholicism.) Most importantly, it is a record of the Catholic Church's early stance on magic (or at least on 'pagan' or non-Christian magic). The bishops were being urged to eradicate pagan magic from their congregations. It was made clear, however, that they could only expel Christians who continued to practise magic after being repeatedly admonished for doing so. Only at this stage could they be regarded as heretics, and it must be emphasized that they were to be punished by being removed from their parishes, not by being tortured, imprisoned, or executed. (Could it be that the authors of the *canon Episcopi* had interpreted Exodus 22:18 to mean thou shalt not suffer a witch to live amongst our community? Or maybe they simply did not heed this command at the time.)

The quote about women riding out on animals with the goddess Diana during the middle of the night is one of the earliest mentions of something like the witches' sabbath, and in that respect, it is a significant early document in the history of witchcraft. That being said, notice that there is no mention of them flying or going to meet with the Devil. Canon law was also clear that this claim of journeying to worship the pagan goddess was a delusion imposed upon the mind by Satan and that the women did not physically travel anywhere. Furthermore, Hutton points out that the women involved reportedly carried out the night journeys to 'complement rather than oppose Christianity and so [were] to be punished with relatively mild penances'.[2] This means that the Church did not consider 'delusional night flying' to be heretical. But during the late medieval and early modern period, despite what would have been regarded as settled law at the time, inquisitors insisted that heretical witches really did fly to secretive nocturnal meetings to worship the Devil.

Ironically, the idea of witches meeting at secret sabbaths likely evolved out of Roman anti-Christian sentiment. In the early days of

Christianity, the Romans accused Christians of meeting in secret places at night to consume the blood of dead children. The reality is, to avoid the attention of the authorities, Christians *were* secretly meeting in caves to practise their religion. And furthermore, when they ate bread and drank wine as part of the Eucharist, they believed they were consuming the blood and flesh of Christ. So perhaps we can see how such rumours might have started because the idea of eating the son of a god does seem somewhat cannibalistic! Christians later chose to repurpose Roman anti-Christian sentiment against pagans and Jews.[3] (The term sabbath is even part of an antisemitic conspiracy theory.) During the medieval era, Christian demonologists (most notably Heinrich Kramer) then repurposed those antisemitic slurs against witches. So now it was witches who got up to unsavoury activities at secret meetings in the dead of night.

Arguably, it was not the Bible which held the greatest influence over the idea of what witches were and what they got up to. For when it came to the development of the satanic-witch stereotype, there is a good deal of evidence to suggest that this figure was born out of the imaginations of the Catholic and Protestant demonologists and the development of subsequent demonological literature. It transpires that many of the early demonologists were Dominican Inquisitors. The Holy Inquisition started in France during the twelfth century to combat religious dissent, and the inquisitors were initially busy hunting heretics, not witches. At this point in time, magic did not really register on the inquisitors' radar. This was because, generally speaking, the practitioner of magic was regarded as a sinner, not a heretic; practising magic was merely a sin amongst many other sins, and so accusations of *maleficium* were usually the concern of the ecclesiastical courts, not the Inquisition. The relationship between magic and heresy was not officially established and defined until as late as the early fourteenth century, and this was in reaction to the widespread practise of magic at the papal court in Avignon in 1320. To combat the problem, Pope John XXII issued a new papal bull, *Super illius specula*, which made ceremonial magic officially heretical.[4] First defined by the Romans as the attempt to bend the will of the gods, ceremonial magic was now redefined as the worship of demons and/or an attempt to conjure and bind demons to the service of the magician. From this point, inquisitors were instructed to act against ceremonial magicians who refused to abandon such practices. They were to suffer the penalties of heresy.

This shift in thinking, where the sin of magic could be turned into the crime of heresy, was crucial for the development of the satanic-witch conspiracy theory. Approximately one hundred years after the link between heresy and magic was established, we see the first major written evidence that the female-led, Christendom-destroying satanic-witch stereotype was taking shape. Between 1408 and 1422, Dominican friars preaching between France and north-eastern Spain pushed the message that magicians needed to be punished as heretics. Henceforth, 'secular courts in the Languedoc area of France . . . began to prosecute individual women for doing homage to the Devil and thus acquiring the power to enter houses through closed doors and poison the inhabitants'.[5] In 1428, in the Italian city of Todi, a woman who allegedly offered forms of love magic and counter-magic was accused of 'riding a demon in the form of a goat . . . to join other people of her kind in revelling and worshipping Lucifer, who ordered her to destroy the children [and suck their blood]'.[6] (This story sounds a lot like the one in the *canon Episcopi*, only the pagan goddess Diana has been replaced with the Devil.) Even though canon law clearly stated that such alleged travel was not a physical reality, this woman apparently flew to a sabbath on the back of a demon. Hutton emphasizes that the one single factor which linked the appearance of all the devil-worship witch trials occurring at the beginning of the fifteenth century 'stretching in an arc from north-eastern Spain to central Italy' was the preaching of friars of the Dominican and Franciscan order.[7] These men had repurposed ancient Roman anti-Christian slurs, mixed them with pagan folklore, added a pinch of misogyny and created a new make-believe enemy of Christendom – the satanic-witch. (Perhaps the concept of the satanic-witch was late to land in the British Isles because the Inquisition never made it that far.)

The most notorious of all the Dominican demonological texts is the *Malleus Maleficarum*. Known in English as the Hammer of Witches, this witch-hunters' manual is often directly linked to the rise of the witch purges in Continental Europe. First published in 1486, it was issued sixteen times in Germany and eleven times in France before 1700, making it almost as popular as the KJV at the time. It was written by German inquisitor Heinrich Kramer (also known as Henry Institoris). The beginning of Kramer's witch trial campaign is said to have started in the small German town of Innsbruck when a wealthy woman named Helena Scheuberin spat at Kramer in the street and cursed him. She had also stood up during one of his sermons to protest that she believed him to be aligned with the Devil. Kramer preached against witchcraft, and the congregation protested that his somewhat unorthodox opinions about witches were a demonstration that he himself was a heretic! The result was that Kramer arrested Scheuberin as a suspected witch, along with thirteen other people who refused to listen to his sermons.

Fortunately for Scheuberin, the Bishop of Brixon, Geog Golser, called off the ensuing witch trials midway through. It is said that his representative at the trial had been unhappy with Kramer's use of leading questions. They also reported that the inquisitor had irrationally focused on Helena's sexuality, constantly asking her about her sexual history, which had nothing to do with the case. Taking Kramer for a madman, Golser ordered the inquisitor to leave the city.[8]

It is often said that Kramer then approached Pope Innocent VIII to complain about the expulsion and the local dioceses' refusal to honour his jurisdiction and that the Pope sided with Kramer. All we know for sure is that a new papal bull, *Summis desiderantes affectibus*, was issued in December 1484. This new bull recognized the existence of witches, declared that they were heretics and explicitly granted Kramer authority to hunt and prosecute them in whatever manner he saw fit. (Which included extracting confessions under torture.) The papal bull declared:

> Many persons of both sexes, unmindful of their own salvation and straying from the Catholic Faith, have abandoned themselves to devils, incubi and succubi, and by their incantations, spells, conjurations, and other accursed charms and crafts, enormities and horrid offences, have slain infants yet in the mother's womb, as also the offspring of cattle, have blasted the produce of the earth, the grapes of the vine, the fruits of the trees, nay, men and women, beasts of burden, herd beasts, as well as animals of other kinds, vineyards, orchards, meadows, pasture land, corn, wheat, and all other cereals; these wretches furthermore afflict and torment men and women, beasts of burden, herd beasts, as well as animals of other kinds, with terrible piteous pains and sore diseases, both internal and external; they hinder men from performing

> the sexual act and women from conceiving . . . they blasphemously renounce that Faith which is theirs by the Sacrament of Baptism, and at the instigation of the Enemy of Mankind they do not shrink from committing and perpetrating the foulest abominations and filthiest excesses to the deadly peril of their own souls.[9]

Armed with and inspired by the new papal bull, Kramer commenced writing. He began his work with a demonstration of why 'the Belief that there are such Beings as Witches is so Essential a part of the Catholic Faith that Obstinately to maintain the Opposite opinion manifestly savours of Heresy'.[10] Here was a terrifying warning to those who would get in the way of his witch purge campaign. Even interfering bishops were now deemed equal to witches and risked being accused of heresy.

The inclusion of the papal bull in the beginning of his book, along with his reliance on antiquated legal ideas, the incorporation of the wisdom of Aristotle, St Augustine, and St Thomas Aquinas, as well as the 'voluntary confessions' of women who had been asked leading questions while being subjected to brutal torture by inquisitors – and had therefore admitted to doing the things they imagined them doing in their misogynistic, somewhat perverted minds – all gave the impression that Kramer was the leading authority on what witches were, what they were capable of, and of how they should be punished. And upon the question of appropriate punishment, he used Exodus 22:18 to defend his position. The *Malleus Maleficarum* called for the total extermination of witches, for the death penalty was deemed to be the only certain remedy against the evils of witchcraft. Kramer whipped up witch hysteria by emphasizing that witches were growing in power, number, and wicked intent. He put flesh on the bones of the satanic-witch by confirming the witches' explicit pacts and nocturnal meetings with the Devil and listing the powers they gained by worshipping him. These powers were: transvection (night riding), birthing the spawn of demons with the help of incubi, preventing men from getting erections, causing sterility and infertility, causing the penis to fall off, shortening the penis to spite a man, changing men into the shape of beasts, assisting with demonic possessions, causing sickness and infestations, posing as midwives to kill children and using their body parts in potions and ointments, injuring cattle from great distances, raising hailstorms and tempests to damage property, and striking men and animals with lightning.[11]

It seems probable that Pope Innocent VIII had been convinced by some of Kramer's outlandish 'evidence' of witchcraft and, fearing that the Devil was getting too powerful in Germany, had issued the bull. However, the bull informs us that, unlike Kramer, the Pope still considered witchcraft to be *maleficium* carried out by men and women, not female-led devil-worship. In Kramer's mind, *maleficium* was an indication that the witch had made a pact with the Devil. He was instrumental in the proliferation of the continental belief that witches were a predominantly female heretical sect who were intent on destroying Christendom. His book would even go on to influence King James VI.

2

This Thou Knowest to Be True

The Witch & the Pedlar

On 18 March 1612, while walking near Colne, Lancashire, a young beggar named Alizon Device cursed a pedlar for refusing to give her pins. The beginning of the Pendle Witch story – the singular event which was the catalyst for the Lancashire Witch Trials – has been retold and reinforced for centuries. (Even those who care little about the Lancashire Witch Trials have probably heard something along these lines before.) Those who have not read Thomas Potts' witch trial pamphlet, *The Wonderfull Discoverie of Witches in the Countie of Lancaster*, might be surprised to learn that there are three accounts of this infamous event. They form the testimony of Alizon Device, the alleged witch; John Law, the alleged victim; and his son Abraham Law, whom we learn was a cloth dyer from Halifax and was not present at the time of the incident.[1] Testimony (referred to in the text as a voluntary confession) was recorded by local magistrate Sir Roger Nowell of Read, Lancashire, during his examinations of the accusers and accused.

We get the precise date of the incident from Alizon's testimony: 'the eighteenth day of March last'.[2] (The Julian calendar was used in England at this time, meaning that 18 March fell on a Wednesday –

the current day of the weekly market in Colne.) The first question we need to ask ourselves is whether Alizon had been able to recall the date of the alleged incident with such precision. This is because, while we are used to using the date/month/year method to account for the occurrence of events, the impression gleaned from reading Potts' pamphlet is that seventeenth-century poor folk conceptualized time differently. When asked when other diabolical events occurred, Alizon and the other alleged witches and witnesses are vaguer with their answers: things happened 'about two yeares agone',[3] 'before Candlemas',[4] 'about Maudlintide next after'.[5] The explanation for this could simply be that they did not remember the exact dates of events which happened further back in the past, only what was happening in their communities at the time. But there is also the possibility that the poorer sort marked their calendar by important festivals and holy days rather than specific days of the month. If this is the case, then this immediately demonstrates that the testimony which was read aloud in court was not a verbatim account of what Alizon had said.

When comparing the three accounts of *what* actually happened, we see some similarities and differences in the following excerpts.

The testimony of John Law:

> Unluckily he met with Alizon Device . . . who was very earnest with him for pinnes, but he would give her none: whereupon she seemed to be very angry; and when hee was past her, hee fell down lame in great extremity.[6]

The testimony of Alizon Device:

> And this Examinate demanded of the said Pedler to buy some pinnes of him; but the pedler sturdily answered this Examinate that he would not loose his Packe; and so this Examinate parting with him: presently there appeared to this Examinate the Blacke Dogge . . . which Black Dogge spake unto this Examinate in English, saying; What wouldst thou have me do to yonder man? . . . [She asked] What canst thou do at him? . . . [He answered] I can lame him . . . [and she said] Lame him: and before the Pedler was gone 40 Roddes further, he fell downe Lame.[7]

The testimony of Abraham Law:

> This Examinate was sent for, by a letter that came from his father, that he should come to his father, John Law, who then lay in Colne speechlesse, and had the left-side lamed all save his eye: and when this Examinate came to his father, his said father had something recovered his speech, and did complaine that hee was pricked with Knives, Elsons and Sickles, and that the same hurt was done unto him at Colne-field, presently after that Alizon Device had offered to buy some pinnes of him, and she had no money to pay for them withall; but as this Examinates father told this Examinate, he gave her some pinnes.[8]

All three accounts agree that the encounter occurred because Alizon wanted pins from John. However, Abraham states that his father gave her pins, John states that he would not give her any (implying that she was begging), and Alizon states that she wanted to buy pins, but John would not sell them to her. There is also some discrepancy regarding who was angrier with whom. And while John and Alizon do both agree that the pedlar fell down, only Alizon's testimony informs us that this happened shortly after they parted. John only says that he fell down after their encounter and does not specify whether this was immediately after. Detail about the fall is absent from Abraham's testimony, as is any reference to a demonic dog.

It is Alizon's revelation about having interacted with a supernatural being in order to cause John harm which turns his fall into an act of witchcraft. When John gets round to mentioning that he had seen a malevolent dog, his testimony is somewhat different from hers: he 'saw a great Black-Dogge stand by him, with very fearefull firie eyes, great teeth and a terrible countenance, looking him in the face; whereat he was very sore afraid: and immediately after came in the said Alizon Device, who staid not long there, but looked on him, and went away'.[9] John's encounter with the creature took place after his fall when he had 'by meanes got into an Ale-house in Colne, neere unto the place where hee was first bewitched'.[10] Alizon's testimony states: 'and this Examinate then went after the said Pedler; and in a house . . . he was lying Lame: and so this Examinate went begging in Trawden Forest'.[11] She does not mention the demonic dog being present at the time of her visit (or why she decided to follow the man she had just cursed). And, although the implication is that the scary dog John saw was the same demonic creature which Alizon had used to lame him, this is not actually stated.

Alizon confessed that she had told the English-speaking dog to lame the pedlar. The word *lame* was commonly used in the 1600s to describe a physical disability, especially in the foot or leg, which affected walking and impaired freedom of movement. It could also be used when referring to an impairment caused by an injury, such as a weak arm after a fall. John says that when in the alehouse, he 'lay there in great paine, not able to stirre either hand or foote'.[12] Alizon's testimony does not go into great detail about John's condition. She only says that when she visited him, he was 'lying Lame'.[13] Abraham received a letter a few days after the incident explaining that his father was 'speechlesse, and had the left-side lamed all save his eye'.[14] But by the time Abraham visited his father, John's speech had somewhat recovered.[15] Potts wrote his own account of John Law's condition when John appeared as a star witness at the trials in August, and it is this account which paints the most vivid image:

> Whereupon it was there affirmed to the Court that this John Law the Pedler, before his unfortunate meeting with this Witch, was a verie able sufficient stout man of Bodie, and a goodly man of Stature. But by the Devilish art of Witch-craft his head is drawne awrie, his Eyes and face deformed, His speech not well to bee understood; his Thighes and Legges starcke lame: his Armes lame especially the left side, his handes lame and turned out of their course, his Bodie able to indure no travell.[16]

Seeking medical rather than superstitious explanations for John's condition, many authors have concluded that the pedlar most likely had a stroke on 18 March. Admittedly, there are similarities with the common symptoms of a stroke, such as facial deformity, weakness and numbness in the arms, loss of speech, confusion, and difficulty understanding. In addition, it is estimated that as many as one in twenty people experience hallucinations and delusions after a stroke, and strokes which cause damage to the midbrain can cause hallucinations which often involve vivid scenes with animals and people.[17] Could this be the explanation for John's claim of having seen a demonic dog standing before him? If

Fig 2.1. A white-faced witch meets a black-faced witch with a demonic creature on a leash. Woodcut, 1720

we suppose that John really had been able to describe the creature in such detail to Roger Nowell less than two weeks after he fell, this would suggest that his health was improving. And yet, when in court some months later, according to Potts, John was worse than ever. So if we take the view that Potts was not exaggerating, perhaps we might be able to explain John's deteriorating condition as the result of him suffering more than one stroke between March and August 1612. Although, the fact that Potts falsely declared that John's condition prevented him from being able to travel, even though he clearly had travelled from Colne to Lancaster, suggests there was a little bit of exaggeration going on.

Knowing little about the real causes of ill health, Abraham Law was adamant that witchcraft was the cause of his father's condition. He heard his father say that 'the hurt he had in his lamenesse was done unto him by the said Alizon Device, by Witchcraft'[18] and that she 'did lie upon him and trouble him'.[19] John's testimony states: 'hee was tormented both day and night with the said Alizon Device; and so continued lame, not able to travell or take paines ever since that time'.[20] The phrase 'lie upon him' is very similar to a phrase used in testimony against Jennet Preston at her witch trial in York. On 27 July 1612, Jennet was accused of using witchcraft to make her victim languish. As he lay dying, 'hee cryed out in great extremitie; Jennet Preston lyes heavie upon me'.[21] While we tend to associate the phrase with feelings of guilt or remorse, at Jennet's and Alizon's trials, the phrase was interpreted to have a magical undertone: the alleged witches somehow affected their victims' physical health without being physically present.

Suppose we were to remove the supernatural elements from the tale of the laming of the pedlar and focus on the parts of the testimony which are concordant. In that case, we could conclude that the following elements of the story are most likely to have some truth to them: John Law and Alizon Device quarrelled about pins, at some point after, John Law fell over, and at some point after that, Alizon visited John while he was feeling unwell in a nearby property. Later in this book, John Law and Alizon Device provide further insight into what really happened on that fateful day.

Hawkers, Pedlars, & Petty Chapmen

As previously stated, the alleged bewitchment of John Law was the catalyst for the Lancashire Witch Trials. For this reason, and because he was a star witness at the trials, the pedlar is one of the pivotal characters in the Pendle Witch story. And yet, despite his significant role, he is often little more than a footnote in texts on the subject. It is the case that hawkers, pedlars, and chapmen have often been overlooked by historians, and it is primarily thanks to the research of historian Margaret Spufford that we can gain better insight into the life and motivations of someone like the elusive John Law. Spufford defined pedlars as 'the chain of distributors who were responsible for much of the supply of cheap goods to rural areas ... mainly the materials for sheets, curtains, shirts, shifts and underclothing'.[1*] Those individuals who sold other types of commodities, such as iron goods or books, were not called chapmen, pedlars, or hawkers, as they were considered to be specialists.[2] In fact, the reality was that throughout the country in the seventeenth century, pedlars 'turned out to carry a remarkably similar mixture of textiles, haberdashery, and ready-made clothing accessories'.[3] While some were wealthy enough to afford a pack horse,

---

* © Margaret Spufford, 1984, *The Great Reclothing of Rural England: Petty Chapmen and their Wares in the Seventeenth Century,* Hambledon Continuum, an imprint of Bloomsbury Publishing Plc. Extracts reproduced by permission of Bloomsbury Publishing Plc.

the majority of small-scale or 'petty' chapmen and women would carry their wares in a wooden trunk, which could be opened up in front of their customers like a mini market stall, or in a pack on their back like John Law.

Fig 2.2. A spectacles seller shows his wares to an old woman on her doorstep. Etching by D Deucher, 1784

For the most part, during the sixteenth and seventeenth centuries, pedlars did not have the best reputations. Unsurprisingly, shopkeepers did not like pedlars; it was suggested that travelling salespeople were one of the leading causes of the decline in trade during the latter half of the seventeenth century.[4] There was possibly some support for this point of view, as the number of travelling pedlars increased sharply during this period.[5] But there is also the argument that the pedlars provided a necessary service to those who did not live near towns and cities and who could not afford shop prices.[6]

Under an English law created in 1597, pedlars were classed as a type of vagrant beggar and could be punished by being whipped 'untill his or her body be bloudye'.[7] In 1618, during King James's reign, a royal proclamation which declared a new licensing procedure for pedlars and petty chapmen was issued. This new proclamation strived to offer some protection to genuine pedlars – those who were earning a living from peddling goods and benefitting the rural communities by selling their wares – and to differentiate them from the thieves and vagrants who often masqueraded as pedlars. Unfortunately for the genuine travelling salespeople, this licensing procedure was quickly condemned and cancelled by the Commons, and instead of protecting pedlars, Parliament put them at greater risk by affirming that *all* pedlars and their like were 'indeed no other but Sturdy Beggars, theeves and absolute dissolutes'.[8]

The U-turn in Parliament can perhaps be explained by consideration of the biggest parliamentary concern of that time: the perpetual fear of the Catholic plot. After the Gunpowder Plot was foiled in 1605, Parliament feared there would be further attempts to overthrow Protestant rule. It had been revealed that there was an underground network of Catholic priests operating in England, often hidden in the homes of their supporters. And it appears there was enough concern in Parliament that pedlars might be part of this papist network, secretly promoting the Catholic faith and the Catholic cause: 'many of them being of no Religion, or infected with Poperie, carry abroad and disperse superstitious Trumperies'.[9] The implication was that the vagrant pedlar, who was often seen travelling door-to-door, might be a Catholic priest in disguise.

It would be easy to assume that Parliament was being excessively paranoid about the idea of 'God's secret agents' roaming the countryside disguised as pedlars. However, the discovery of an intriguing object has demonstrated that this really *was* happening in Lancashire. In the 1800s, a pedlar's trunk was discovered behind a wall in Samlesbury Hall, where it had lain hidden for 200 years. (Samlesbury Hall is reported to have at least three priest holes.) The trunk contained many items that might appeal to a Jacobean woman, such as beads, coloured silks, and linen fabric. But these items were never intended to be sold, for they are now understood to have been the illegal vestments and rosary beads of a Roman Catholic priest, cunningly disguised as women's clothes! In fact, the trunk contains everything a priest would need to be able to say Mass door-to-door, including a pewter cup for holy communion and an altar stone, and it is intriguing to discover that this illegal activity was happening close to the Pendle Forest. (Saint Edmund Arrowsmith is one of the Catholic priests who has been linked to the trunk. He was eventually betrayed to the authorities and hanged, drawn, and quartered in Lancaster on 28 August 1628.)[10]

The Wonderfull Discoverie tells us nothing about John Law's religious beliefs; it tells us very little about him, full stop. However, the way in which John chose to describe his symptoms can perhaps tell us something about his background. Some days following the incident, when talking to his son, Abraham, John described the pain he was feeling by likening it to being 'pricked' by various tools: 'Knives, Elsons and Sickles'.[11] This interesting choice of simile demonstrates some knowledge of tools which are particular to certain trades. Obviously, a knife had a place both domestically and in many types of work, but the sickle was particular to agriculture, where the small curved blade was ideal for harvesting grain. Is it possible that John had once been a farm labourer or perhaps grew up on a farm? An elson (or elshin) was a name for a shoemaker's awl. Little changed in the way of shoemaking tool design until mechanization in the nineteenth century. Two types of awls were used by the shoemaker: a straight-bladed stitching awl, used for making holes through leather, and a curved blade closing awl, used for joining the sole to the upper.[12] The elson is mentioned in a Scottish verse called *An Ode to Mr Forbes*, written before 1759 by Allan Ramsay: 'Nor Hynds [farm-servants] wi' elson and hemp Lingle [shoemaker's thread], / Sit solling Shoon [shoes] out o'er the Ingle'.[13] Having already established that a petty chapman would not sell these types of wares, we cannot use his occupation as a pedlar to explain his knowledge of elsons. Had John perhaps found employment as a shoemaker in the past, therefore?

Joseph Wright's nineteenth-century dialect dictionary, *The English Dialect Dictionary*, shows that the word elson was used predominantly in Scotland and the Northern Counties of England, including Yorkshire and Lancashire. It does not show evidence of the word being used in the south or the west, and it seems that shoemaking awls were known by a different name below the East Midlands.[14] Consequently, John's use of northern dialect helps to give us a broad sense of where he came from. Spufford emphasizes that the abodes of the chapmen are notoriously difficult to trace, and it was common for pedlars to die miles away from their homes. One record of a pedlar of whom she could find adequate information showed that 'In 1677 James Hutcheson of Annandale in Scotland died at Marnock in Somerset.'[15] Similarly, another Scottish pedlar, John Carde of Galloway, died a long way from home at Portsmouth in 1681.[16] Intriguingly, through her research Spufford came to realize that many pedlars hailed from Scotland. And evidently, some pedlars were prepared to travel extensively for work. She notes that as early as 1537, the King of Poland legislated against Scottish pedlars; by 1621, around 30,000 Scots were living in Poland.[17] As for the abodes of pedlars, these varied considerably. While some might own or rent a home, many others rented a room in a property or were of no fixed abode.[18]

There was a hierarchical structure of pedlars, beginning with the very poor with his or her pack, a man or woman with a beast of burden, a man or woman with a market stall, and the shopkeeper who might also sell wares door-to-door locally or in other areas.[19] Many young people started out with packs on their backs, hoping to have a stall or shop in the future. John Law, the 'Pettie Chapman',[20] appears to have been on the lowest rung of the ladder, and yet he was not particularly young himself for the period; we know he had a son of working age.[21]

Irrespective of their social positions, their business methods remained similar: 'The chapmen bought on credit, and they also sold on credit.'[22] (Pedlars typically died owing and being owed various degrees of debt.) This business knowledge possibly helps to support Alizon's claim that she was not begging for pins when she met with John Law, as she would have understood that pedlars offered credit. Maybe her family were used to buying from them in this way. (There is a record of a shop in St Albans selling pins priced at 6d a thousand in 1607.[23]) This method of business was, of course, high risk for the seller as they could incur bad debt expense if the buyer did not eventually pay the full amount owed. Maybe this was part of John's reason for refusing to sell his wares to Alizon: perhaps the Devices were bad customers.

Surviving inventory records show that debts owing to deceased pedlars typically belonged to people who lived within a twelve-mile radius.[24] This suggests that although prepared to travel long distances for business, pedlars also relied on repeat business near their homes, in the nearest market towns, and the surrounding hamlets. It becomes clear that pedlars must have visited the same areas frequently in order to collect debts owed, as much as to sell goods, and this helps us narrow the search for John Law's home. Because John Law was getting on in years by seventeenth-century standards and did not have a pack horse (as far as we are aware), it seems highly likely that he lived within a twelve-mile radius of Colne. Evidence which can offer further support to this theory is that pedlars tended to travel for work between April and October, coinciding with the dates of the fairs around the country.[25] (A lot of this data has been obtained by examining the birth dates of their children!) So, the fact that John was selling his wares near Colne on a Wednesday in March indicates that he was probably working on his home turf at the time.

On the Highway Called Colne Field

Fig 2.3. A narrow track near Trawden

There has always been an element of mystery surrounding the location of the incident occurring on 18 March 1612. John's account states 'thorow [through] Colne-field',[1] Alizon's account states 'on the high-way, called Colne-field, neere unto Colne'.[2] The problem is there is no longer a road or area called Colne Field, but fortunately, some sources from the past can help narrow the search for the likely meeting place of Alizon and John.

By 1612 Colne was a vital market town adjoining the modern-day Pendle parishes of Foulridge, Laneshaw Bridge, Trawden Forest, Nelson, Barrowford, and Blacko. The weekly markets were originally held in St Bartholomew's churchyard, which was the centre of activity for many years and was even the site of the town's wooden pillory. The churchyard was only enclosed with railings and gates in 1820, following a prolonged period of vandalism and a complaint by the Bishop of Chester that the graveyard was in terrible condition. In the latter half of the nineteenth century, local author James Carr, when writing about the town's history, mentioned that the graveyard had long been the playground of the locals – people had even gathered there to watch wrestling matches! (In 1815, this even led to the death of one of the wrestlers.)[3]

At the time of composing his work, Carr noted that the town still lacked a 'market house', so 'dealers and hawkers who frequent[ed] the town on market days, expose[d] their goods for sale with impunity, either on stalls erected in the street, or not infrequently on the ground'.[4] We can get a sense of the type of goods available to buy in Colne during the early part of the seventeenth century by studying household and farm accounts belonging to the Shuttleworths of Gawthorpe Hall. In 1612, they noted the purchase of sack and white wine, and between 1618 and 1619, they recorded the carriage of iron, soap, sugar, garden seeds, and 'a great pye' to Colne.[5]

St Bartholomew's Church, situated on top of the ridge on Church Street, is one of the town's oldest existing buildings; it is mentioned in the 1122 charter (though it has undergone extensive restoration over the centuries). St Bartholomew's only became a parish church in 1867. Prior to this date, Colne was part of the ancient parish of Whalley, and it was the Cistercian monks of Whalley Abbey who originally provided chaplains for the church.[6]

The town has a well-known history of textile production. The Industrial Revolution led to an increase in population, and many mills and houses were built during this time of expansion. By 1900 there were fifty-five cotton mills, many of which were situated alongside Colne Water.[7] The actual length of the historic relationship with textiles stretches back much further than many people might realize, as Colne had a fulling mill as early as 1311. It probably stood on the site of what is now Walk Mill.[8] We also know that by 1596 the town had at least one corn mill. A recent archaeological study has uncovered the remains of a medieval corn mill that once stood in Greenfield Nature Reserve to the west of Colne. It is thought to have dated back to the 1200s and survived as a corn mill for centuries before being converted into a cotton mill in the nineteenth century.[9]

Carr states that St Bartholomew's churchwardens were the 'authorities of the place' during his lifetime.[10] As church service started on a Sunday, the churchwardens would exit the church 'preceded by the constable, and followed by the sexton, whip in hand, onward through the main street, and down to Waterside and back, they went, driving all idlers they could catch back with them to church'.[11] It was also part of their weekday duties to attend the market 'and see that the butter was the correct weight, for, if found to be otherwise, it was distributed amongst the poor'.[12] Around 1601, churchwardens had been most aggrieved that the locals were not respecting their authority: Colne parishioners were 'burying their dead without payment of the customary fees'.[13] To ensure this did not continue, the churchwardens held a meeting which the principal inhabitants of Colne attended. The outcome was that those wishing to bury their dead at St Bartholomew's would now be forced to make payment upfront: 'whosoever, from henceforth, shall bury their dead within the church, shall pay for a child that is brought uppon a woman's heead Twenty pence, and for every other person upon a beare, whether it be a man or a woman, or aine woman dying in childbeed . . . shall pay . . . the Churchwardens of that circuit before the burials'.[14] (It was standard practice for a parish to buy a bier, a type of cart used to transport the corpse to the graveside.) Whether the failure to pay their debts demonstrates that the friends and relatives of the deceased could not afford to pay the burial fees, or were merely unwilling to pay, is open to debate.

St Bartholomew's churchyard is not particularly large, yet Carr noted that the parish burial register which began in 1599 showed that nearly 27,500 burials had taken place since this date.[15] (The larger cemetery to the east of Colne was not consecrated until 1860.) It transpires that the graveyard was only able to accommodate such a great number of bodies because of the addition of a bone house: 'This was a roofless semicircular building, some 8 feet long, abutting the west end of the church tower. In it, the sexton deposited the bones and fragments of coffins which came in his way when preparing fresh graves.'[16] (This might have been one way for a budding witch to obtain bones and teeth relatively easily!) 'About the year 1830 it had become so full, and, from its position, so exposed to view and offensive, that a new subterraneous bone-house . . . was built within a few yards . . . of the Grammar School.'[17]

From this little glimpse into the history of Colne, we get a sense of the types of public rights of way which would have been essential for the inhabitants of the town and the surrounding areas. They would have required access to their abodes, the mills, the church, the market, their fields, and the common land. In 1555, an Act of Parliament passed the burden of maintaining England's network of highways onto individual parishes. Under the Highways Act, every parish was to select two 'honest persons' to survey the highways in their parish which ran into market towns. The two individuals would be chosen during the Easter week. Following their assessment of these roads, the locals would be expected to carry out any necessary work for four days each year without pay. This increased to six days in 1563. (Any 'able-bodied' member of the community who did not fulfil this obligation could be subject to a fine.)[18] It makes sense that the monarch focused on maintaining the highways that led to markets, for these roads were vital for trade and the economy. Such roads would have to be sturdy enough to accommodate a large footfall, packhorses, waggons, carts, and droves of livestock. Because of the importance of these roads, the surveyors were permitted to take 'rubbish' from quarries and dig for gravel without the permission of the owners.

Around 1554, during the reign of King Edward VI, a land survey of the Colne area was undertaken. It was noted that the wasteland surrounding Colne was not wholly impassable but that the west side was the most accessible. The land to the east of Colne was reportedly in an 'indifferent state of cultivation.'[19] This land was named 'the Colne Fields.'[20] From references in Carr's *The Annals of Colne*, we know that during the latter half of the nineteenth century, Colne Field encompassed Horsfield Cricket Ground, which is presently part of Horsfield Ward. After consideration of Ordnance Survey and tithe maps, it seems likely that Colne Field stretched from the eastern edge of Colne town (roughly the western end of Market Street) across to Swanfield in 1612. The northern boundary roughly followed the route of what is now Byron Road (which was built relatively recently). Colne Field stretched as far south as Colne Water.

Carr states that 'The present road on Colne Field opened [in 1812].'[21] An Ordnance Survey map published in 1895 shows there was only one road in Colne Field at the end of the nineteenth century; this was Keighley Road, which was a continuation of Market Street.[22] (This must have been the road Carr was referring to.) Keighley Road runs east to west along the southern boundary of the cricket ground and cuts through the centre of what used to be Colne Field. The 1842 tithe map for the township of Colne shows that the land in the Colne Field area was gradually improved and enclosed. Four enclosed fields bear the name of Colne Field Meadow, three of which are situated above Keighley Road and one below. The smallest of these fields was located in what is now the eastern part of Colne Cemetery. The largest is now covered in houses and streets: Granville Street, York Street, Gordon Street, and Charles Street. Rutland Street is now on the site of the second largest field, and a property called Colne Field House, which had a garden and stable, was also built on this site. The fourth field, whose full name was Swan Field/Colne Field Meadow, is now the site of Colne Park Primary School. Another field is marked as Colne Field Pasture, and this former pasture land is now Dudley Street and Sefton Street.

In the seventeenth century, the majority of rights of way in Colne Field would have been field ways, or in other words, simple field tracks, which allowed tenant farmers to gain access with their carts onto their rented fields. In 1922, local author Fred Bannister wrote about the history of neighbouring Trawden Forest. By studying the Colne Halmot Records of the 1500s, Bannister discovered just how

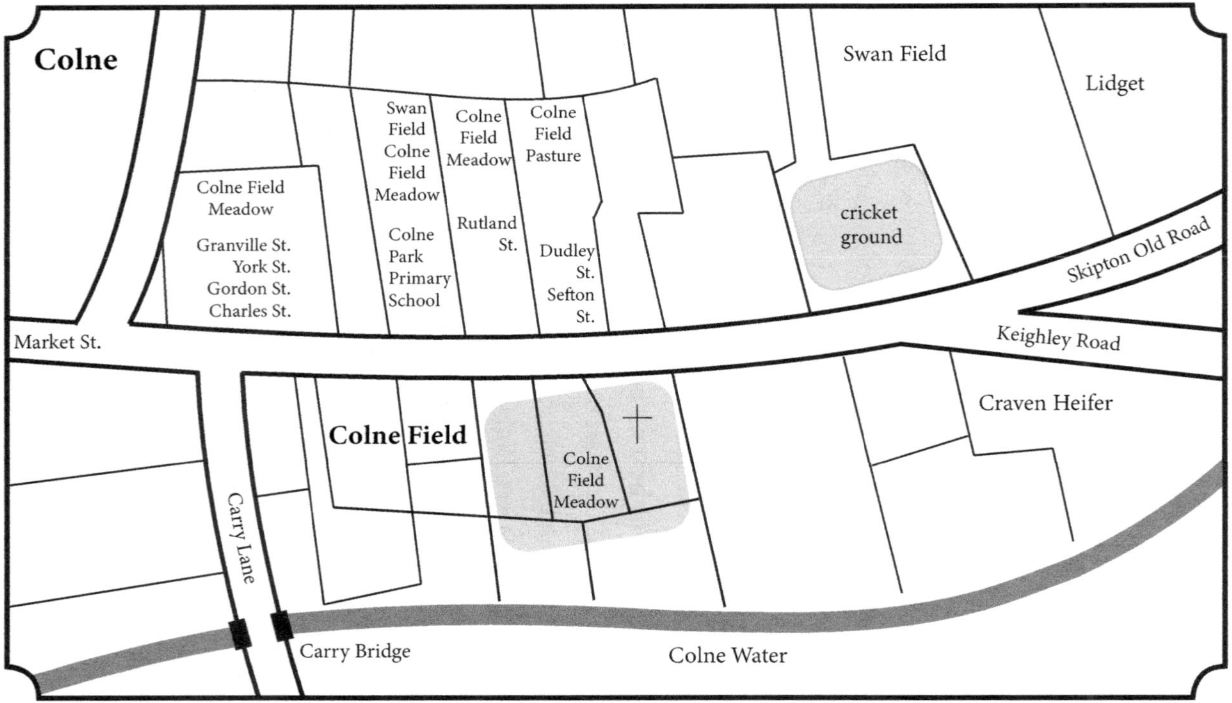

Map 1. Map of Colne Field, showing present-day street names alongside field names as they appear on the Colne tithe map surveyed in 1842

frequently tenants argued about these types of rights of way. It was typical that a grievance would be raised because one tenant had tried to block the access of another. For example, in 1532, Geoffrey Folds (from Trawden) complained that John and James Herteley had destroyed and ploughed his field way, preventing him from accessing his land.[23] It is easy to see that pinching a bit more land here and there would always have been a temptation, and as more land started to be enclosed, these types of complaints multiplied around the country. In 1522, following opposition to such land changes in the Beardshaw Booth area, the Halmot Court ordered a priest called Nicholas Hartley to leave access for all tenants coming and going with their carts. In addition, a field way nine feet in width was to be created to ensure that all tenants had access to the common pasture.[24]

Although John and Alizon could have met on a field way in Colne Field, another more likely possibility exists. Given that Alizon was (according to Potts) heading to Trawden Forest on 18 March, and because she refers to a highway, it is more likely that she met with the pedlar on Carry Lane. Carry Lane sits to the west of the 1860 cemetery and runs north to south alongside the western edge of Colne Field. This lane is known to be one of the oldest roads into Colne from Trawden, was used frequently by drovers, and would have been a substantial and essential highway maintained under the Highways Act. Carry Bridge, which stretches over Colne Water, is mentioned in the court roll of 1546 as Carry Hey Bridge, and prior to its construction, a ford stood in its place.[25] As Carry Lane continues south-east over Carry Bridge into Trawden Forest, it begins to climb up into Carry Heys and becomes Coal Pit Lane. (Bannister notes that the coal pits around Carry Heys were some of the earliest in the area, and there is a record of Trawden coal being sold as early as 1296.[26]) Coal Pit Lane then becomes Mire Ridge, and this name suggests that it was a route across an area of wetland. Bannister also highlights that in 1538, Carry Heys was written as Carre Heyez and that the word carr was an old word meaning a marsh or marshy place. Carry Heys, to his reckoning, meant the edge of the marshy place.[27] If you walk down Carry Lane, cross over Carry Bridge and continue a short distance further, you will notice a stone gate post opening next to some agricultural buildings on the right-hand side. This is the beginning of a partly paved footpath which cuts out Coal Pit Lane and leads across fields before joining the Mire Ridge road. It is said that this footpath is known locally as the Trawden Flags because the path was used frequently by Trawdeners visiting Colne.[28]

In 2020, Colne Town Council compiled a record of Colne's historic buildings, and one of the oldest buildings sits at the top of Carry Lane, at the Keighley Road junction. According to the record, terraced houses numbered fourteen and sixteen Keighley Road were once an inn and ancillary buildings. Most intriguingly, the report states that this property is infamous as the inn where the pedlar was taken to recuperate.[29] However, the report was updated in 2022, this detail was removed, and the house numbers were also amended to fourteen to eighteen. Usefully, the amended report does highlight that the houses are situated in what used to be Colne Field and that this area became known as Carry Lane Head later on.[30] Another theory (promoted by enthusiastic tour guides) is that John Law was taken to an inn called The Greyhound, which is believed to have been located somewhere on the eastern end of Market Street. (It was demolished in the 1700s.) The location of John's place of recuperation is not stated in *The Wonderfull Discoverie*, but one important point to make here is that John refers to an alehouse rather than an inn, and there was a difference between these establishments in the seventeenth century. Inns were generally seen as more respectable than alehouses, and it tended to be the wealthier sort who stayed overnight in inns. Alehouses were a cheaper alternative, with some offering a 'put me up' style of lodging.

The world of seventeenth-century alehouses is somewhat tricky to navigate, for an individual might have opened their house on occasion to sell domestically brewed ale (albeit often illegally). As Alizon used the phrase 'a house' rather than alehouse, perhaps we might consider that this was the type of drinking establishment which John had been taken to. It is curious that she did not mention whose house it was, however, which would seemingly have been a natural response. This might suggest that Potts or Nowell had omitted this detail from the testimony. Equally, if John was taken to an inn or legal alehouse, then it is strange that neither he nor Alizon referred to the property by its name rather than function, such as The Greyhound Inn, The Red Lion, The Black Bull, etc. In 1393, King Richard II passed an Act making it compulsory for alehouses and inns to hang a sign outside to make them clearly identifiable. These signs would often display an illustration rather than a name, as the majority of people were illiterate.[31] Before 1619, justices of the peace vetted would-be proprietors 'possessing full discretion to license alehouse keepers by taking bonde and suretie from tyme to tyme by Recognizance'.[32] Officially, no licensed alehouse keeper could allow anyone 'to lodge above one day or one night without first giving their names to the constables, unless the alehouse keeper knew them and would be responsible for their behaviour'.[33]

Anyone who has walked up Carry Lane to the Keighley Road junction will have noticed the steep gradient. At least sixteen buttresses were placed along the side of the road to support horses carrying heavy loads up the hill. (Cartwheels were backed against the buttresses, thus taking the weight of the shafts, enabling the horse to rest.)[34] If John Law had suffered a stroke near the bottom of Carry Lane, he would have needed assistance to get to the inn at the top of the lane or the inn on Market Street.

Fig 2.4. View of Colne Cemetery, formerly part of Colne Field

Fig 2.5. The buttresses on Carry Lane. The property at the top of the lane is reported to be the inn to which John Law was taken

3

The Superstition Epidemic

Pigeon Slippers & Other Medicaments

> The universities do not teach us all things, so a doctor must seek out old wives, gipsies, sorcerers, wandering tribes, old robbers, and such outlaws and take lessons from them. A doctor must be a traveller. . . . Knowledge is experience.
>
> Paracelsus (1493–1541)

The obvious flaw with seventeenth-century academic medicine was that it was based on an incorrect understanding of human physiology. University-educated physicians typically subscribed to the Ancient-Greek theory that disease was an imbalance in the four humours: blood, phlegm, yellow bile, and black bile. (According to Galenic humoral theory, each bodily fluid had one of four qualities: hot, dry, cold, or wet.) Qualified seventeenth-century doctors saw the human body as a microcosm of the universe (the macrocosm) and were astrologers as much as they were physicians, believing our health was affected by astrological activity. (Signs of the Zodiac ruled over parts of the body, and planets ruled over the organs and systems.) Diagnosis often involved knowing the exact time the patient became ill, after which the astrologer-physician would cast retrospective horoscopes to identify the configurations of the planets that had caused the humoral imbalance. Alternatively, some physicians preferred to compare the colour of their patient's urine against various astrological urine charts. Having established which of their patient's humours were in excess or lacking, physicians always agreed that purging was the best form of treatment. Bloodletting, usually by venesection, scarification, or the application of leeches to the skin, was a common way to redress the humoral balance; vomiting and sweating might also be induced. Internal medicine and other external medicaments were also added to the body to redress the balance of the humours.[1]

As early as 1421, the university-educated astrologer-physicians had petitioned Parliament, requesting that only those with appropriate qualifications be allowed to practise medicine. Unqualified practitioners, they argued, caused 'great harm and slaughter of many men'.[2] Virtually anyone could set themselves up as a healthcare practitioner in the fifteenth century. On market day in your average town, amongst the food and cloth stalls, you would likely find tooth pullers, bone setters, and quacks selling various pills and potions. (People who pretended to be qualified or skilled in medicine and delivered healthcare and entertainment at the same time!) While the concerns of the fifteenth-century physicians might have been genuine, the cynical would say that a financial incentive likely lay behind the petition; by cutting out the competition, their profit was bound to increase. (The unqualified practitioners of medicine had broad appeal, not necessarily because their treatments were more successful, but mainly because they were more affordable.) Furthermore, while there was, undoubtedly, some truth to the physicians' argument that unregulated healthcare was causing harm to the public, it can hardly be said that their own methods (particularly their insistence on opening up veins) safeguarded the life of the patient. (The methodology employed by the physicians during the bubonic plague epidemic in the 1600s was as dangerous as it was barbaric. To 'draw out' the disease from the body, they often resorted to opening up buboes, either with a vein opener or a red-hot poker, causing excruciating pain and aiding the spread of deadly bacteria at the same time.)

In 1511, almost one hundred years after the original petition, an Act of Parliament was passed to put an end to the 'great Multitude of ignorant Persons' that were carrying out 'the Science and Cunning of Physick and Surgery' in and around London (within a seven-mile radius).[3] This was the first real attempt by the State to regulate the healthcare profession. Now physicians were prohibited from working in the specified area unless they had been approved by the Bishop of London. That being said, there is little evidence to prove how effective this Act really was. And the truth is that, even if they had been capable of doing so, there were simply not enough qualified physicians to maintain the health of London's population. One reason for the shortage of physicians was that it took eleven to fourteen years to obtain a medical degree. (As well as learning physic, the medical student also had to learn astrology and astronomy (which were not totally differentiated at this point), and mathematics.)[4] And so, recognizing that there was much need for medical assistance, the new law did allow some unqualified *men* to practise physic in districts where no fully trained doctor existed, so long as they could demonstrate that they had gained medical knowledge by reading medical texts.[5] The all-male signatories of the 1421 petition had specifically asked the monarch to make it law that 'no Woman use the practise of Physic'.[6] From our perspective, this request can be seen as both misogynistic

Fig 3.1. A man consults a physician who examines a flask of his urine. Engraving by Joannes Jonstonus, 1644

and a shrewd business move, for surely the quickest way to increase business was to ban half of the population from practising medicine. To the delight of sixteenth-century university-educated physicians, the 1511 law was clear that female healthcare providers came firmly under the category of ignorant persons.

The Physicians and Surgeons Act was created during King Henry VIII's reign. Henry had been untrusting of unqualified medical practitioners, and the Act informs us that, thirty years before he saw the need to create the first Witchcraft Act, he regarded them as quacks and, more importantly, *witches*. The Act accused smiths, weavers, and *women* – people who, according to the Act, could not read and consequently lacked any real medical knowledge – of carrying out 'great Cures and Things of great Difficulty, in the which they partly use Sorcery and Witchcraft, [and] partly apply such Medicines unto the Disease as be very noious [noxious] . . . to the high displeasure of God, great Infamy to the Faculty, and the grievous Hurt, Damage, and Destruction of many of the King's liege'.[7] This Act of Parliament officially linked unqualified practitioners of medicine to witchcraft and portrayed them as wicked and threatening. The State had demonized them. During the sixteenth century, unqualified healthcare practitioners became commonly referred to as cunning folk: people who, in addition to offering healthcare services, might also use supernatural means to find lost treasure or property, identify thieves or foresee the future. (Activities which became formally recognized as acts of witchcraft in 1542.)

It is evident from the 1421 petition that the medieval university-educated physicians had referred to the unqualified physicians as the 'un-cunning', meaning lacking in true knowledge or expertise.[8] They reserved the title of cunning for themselves: it indicated that they were the experts in their field:

> High and mighty Prince . . . for so much as man has three things to govern, that is to say, Soul, Body, and [worldly] Goods, the which ought and should be principally revealed by three Sciences, that be Divinity, Physic, and Law, the Soul by Divinity, the Body by Physic,

> worldly Goods by Law, and these cunnings should be used and practiced principally by the most cunning men in the same Sciences.[9]

Although incomprehensible to us today, seventeenth-century physicians were natural philosophers, meaning that most of their 'knowledge' about health, disease, and the functionality of the body was based on postulation rather than physical experimentation. Ideas about physiology were simply assumed to be correct. (Especially if they were written down.) In 1653, herbalist Nicholas Culpeper expressed his dissatisfaction with the profession, complaining that the majority of 'young novices' (student doctors) were taught physic 'just as a parrot is taught to speak'.[10] In his opinion, the only explanation a physician could give as to why they were prescribing a particular form of treatment for their patient's health complaint was that 'an Author says so, therefore it is true'.[11] And when it came to academic texts on medicine, he exclaimed that they were 'full of nonsense and contradiction as an egg is full of meat'.[12] Unlike most of his peers, Culpeper saw an issue with the fact that the medical texts physicians relied upon contained contradictory treatments and cures.

While there were some attempts by medical professionals to carry out practical experimentation in the 1600s – to test theories in the way modern scientists would do today – such attempts were controversial and rare. The most well-known experiment was carried out by maverick physician William Harvey, who, through the vivisection of live animals, discovered the circulation of the blood.[13] Unfortunately, most physicians failed to recognize Harvey's great scientific achievement and, for a considerable amount of time, stood by the archaic Galenic postulation that the blood moved through the heart much like the tides of the sea. (Also, it is important to stress that Harvey understood the human body via the microcosm/macrocosm model. The heart, he said, was like the sun and comprised of heat and fire. The proof was that the body became cold once the heart stopped working.)

A team of Cambridge University scholars recently concluded a decade-long project, examining 80,000 seventeenth-century consultations belonging to astrologer-physician Simon Forman (who turned to medicine after claiming to have cured himself of the plague in 1592) and his protégé, the Anglican rector and astrologer-physician, Richard Napier. This extensive research project has uncovered what can only be described as a list of questionable medicinal treatments by modern-day standards. Some of the strangest remedies Napier prescribed were those in the category of external medicaments. For example, as a cure for hot red eyes, coughs, and at least thirty other ailments, he recommended that pigeons be 'slit' and applied to each foot.

It turns out that Napier was not the only physician to recommend that pigeons be applied to the body; even physicians educated at Montpellier were taught to put a pigeon on their patient's chest to bring comfort to the heart. And in 1612, Prince Henry, the son of King James I of England, had pigeons placed upon his head and feet by the royal physicians.[14] Whatever the complaint had been, the prescribed treatment failed to treat it, and it is interesting to note that King James regarded academic medicine as useless conjecture.[15] The reputation of academic medicine was damaged even further by Thomas Sydenham, one of the most famous astrologer-physicians of the seventeenth century. He considered that it would have been better for many patients if the art of physic had never been invented and declared that many poor folk owed their lives to their inability to afford the services of university-educated physicians.[16]

Even though the State had demonized uneducated-physicians, many patients (rich and poor) preferred to be treated by the cunning folk because their medicinal knowledge had been obtained through practical experience rather than by reading a book or two. Even Thomas Hobbes stated that he would rather be treated by an experienced old woman who had been at many people's bedsides than by a learned but inexperienced physician.[17]

We see from the quote at the beginning of this chapter that Swiss astrologer-physician Paracelsus recognized the limitation of his purely academic sixteenth-century education in physic. As a result, he actively sought out the cunning folk in order to expand his medical knowledge. Paracelsus presented the first significant challenge to humoral theory, believing disease was a type of poison brought by the stars, not a humoral imbalance. He also considered that disease could be cured by medicine similar in nature to the disease. This was seemingly contrary to Galenic humoral theory which promoted using opposite qualities as treatment. (For example, if a person had a fever which was regarded to be a hot condition, Galen would have treated the health complaint with the application of something cold to redress the humoral imbalance.)

Paracelsus had observed the everyday use of like-for-like medicine by the common folk. The Doctrine of Signatures, or the theory that every plant has characteristics (signatures), such as a particular shape or colour, which are indicative of the disease they can cure, was incredibly popular at a grassroots level. We would assume that selecting plants based on their appearance alone must have yielded little medicinal success, and yet, the popularity of the concept of signatures can be observed in the common names of many plants and herbs. Toothwort, for example, was used for tooth ailments, and lungwort was used to treat pulmonary conditions. Feverfew was used to treat fevers.

In May 1600, Napier recorded in his case studies that someone referred to as Mother Gale was convinced that a young boy suffering from burning shoulders, swollen knees, and back pain had been bewitched.[18] As you might have guessed, he treated the boy by applying a slit pigeon to his body. (The difference was that this time he put the freshly slit bird on the boy's face, not his feet.) We do not know why Napier used this form of treatment during this (or any other) consultation. But it is interesting to note that there is an ancient superstition that cockerels can cure illness if rubbed against the bodies of the sick and then removed from the parish.[19] This type of superstition stemmed from the ancient folklore that you could only be cured of an affliction by transferring it to someone or something else. So, for example, a person might remove a wart from their finger, and to prevent its return, wrap the wart up in a small piece of fabric, tie it onto the low branch of a tree, and hope that some curious passer-by will be tempted to examine the contents and become the new host of the affliction! (This is possibly where the phrase 'get lost' comes from.) Such a notion dates back to Anglo-Saxon times (if not before), and superstitious 'get lost boxes' were even found on country lanes in Cornwall as recently as the twentieth century.[20] Maybe Napier believed he was transferring the curse to the dead bird. Or perhaps he was doing what Culpepper accused all physicians of, namely copying something he had read without being able to justify why he was doing so.

Witch trial pamphlets suggest that some of those who were formally accused of witchcraft specialized in counter-magic medicine, or in other words, medicine which removed or transferred harmful magic (like curses) or which protected against witchcraft. Counter-magic might take the form of physical medicines or spoken words or charms. Counter-magic practitioners were frequently sought out by those who had convinced themselves that either they, their animals, or their goods had been bewitched. It is safe to say that fear of bewitchment was common in the seventeenth century. Culpeper's book of botanical medicine even includes those herbs deemed 'excellently good to remove witchcraft in both men and beasts'.[21] It must also be emphasized that the astrologer-physicians (like Napier) also made this type of diagnosis. In fact, witchcraft would appear to have been the standard explanation for illness when a qualified doctor had failed to find any other possible cause.[22]

It is perhaps also true that the unqualified medical practitioner and the university-educated practitioner alike could just as easily have concluded that God (not a witch) had caused the illness from which a patient was suffering. This is because the Christian belief that God could inflict disease as divine punishment ran alongside the aforementioned theories about illness. Author John Raach even concluded that the main reason medicine was late to establish itself as a profession was because of the widespread belief in the Middle Ages that disease had been imposed by God as punishment for sin and was therefore to be endured.[23] Be that as it may, there was increased interest amongst those ordained by the Church in botanical medicine during the fourteenth century. The first major work in English on the subject was the *Rosa Medicinae*, written by a monk in the early 1300s. (It combined Greek, Arabic, Jewish, and Saxon medical writings and included observations based on personal experience.) This type of written text became known as a herbal.[24]

Herbals were originally designed to be used by physicians to aid their work, and they were also sold to wealthy men (not women) to benefit the health of their households. (The cost of the books alone meant that only the wealthiest members of society could utilize them.) Although they were not supposed to, there is evidence that wealthy women consulted these books; their handwritten names are present in many original editions, and sometimes they even wrote recipes in the page margins. As the maintenance of the household, including the health of the occupants, was the woman's responsibility, it makes sense that women would have valued this type of book.

Many wealthier households would have their own physic garden. This was an area of land dedicated to growing medicinal plants and herbs. If a family member suffered from a common ailment such as 'dropsy' (water in the legs), they would ensure to grow herbs believed to offer relief for this condition. If they had some knowledge of Galenic humoral theory, they might grow hot and dry herbs, like rosemary, to rebalance the wet and cold symptoms of dropsy. Or perhaps, if, like many common folk, they were influenced by the Doctrine of Signatures, they would grow herbs which they thought physically resembled the illness in some way.[25] If their home remedies failed, they could always seek the expertise of the physicians or the cunning folk.

Medicines made from one plant were often known as simples. Even the poorest household could make this type of medicine by boiling the plant over an open fire. Those not fortunate enough to have a physic garden could scour the countryside for plants growing naturally on common land and in hedgerows. It is difficult to establish how many households made more complex medicines at home using a pestle and mortar or vial. But just like it makes sense for us to have some kind of medicine store in our own homes, such as a reserve of paracetamol or cough syrup, it is most likely that seventeenth-century households would have had some ready-prepared medicine on hand in the form of salves, oils, and ointments, or at least some key ingredients which could be easily turned into medicine. Wealthier people living near

The Book of Knowledge. 11

Some would confound Aſtronomy and Aſtrology together, which are in Truth different Things: And both have their particular Uſe and Excellency: Aſtronomy teaches the various and different Motions of the Planets, and Aſtrology ſhews us their Influences and Effects: But I ſhall treat of the Signs and Planets more diſtinctly: And firſt of the twelve Signs of the Zodiack, which govern the ſeveral Parts of Man's Body; which are ſumm'd up in Verſe:

VI. *A Deſcription of the Twelve Signs in the Verſe, ſhewing what Part of the Body each rules.*

MAn's Head and Face Heaven's Ram obey,
His Neck the Neck-ſtrong Bull doth ſway;
The Arm-twining Twins guide Hands and Arms,
Breaſt, Sides and Stomach Cancer *charms;*
The Lion rules his Back and Heart,
Bowels and Belly's Virgo's *Part;*

B 4 *Rein*

Fig 3.2. The signs of the zodiac and the parts of the body they influence. A page from The Book of Knowledge, Treating of Wisdom of the Ancients, printed in Glasgow in 1794

towns and cities might have obtained more complex medicine from apothecary shops and other shops which sold some medicaments amongst their wares. The inventory of a Welsh apothecary from Wrexham demonstrates that in 1681 he was even selling 'chemical medicine' in the form of 'Egyptiacum', or 'Egyption ointment'.[26] The recipe for this exotic-sounding ointment in Culpeper's herbal shows that it was made by boiling finely powdered verdigris (the green patina which forms on oxidized copper) with honey and vinegar. Culpeper noted that it 'cleanses filthy ulcers and fistulas forcibly, and not without pain, it takes away dead and proud flesh, and dries'.[27]

Ill health was something to be very fearful of in the days before antibiotics and vaccines. Seventeenth-century people would have been acutely aware of their own mortality. And as Jean Walton, a local author from Blacko, once said: 'The will to live is a primitive urge which is shared by all animate things, animal or vegetable.'[28] Recognizing this drive for survival, she did not condemn the remedies based upon superstitions (as she saw them) which were still being used around Pendle in the early to mid-twentieth century. She had witnessed the common practice of placing red beads around a baby's wrist 'to ward off evil spirits' and 'keep the child free from disease'.[29] Children suffering from rickets were rolled in early morning dew and clothed in a vest made of red flannel,[30] and a child suffering from an infectious disease would have raw meat suspended around its neck in a piece of red flannel: 'The idea was that as the meat decayed it absorbed the fever from the child. The more potent the smell the more effective the remedy, as the smell drove off the evil spirit that caused the fever.'[31] This latter method of treatment would not be out of place in Napier's case studies, for it has a whiff of pigeon slippers about it! (This penchant for using red objects to treat ill children can be traced as far back as the thirteenth century, for the author of the *Rosa Medicinae*, John Gaddesden, wrote that he cured King Edward the II's son of smallpox by wrapping him in a red cloth.)[32] Walton recalled that if the 'old wives' in her village could not find a remedy or a reason for a condition, such as a birthmark or cleft palate, they would satisfy themselves by reasoning that it had been caused by the wrath of God or the Devil, and was therefore beyond their capabilities.[33] Even though the germ theory of disease supplanted humoral theory in the nineteenth century, it is apparent that many people still believed in superstitious explanations and cures for disease.

The Signature of All Things

I knew well enough the whole world, and everything in it, was formed of a composition of contrary elements, and in such a harmony as must needs show the wisdom and power of a great God. . . . I knew those various affections in man, in respect of sickness and health, were caused naturally . . . by the various operations of the Microcosm; and I could not be ignorant, that as the cause is, so must the cure be; and therefore he that would know the reason of the operation of the Herbs, must look up as high as the Stars, astrologically.

Nicholas Culpeper, *The Complete Herbal*

As previously stated, university-educated physicians were natural philosophers, meaning they were people who postulated about their natural world. But natural philosophy often overlapped with occult philosophy: the study of the powers said to be hidden in the natural world. The Doctrine of Signatures, as well as being an example of like-for-like medicine, is also an example of occult philosophy, and many people reasoned that the healing properties of plants had been supernaturally imposed by God. (Culpeper refers to these occult healing properties as the 'virtues of the herbs'.[1]) Using God's herbs as medicine was considered by Bishop William of Auvergne, in the thirteenth century, to be a form of natural magic: magic which made use of the powers inherent in the natural world.

During the European Renaissance, scholarly interest in magic exploded. The crucial point to note is that university-educated men did not only read about magic, they also *practised* magic – profusely. (Paracelsus himself had a keen interest in magic.) Scholarly interest in magic can be broken down into the exploration of three interconnecting categories – natural magic: using the hidden/occult properties in the natural world; celestial magic: exploiting the influence of the stars; and ceremonial magic.[2] By the seventeenth century, ceremonial magic was considered to be ritual magic involving the invocation of demons. However, demons were not the only supernatural beings which scholars attempted to invoke.

We already know that ceremonial magic was made heretical from the fourteenth century, meaning that anyone practising this form of magic risked being burnt at the stake. Possibly because of this fact, in 1486, Italian philosopher Pico della Mirandola (a pious Christian) attempted to justify practising ceremonial magic by splitting it into two forms, essentially a good form and a demonic form. The good version was theurgy, which he argued was the highest realization of natural philosophy. This was magic reliant upon an alliance with divine supernatural beings such as angels. The demonic form was goetia, which consisted 'wholly in the operations and powers of demons'.[3]

To the mind of William Perkins, one of the foremost leaders of the Puritan movement in the Church of England during the Elizabethan era, there was no such thing as good invocation. Perkins, as a Christian, did not deny the existence of angelic or demonic beings. But he argued that the so-called angelic communications of theurgy were really delusions created by the Devil. In 1608, he published *A Discourse of the Damned Art of Witchcraft*, a book which aimed to challenge those who were sceptical about the existence of witches. Scot might have argued that witches were merely deluded individuals, but Perkins' counter-argument was that they had been deceived by the Devil himself. Only God, he emphasizes, can change physical substance, but the Devil is capable of making people believe that they are seeing, hearing, or touching something that is not really there. According to his theory, even though a witch might think they are working in God's name, they are ultimately being tricked by the Devil.[4]

Perkins is keen to stress that 'in the practises of sorcerie and Witchcraft, the Devil can doe so much onely as God permits him, and no more'.[5] Because Christians consider that no other entity is more powerful than God, it must follow that the Devil cannot be more powerful than the Almighty, and according to Perkins, God actually controls how much power the Devil has. But if God can control the Devil's power, and moderate his behaviour, then the question is, *why* would God allow him to carry out diabolical acts of witchcraft, such as deluding Christians into believing they are seeing angels in the first place? Perkins attempts to resolve this conundrum:

> [God allows witchcraft] for the punishment of unbelievers and wicked men: for oftentimes God punisheth one sinne by another, as the antecedent sinnes by the consequent. This Paul plainley sheweth . . . that because men received not the love of the truth, therefore God would send upon them strong illusions, that they should believe lies. . . . God suffereth the practises of Witchcraft, to be so rife in these our dayes, to punish the ingratitude of men, who have the truth revealed unto them, and yet will not believe and obey the same, but tread it under their feete.[6]

The major problem with this whole argument is that it transpires that witchcraft is ultimately God's work, not the Devil's. Consequently, it does not make much sense to maintain the opinion that the Devil is against God when he is working on God's behalf.

In further elaboration of the operations of the Devil, Perkins theorizes that the arts of Satan had been passed directly to 'wicked and ungodly persons of ancient time' who then shared the art with others.[7] This is how the practice of witchcraft had spread. Apart from making an appearance to teach his original recruits, Perkins states that he then

Fig 3.3. Herbalist Nicholas Culpeper. Engraving by unknown artist

chose not to continue to do so because the Devil 'finds in experience, that things are far more welcome and agreeable to the common nature of mankind, which are taught by man like unto themselves, then if the Devil should perfectly deliver the same, to each man'.[8] And yet, if we are to go by *The Wonderfull Discoverie*, it would appear that the Devil was popping up frequently in Pendle in the sixteenth and seventeenth centuries, evidently on a bit of a recruitment drive.

Perkins believed in the satanic-witch conspiracy. He considered that people were tempted into witchcraft and making compacts with the Devil for two reasons: to better their position and status and to know the secrets of the macrocosm (that which God wanted to remain hidden from mankind). To demonstrate that he was correct in his opinion, he used the following example as an illustration:

> Certain Popes of Rome, as Sylvester the second . . . for the attaining of the Popedome (as histories record) gave . . . [himself] to the Devil in the practice of Witchcraft, that by the working of wonders [the Devil's magic, a lesser form of miracle] . . . [he] might rise from one step of honour to another, until . . . [he] had seated . . . [himself] in the chair of Papacy.[9]

This tale had started to circulate around the twelfth century. Pope Sylvester II was both a devout Catholic and a man with a remarkable ability to understand astronomy, mathematics, and many other learned subjects, which he then went on to teach. After he became the head of the Catholic Church in 999, rumours abounded of his dealings with the Devil, and it was alleged that he had studied sorcery and owned a book of magic spells. It is incredible to think that, at one point, even the head of the Catholic Church was demonized for seeking or having greater knowledge of the universe than is provided by Scripture alone. But perhaps the reality is, like on other occasions in the past, the accusations of sorcery were levied as part of a cunning plot to swiftly remove a political adversary. (There were, after all, many cardinals who coveted the papal crown.)

During the European Renaissance, many learned-Christian-men had a great desire to explore and unravel the mysteries of God's Universe, and as part of this desire, there was a renewed philosophical and theological interest in Hermetic texts and Neoplatonism (or new-Plato philosophy). In the third century AD, the philosopher Plotinus (continuing the work of Plato) wrote a philosophical treatise about 'the One': a non-physical source from which all existence descended. His successors often incorporated religion into Neoplatonism, making it the belief in a cascading realm of spirit and physical forms. Early Christians, or Gnostics, saw the One as a purely spiritual, divine entity which 'thought' ideas. Below the One was the Demiurge (Greek for craftsman), a lesser God-like spirit who took the ideas of the One and made them a physical reality. So, for example, if the One had the idea of a planet, the Demiurge made the physical planet. Likewise, if the One had the idea of a giraffe, the Demiurge made the physical giraffe. The next realm was that of the spirits. In a Christian context, this would be understood as the realm where the angels and demons dwelled. Humans were in the next realm, followed by the realms of animals, plants, minerals, and finally, non-being (or nothingness).

Everything above human is spirit. Everything below is physical. But humans are unique because they have a soul and a body, making them both spirit and physical. (It was believed that animals did not possess souls, which might explain why people had no qualms about wearing pigeons as slippers.) Hermeticists believed that we could transcend the physical realms and be united with the One because of our unique position. During the European Renaissance, many Christian scholars incorporated Neoplatonic philosophy into their faith and began to practise magic in an attempt to gain greater knowledge of the Christian universe.

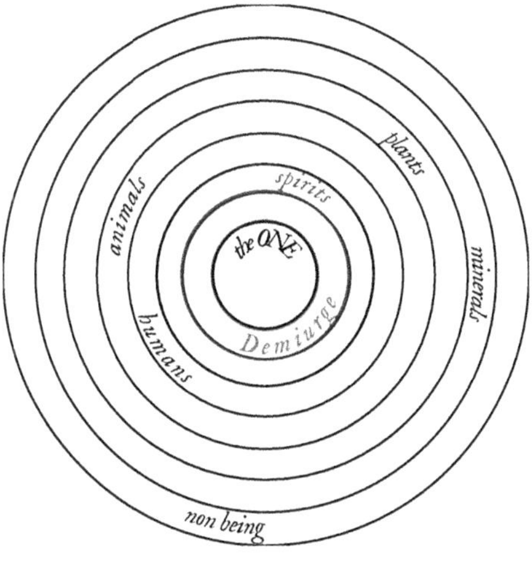

Fig 3.4. The Neoplatonic realms from the Gnostic perspective

The Neoplatonic world was the world the Pendle Witches were born into. Everything, from stars, planets, plants, animals, metals, landscapes, words, and letters, had occult properties which bore sympathetic correspondences with each other.[10] You might have heard the often-quoted fundamental principle of Hermeticism: 'As above, so below'. This cryptic paraphrase is often interpreted as 'the macrocosm influences the microcosm'. Such a principle inspires the idea that it is not only the human which is a microcosm of the universe, as was the view of the physicians, but that a body part could be a microcosm of the man. One could therefore read a person's palm to understand the inherent qualities and character of the person, for example. Jacob Boehme, the mystic, theologian, and philosopher, wrote: 'The whole outward visible world with all its being is a signature, or figure of the inward spiritual world; whatever is internally, and however its operation is, so likewise it has its character externally.'[11] Like-for-like medicine, such as using a plant that looked a bit like teeth to cure toothache, was a type of sympathetic cure. Similarly, treating a condition of the eye which, according to Culpeper, is influenced by the sun and moon, with a herb governed by the sun and moon, was also a type of sympathetic cure for disease.[12] There were some scholars who contested the idea of signatures and sympathetic correspondences, but Oxford University upheld the reality of cures by sympathy as late as 1653.[13]

Even Reginald Scot had some belief in cures by sympathy:

> Those amulets, which are to be hanged or carried about one, if they consist of hearbs, rootes, stones, or some other metall, they maie have diverse medicinable operations; and by the vertue given to them by God in their creation, maie worke strange effects and cures: and to impute this vertue to anie other matter is witchcraft.[14]

Scot distinguished objects in the natural world which were part of 'physicke', 'philosophie', or natural magic, from the objects and methodology the Catholic Church imbued with virtues, such as 'a naile taken from a crosse, holie water, and the verie signe of the crosse'. This was merely 'popish stuffe',[15] or, in other words, what the Protestant Church considered to be superstition and nonsense.

We can see that the Catholic Church had been a rather unwitting witchcraft influencer. For example, according to the testimony of James Device, his grandmother Elizabeth Sowthernes had once 'bid him this Examinate goe to the church to receive the Communion . . . and then not to eate the Bread the Minister gave him, but to bring it and deliver it to such a thing as should meet him in his way homewards'.[16] According to Thomas, the congregation believed communion bread had magical power and that the person who did not swallow the bread was in possession of that power. Some anecdotes show people using communion bread to cure fevers, restore eyesight, and keep caterpillars away from their crops. More generally, the bread was seen as a source of protection against misfortune.[17]

It is evident that even after the Reformation and the Protestant declaration that the consumption of bread and wine as part of the Eucharist were merely symbolic actions to remember the sacrifice of Christ, the belief in the Church's ability to bestow magical power or occult/hidden properties onto material objects endured in the minds of many. The Protestants erased much of what they labelled popish superstition from their religious methodology, but as English clergyman and naturalist Gilbert White noted:

> It is the hardest thing in the world to shake off superstitious prejudices; they are sucked in as it were with our mother's milk; and, growing up with us at a time when they take the fastest hold and make the most lasting impressions, become so interwoven with our very constitutions, that the strongest sense is required to disengage from them.[18]

When communicating with the Device family about the subject of seventeenth-century medicine, the family informed us that, during their lifetime, they knew people who wore a rabbit's foot on their person as a type of external medicament to increase fertility. We can see both sympathetic and Galenic influences at play here. Someone in the seventeenth century who could not conceive a child would likely seek a remedy. From the Galenic perspective, they were 'lacking' in fertility and needed to 'add' fertility to the body. Because the rabbit is renowned for its ability to reproduce, the animal was perhaps a logical sympathetic medicinal choice of the age for infertility. Scot noted that some people believed carrying a rabbit's foot on their person would ease arthritic pain. It is not difficult to imagine why a person who lacked agility might try to redress the imbalance by adding a rabbit's foot to their person; the bouncing nature of the rabbit gives it the appearance of having very strong and flexible joints.

Diarist Samuel Pepys' use of a hare's foot is perhaps more difficult to understand, for he wore it to cure colic, and any obvious link is less forthcoming. Pepys noted with surprise, on 20 January 1665, that a hare's foot remedied his condition. Sir William Batten, an English naval officer and politician, had recommended using a jointed hare's foot, assuring Pepys that since he had carried such an object on his person, he had not been troubled by colic. Pepys notes continue: 'and it is a strange thing how fancy [imagination] works, for I no sooner almost handled his [hare's] foote but my belly began to be loose and to break wind . . . I became very well, and so continue.'[19] As amusing as this account might be, what is particularly interesting about this statement is that the diarist seems to express the belief that one's imagination alone can bring about physical changes in the body. This is particularly insightful because Neoplatonists believed that the imagination influenced the body and the mind influenced matter. As we shall go on to see, the Device family also greatly believed in this idea.

The Charms of Daft Wives

Learned magicians left a great deal of evidence of their attempts to: summon and bind angels and demons, use celestial magic to predict the demise of kings and popes, use magical means to find lost treasure, and intentionally inflict harm upon their adversaries. This evidence was not only in the form of physical objects, such as paper talismans and scrying mirrors, for many had written about their exploits, even daring to publish texts on hermetic philosophy, alchemy, theurgy, and goetia. And yet, despite the vast trail of evidence of their having practised witchcraft, the prosecution of learned-men did not happen that much in comparison to the prosecution of peasant women who, at the exact same time, were being tortured, burned, and hanged in their thousands, based on very little (if any) physical evidence of their having practised witchcraft whatsoever. So, while it was true that exploration into the realm of magic could bring anyone under suspicion of being a witch, the odds were clearly stacked so that men – specifically wealthy educated men – would get away with it, and women would not.

When Roger Nowell ordered constable Henrie Hargreives to search the Device family home for evidence of witchcraft, there was little hope of him finding a paper talisman or magical text secreted somewhere. This is because, whether practising witches or not, the poorer sort were illiterate and passed their information on orally. And in addition, books were expensive luxury items in the seventeenth century. Hargreives did unearth some clay and teeth which Nowell would claim were used to perform witchcraft. (This will be discussed later in this book.) Still, he needed more evidence, and so during his examinations of the accused, he attempted to extract confessions of their having used oral charms. In *Daemonologie*, King James VI refers to 'such kinde of Charmes as commonlie daft wives uses, for healing of forspoken goodes, for preserving them from evill eyes . . . or doing of such like innumerable things by wordes, without applying anie thing, meete to the part offended, as Mediciners [qualified physicians] doe'.[1]

According to her own testimony, as written in *The Wonderfull Discoverie*, Anne Whittle (alias Chattox) confessed 'That she was sent for by the wife of John Moore, to helpe drinke that was forspoken or bewitched: at which time shee used this Prayer for the amending of it, *viz.*

A Charme

Three Biters hast thou bitten,
The Hart, ill Eye, ill Tonge:
Three bitter shall be thy Boote,
Father, Sonne, and Holy Ghost
a God's name.
Five Paster-nosters, five Avies,
and a Creede,
In worship of five wounds
of our Lord.

After which time that this Examinate had used these prayers, and amended her drinke, the said Moores wife did chide this Examinate, and was grieved at her.'[2] If we assume that Anne's testimony has a grain of truth within it, then it would appear as though Anne Whittle's neighbours believed she had some skill in counter-magic. But why

Fig 3.5. A witch holding a plant in one hand and a fan in the other. Woodcut, c.1700

would John Moore's wife have asked Anne to heal bewitched drink (beer or ale) and then have scolded her for doing so? Alizon Device's testimony also includes an account of the argument about spoiled drink, but the version of the story she relayed was quite different to Anne's: 'about two years agoe, she, this Examinate hath heard, That the said Anne Whittle, alias Chattox, was suspected for bewitching the drinke of John Moore of Higham.'[3] Was the truth that John Moore's wife scolded Anne because she thought she was behind the bewitchment?

A neighbour called James Robinson also accused Anne of bewitching drink. According to *The Wonderfull Discoverie*, around 1606, Anne had helped his wife to card wool for a couple of days in their home. During this time, Anne had helped herself to drink which his wife had brewed. When his wife came to brew a new batch of beer or ale, she had little success 'for some eight or nine weekes'.[4] James Robinson quickly reasoned that Anne had bewitched it. He went on to affirm in his testimony that 'Anne Whittle, alias Chattox, and Anne Redferne her said Daughter, are commonly reputed and reported to bee Witches.'[5] It is safe to say that witches were not typically born overnight. It could take years for an individual to gain the reputation of being a witch, and it appears that Anne Whittle had gained a reputation for using charms to harm goods as well as to heal them. It is perhaps true that the individual who offered the service of counter-magic gained in the short term, receiving some form of payment for their assistance. But they were putting themselves at great risk in the long term, for if they were deemed powerful enough to remove bewitchment, their neighbours would surely believe they were also powerful enough to bewitch.

Although King James considered charms to be the work of women, Reginald Scot observed that it was not only 'daft wives' who used word magic as a form of medicine: 'There be inumerable charmes of conjurers, bad physicians, lewd surgians, melancholicke [deluded] witches . . . for all diseases and greefes; speciallie for such as bad physicians and surgions knowe not how to cure, and in truth are good stuffe to shadow their ignorance.'[6] Scot viewed charms as quackery and argued that their use in place of physical treatment put the patient at greater risk of loss of life.[7]

The charm which Anne Whittle allegedly used to un-bewitch drink contains obvious Catholic phraseology. The pronunciation of Catholic prayers was commonplace in magical practices both before and after the Reformation. For example, in 1528, a practitioner of magic named Margaret Hunt admitted that she instructed her sick clients to repeat certain amounts of Pasternosters, Aves, and Creeds.[8] In 1622, London empiricist Robert Booker even used a version of the same charm to treat a man whom he believed had been bewitched. Thomas states that the *Three Biters* charm emphasized that the forces of religion were strong enough to deal with the three sources of witchcraft: concealed malevolence (the heart), bitter words (the tongue) and ocular fascination (the eye).[9]

While those who prosecuted the alleged witches at the Lancaster Assizes accused them of using charms, which implied that they were commanding assistance from demons, in the testimony supplied by the alleged witches themselves, they referred to such verses as prayers, which implied that they were petitioning God for help. Those accused of charming often denied the charge, claiming they had only used prayers to help people or animals, not magic.[10] But by the seventeenth century, anyone using Catholic phraseology to pray to God was circumspect because Catholicism was illegal and because the Protestant Church had demonized the faith. Consequently, a Protestant juror might be more inclined to believe that someone who recited Catholic phraseology was attempting to invoke demons.

Ironically, the most common prayer used by Protestant Christians, *The Lord's Prayer*, is a command, not a petitionary prayer. The reciter is not *asking* God for their daily bread – God, can you give us some bread, please? – they are instead literally *commanding* it. This is evident by the use of an imperative verb: '*Give* us this day our daily bread' (Matthew 6:11). The prayer continues with its demands: '*Forgive* us our trespasses' (and so on and so forth). It seems that Tyndale coined these well-known phrases when translating the New Testament into English in the early sixteenth century, and they have been recited ever since. Author David Daniell, in his book on the history of the translation of the Bible into English, includes the following parody of what the translation might have been if Tyndale had not made his abbreviations: 'We should be obliged [grateful] for Your attention in providing our nutritional needs and for so organising distribution that our daily intake of cereal filler be not in short supply.'[11] By simplifying *The Lord's Prayer*, Tyndale had inadvertently made it appear as though Protestants did the very thing the early Christians had assured the Romans they did not do – practised ceremonial magic to bend the will of their God. (Notably, such imperative verbs are lacking in Anne's charm.)

Alizon Device

It should not come as a great surprise to learn that the Device family did not, and do not, consider themselves to be witches. In fact, they had been *fearful* of the supernatural. Just like many Pendle folk, they had been very superstitious people when they were alive. This meant they believed in the reality of good and bad luck and were quick to determine that many things happened due to supernatural causes.

This book does not go into the 'mechanics' of how mediums communicate with spirits, but it is necessary to affirm that mediums cannot work without the aid of their spirit guides. Guides help other spirits communicate with the medium (especially those new to communicating with mediums). Spiritualists believe we all have spirit guides who accompany us throughout our lives. They are evolved spirits who have experienced life in the physical world and have our spiritual growth and welfare at heart.

On the subject of belief, and in response to the question of what the Device family believed in, the spirit guide who helped to create this book shared the following philosophy with the Spiritualist medium, along with the accompanying message:

In the beginning was thought, and thought is a living thing.

Fig 3.6. A female biscuit seller carrying two baskets of Dutch biscuits. Etching from The Cryes of the City of London Drawne after the Life. After M. Laroon, 1688

Alizon Device and her family believed in the power of thought. More specifically, that some people had the ability to think deeply and meaningfully about something and make it manifest. This was not a belief unique to her family, but one shared by many poor people; those who needed more, to survive.

Having confirmed that Alizon and her relatives believed it was possible to effect a physical change through thought alone, we see evidence when we read *The Wonderfull Discoverie* that she felt her grandmother had some skill in manifestation. For example, on one occasion, Alizon seems to have believed that her grandmother had made milk turn into butter without physically churning it:

> And further, this Examinate sayth, that about two yeares agon, this Examinate having gotten a Pigginfull of blew Milke by begging, brought it into the house of her Graund-mother, where (this Examinate going foorth presently, and staying about halfe an houre) there was Butter to the quantity of a quarterne of a pound in the said milke, and the quantitie of the said milke still remayning; and her Graund-mother had no Butter in the house when this Examinate went foorth: duering which time, this Examinates Graund-mother still lay in her bed.[1]

The Device family sometimes practised manifestation to bring much-needed sustenance into the house. But they also relied upon prayer. Their reliance on supernatural intervention as a survival technique can be seen as a demonstration of the level of poverty and desperation they had come to find themselves living in. In testimony given by young Jennet Device, it is stated that her mother had taught her a prayer to get drink: '*Crucifixus hoc signum vitam Eternam. Amen*'.[2] According to Potts' pamphlet, Jennet's brother, James, 'confessed' to her 'that he by this Prayer hath gotten drinke: and that within an houre after the saying the said Prayer, drinke hath come into the house after a very strange manner'.[3] The 'strange manner' by which the drink arrived is not stated, suggesting that Nowell had added this sentence to convince the jury that James had uttered a charm rather than a prayer, and so had practised witchcraft. But because both the Catholic and Protestant Church had reinforced the idea that Christians should pray to God to answer their needs, it seems more reasonable to conclude that James had prayed to God for drink, and believed He answered his prayer than to conclude that he said a charm, and believed that the Devil had obliged him. Perhaps, in the end, it was the fact that James had used Catholic phraseology which led the jury to believe that James had sought assistance from Satan on this occasion.

As part of their belief in the power of thought, the Device family (like many who lived during the seventeenth century) also believed that some people possessed the ability to curse: meaning that they could cause physical harm to another person at a distance, through hostile words alone. But that being said, the Device family did not necessarily believe that cursing was an act of witchcraft. This was because they did not consider that the person attempting to curse someone was always using demonic power to do so. We know that their opinion was contrary to the opinion of those who prosecuted witches. As far as magistrates were concerned, successful cursing was a 'sufficient proof' of witchcraft. The Church had stipulated that *maleficium* carried out by witches was *always* aided by demons, and curses were evidence of the witch's association with demonic entities.

Many people do not realize that before the first Witchcraft Act was created (thereby turning cursing into a criminal act) and even after the law was implemented, Christians often perceived cursing to be a form of divine justice. When someone was deemed to have been successfully cursed by a neighbour, members of the community sometimes believed God had enabled them. Above all, the curses made by the poor and injured against those who had harmed them were believed to be the most likely to come to fruition. If a curse was successful, it was proof that the perpetrator had acted unjustly against the individual who had wished the curse upon them and was deserving of God's punishment.[4]

The Device family believed cursing was principally an innate supernatural ability. This belief likely stemmed from contemporary ideas concerning occult properties. Seventeenth-century people generally accepted that everything in God's universe, including stars, plants, rocks, metals, and animals, was bestowed with hidden supernatural qualities, so why wouldn't they have believed that humans were bestowed with these qualities too? What we know for certain is that the Device family believed some people had more powerful minds than others and could do things – supernatural things – (be they good or bad) which other people with less powerful minds could not.

§

Alizon Device (unlike her mother) had never been overly concerned about the future. But that all changed in March 1612. She spent the last months of her life living in total fear. When we asked Alizon to show us what really happened between her and the pedlar, she made it clear that she 'had no deep intention to kill or lame the pedlar, for the refusal of pins'. She admits that she could be rude to people and that she spoke coarse words to John Law out of anger and frustration for his having ignored her. But their exchange was not extraordinary, in as much as they had spoken to each other in the same abrupt manner in which all poor people spoke at the time. On the day she met the pedlar, Alizon had not been into Colne town, but from Blacko, had walked along the town outskirts to the west, then across fields on the Trawden Forest side of Colne Water, before arriving on the highway via the footpath now known as Trawden Flags (near to Carry Bridge). She had spotted the pedlar approaching in the distance, and because

Fig 3.7. 'Trawden Flags', Colne. The meeting place of Alizon Device and Jonn Law

she had wanted some pins to help her carry out work with clothes and cloth, she had waited for him. As he drew near, she asked him for pins, but the pedlar was dismissive of her. She stood shouting at him in response, and he grumbled back at her as he continued walking on by. She then turned her back on him and began heading along the highway, in the opposite direction. After walking only a short distance, she became aware of raised voices. Looking over her shoulder, she saw that the pedlar was lying face down on the ground. She waited a little while, watching as two men helped him to sit upright. She then carried on walking.

On her return journey home from Trawden Forest on 18 March, Alizon was intent on walking through Colne town. As she crossed Carry Bridge and turned left, some local women came rushing to speak with her. She quickly learned from them that the pedlar was lying ill in a property nearby (which she refers to as The Dog). People had already started to gossip that she had been involved, and they were most eager for her to share what had happened. Alizon, most perplexed by the attention she was getting, replied that she honestly did not know what had happened to John Law. In truth, she had not given John's fall any thought. But now, curious about his affliction, she decided to see the pedlar for herself.

After doing so, while walking home, she was in the frame of mind to feel a bit sorry for John, and at the same time, she also started to worry a little about whether some of the women were right and his affliction was down to her; had *she* cursed him? She began to question whether she had the power in her mind to harm him; however, she had a lot of doubt about this. As she arrived home, her mood lifted, and she started to feel a bit proud of herself, deciding that what had happened had been a good thing anyway because now people would no longer ignore her and would take notice when she spoke.

§

Alizon was a pretty young woman with medium brown hair, large blue eyes, a round face, and rosy cheeks. The encounter between herself and John indicates that she did have a temper. She was, nevertheless, normally of a happy disposition. While out and about looking for work opportunities, she enjoyed strolling through the countryside. (She says that none of the family liked being indoors very much, for their home was not particularly comfortable.) She typically got on well with her family, although her brother did have the ability to rile her, for (as we will see) James could be rather 'naughty'. Although Potts portrays her as a beggar, Alizon did try to earn a living, and one method of doing so was via the production of homemade soap (which she was very proud of).

Nowadays, it is very easy for us to purchase all manner of cleaning materials, which are produced on a massive scale, but in the early seventeenth century, many households made their own. Because this was a somewhat time-consuming, physically demanding, and dangerous process requiring a good degree of know-how, households which could afford to might choose to buy soap from a local maker instead. Soap was used for cleaning the skin and hair, clothes and bedlinen, plates, and various other kitchen items and had to be able to remove both dirt and grease. It was produced in liquid form or made into a cake (or loaf), which you could take a few shavings off as and when needed. (Some anecdotal records suggest that pretty-looking soaps were often displayed in the home.) The soap-making process began by running water through pot ash to produce lye (sodium hydroxide). (Every home with a hearth would have access to ash, which due to its alkaline nature, is a hazardous caustic material that can easily burn the skin.) The lye would then be heated and left to cool slightly. While waiting for the temperature to decrease, animal fat was melted over a fire, and then the lye was added to it and stirred until it started solidifying. The hot soap was then put into a mould and left to cool. Sometimes fragrances would be added to the mixture, and Alizon liked to add flower petals to her soap. She had learned about plants and herbs from her grandmother Elizabeth Sowthernes. If they spotted some useful herbs or flowers on their travels, they would often pick them and carry them home in their coifs.

Fig 3.8. 'The ghost in the lamp'. Carry Bridge, Colne, c.1900

4
The Wonderful Discovery of Witches

The Age of the Pamphleteer

We know of the Lancashire Witch Trials of August 1612 because of Thomas Potts' witch trial pamphlet, *The Wonderfull Discoverie of Witches in the Countie of Lancaster.* Published in 1613, it is the only contemporary historical source we can draw from to gain insight into the nature of the prosecutions. (Unfortunately, the original indictments and gaol records have been lost over time.) Had the pamphlet not been commissioned, it seems highly likely that we would never have heard of the likes of Demdike or Chattox. Like many executed under witchcraft legislation, they would have been forgotten. When Potts put quill to parchment more than 400 years ago, he could not have imagined that his work would still be in print in the twenty-first century.

American historian Wallace Notestein observed that twenty-eight major English witch trials were recorded in contemporary pamphlets between 1558 and 1718.[1] Arguably, *The Wonderfull Discoverie* is the most famous of all. Perhaps the sheer amount of accused individuals involved, coupled with the fact that this was the first trial to record an oral compact with the Devil, ensured its place in history. It went on to influence the Witch-finder General, Matthew Hopkins, later in the seventeenth century and even influenced judicial proceedings in the USA during the infamous Salem Witch Trials; across the pond, Thomas Potts became revered as an authority on witches.

Despite receiving great renown for doing so, writing a witch trial pamphlet had not been Potts' idea. He was appointed the task by the two northern-circuit judges who had administered criminal law at the Lancashire Assizes: Altham and Bromley. Sir James Altham was born around 1555 in Essex. He was appointed a Baron of the Exchequer in 1606. Sir Edward Bromley was born around 1563 and lived in Shropshire. He became a Baron of the Exchequer in 1610.[2] Of the two men, it was Judge Bromley who had presided over the witch trials, and our spirit guide has confirmed that he was the driving force behind the pamphlet. Even though it is usually only attributed to Potts, Bromley revised and corrected his work before publication.[3] Consequently, we must consider that the pamphlet really had two authors.

Potts had been employed as a clerk during the trials of the Northern Circuit Assizes.[4] He wrote the pamphlet while lodging in Chancery Lane, London. Upon completion, he dedicated it to MP Lord Thomas Knyvet, 1st Baron of Escrick, and his wife, Lady Elizabeth Knyvet.[5] It is often alleged that by 1612, Knyvet, who had been instrumental in the foiling of the Gunpowder Plot in 1605, had fallen out of favour with King James I. This has led to speculation that Knyvet himself was behind the sensational claim that the Pendle Witches had conspired to blow up Lancaster Castle. Some authors believe this was a fabricated detail, shoehorned into the text at the last minute to remind His Majesty that he needed to keep men like Knyvet around. We will soon see that this idea has no merit.

The Wonderfull Discoverie is purported to be an accurate account of each indictment, arraignment, plea, and verdict accompanied by correlating witness testimony obtained either during or prior to the trial. And Judge Bromley affirms that he double-checked Potts' work to ensure that 'nothing might passe but matter of Fact, apparant against them by record'. He continues:

> It is very little he [Thomas Potts] hath inserted, and that necessarie, to shew what their offences were, what people, and of what condition they were: The whole proceedings and Evidence against them, I finde upon examination carefully set forth, and truely reported, and judge the worke fit and worthie to be published.[6]

But contrary to Bromley's assertion, during communication with the spirit of Thomas Potts, it was revealed that Potts and Bromley were prepared to add just about anything to the text to attract as many readers as possible and make the trial appear more impressive – to the King in particular. In his new role as author, Potts set out to enthral the reader with his tale of a county filled with diabolical witches, discovered by God's grace and delivered to justice by his divine instruments.

Bromley and Altham were ambitious men, but a judge could only advance in his career if their work impressed the reigning monarch. According to author Philip C. Almond, the advancement many judges sought was promotion to one of the more prestigious southern circuits. He also suggests that the northern circuit was the least desirable of the six judicial circuits, mainly because the work involved an unenviable amount of arduous and dangerous travel – judges often required the accompaniment of an armed escort.[7] Lancaster was also far from court, making it more difficult for judicial triumphs in the north to reach the King's ear. And so, creating a sensational witch trial pamphlet which appealed to King James's interests was a canny move on the judges' part. And cannier still was their attempt to procure advancement by massaging the King's ego, for the trial had proved that everything the King had purported to be true about witches was true.

Many people do not realize that *The Wonderfull Discoverie* is two pamphlets combined. The last account at the end of the work is the arraignment and trial of Jennet Preston of Gisburn, who was tried at the York Assizes in July 1612.[8] This account has a title page of its own, contained amongst some blank pages.[9] It also has a print date of 1612, leading some authors to conclude that Potts' pamphlet includes a reproduction of an earlier commissioned work. However, copies of the original publication have never surfaced, and Almond highlighted some evidence which suggests that it was never printed separately: *The Arraignement and Triall of Jennet Preston* was never registered in *The Stationers' Register.*[10] In 1557, The Stationer's Company of London were given a Royal Charter to regulate the professions associated with the publishing industry. The register was part of that regulation, allowing publishers to document their claim to print a particular work. On 7 November 1612, publisher John Barnes paid a fee of 6 pence to register *The Wonderfull Discoverie* only. The working (and not so catchy) title for which was:

> *The great discovery of Wytches in the County of Lancaster with the Array[g]nement and triall of 19 notorious witches at th[e] assizes and general gaole Delyverye at the castell of Lancaster the 17. of August 1612, and of JENNET PRESTON at th[e] assizes at York the 27 of*

July [1612] codem Anno with her execucon for the murther of Master LYSTER by Wytch-craft.[11]

In April 1612, gentlemen of the jury in Yorkshire reached a verdict of not guilty against the alleged witch Jennet Preston. But only three months later, during the July Assizes, Jennet was found guilty of another witchcraft charge and subsequently hanged. Judge Bromley had presided over the first trial and Judge Altham over the second.

Notestein observed that witch trial pamphlets often followed the same format: 'It was of course a partisan document, usually a vindication of the worthy judge who had condemned the guilty, with some moral and religious considerations by the respective and righteous author.'[12] It seems most likely that the York witch trial pamphlet had been commissioned by Altham to clear his name following an outcry by Jennet's family that she had been falsely accused and wrongly condemned.[13] However, we shall go on to see that the York and Lancashire trials are connected. And because Judge Bromley decided to commission a pamphlet about the Lancashire Witch Trials (for self-promotion and career advancement), Altham changed his mind about the Preston pamphlet. From his perspective, it would be far more beneficial for his reputation if the Preston trial was incorporated into *The Wonderfull Discoverie*, proving that Jennet Preston had conspired with notorious witches over in Lancashire. Who then could dispute that she had been a witch?

Knowing that witch trial pamphlets were often contrived as a form of damage limitation to justify a judge's decision to condemn an alleged witch, it seems remarkable that Potts implied the judges commissioned this second pamphlet, not due to an outcry of injustice at the loss of so many innocent lives, but because there was an outcry that they simply had not hung enough. Potts claims that many 'came to prosecute against many of them that were not found guiltie, and so rest very discontented, and not satisfied'.[14] (This would appear to be a reference to the Samlesbury Witches, who were found innocent of the witchcraft charges against them.)[15] At the time, the official explanation the judges gave for producing the pamphlet was that there were 'divers uncertaine reportes and relations of such Evidences, as was publiquely given against them at their Arraignement'.[16] During the summer of 1612, the instruments of God were carrying out their work on a grand scale, and everyone was talking about it. As a result, there were many inaccurate accounts in circulation, and the judges deemed it 'necessary' to make the truth known (and profitable, of course).

Studying surviving English court and gaol records allows us to estimate how many English people were prosecuted under the Witchcraft Statutes. In his book *Witchcraft in Tudor and Stuart England: A Regional and Comparative study* author Alan Macfarlane demonstrates his findings for the county of Essex: 'The Essex Assize records contain some 503 indictments for offences under the Witchcraft Statutes in the years between 1560 and 1680; an average of over four cases a year for 120 years.'[17*] Comparatively, in one month alone, we see that nineteen alleged witches were indicted at the Lancashire Witch Trials of August 1612. (Elizabeth Sowthernes died before her trial.) Potts emphasizes that the number of accused witches at Lancaster was unprecedented: 'the number of them being knowen to exceed all others at any time

* Reproduced with permission of the Licensor through PLSclear, © Alan Macfarlane, 2nd edn., 1999, *Witchcraft in Tudor and Stuart England: A Regional and Comparative Study*

heretofore'.[18] This remarkable number of accused individuals had drawn much attention and anticipation: 'upon the caryage, and event of this businesse, the Eyes of all the partes of Lancashire, And other counties in the North partes thereunto adioyning it were bent: And so infinite a multitude came to the Arraignment and tryall of these Witches at Lancaster'.[19]

§

Thomas Potts wants it to be known that even as a small child, he had a great desire to achieve something with his life, and the authorship of *The Wonderfull Discoverie* resulted in the fulfilment of this ambition. He made a name for himself by writing the pamphlet, and it was his *greatest* achievement. When the medium asked Potts whether he has any remorse, he said that he has 'some', acknowledging that what he wrote about the Lancashire Witch Trials was not always the truth and had caused harm to those who should have been able to trust the men in positions of judicial authority. But he also wants it to be understood that he did not volunteer to write the text – it was considered by the judges to be part of his job. Indeed, Altham and Bromley do state in the text that they 'imposed the labour of this Worke upon this Gentleman, by reason of his place, being a Clerke at that time in Court, imploied in the Arraignement and triall of them'.[20]

Our spirit guide has emphasized that even at the time of its commission, the ambitious and fame-hungry Bromley had a great desire for the pamphlet to go down in history. Although it seems he got his wish, perhaps with hindsight, he should have considered the old adage that we should be careful what we wish for. Few today have a high regard for those who condemned innocent men and women.

Beyond the Border

> This Jennet Preston being Prisoner in the Castle at Yorke, and indicted, for that shee felloniously had practised, used, and exercised diverse wicked and devilish Arts, called Witchcrafts, Inchauntments, Charmes, and Sorceries, in and upon one Thomas Lister of Westby in Craven in the Countie of Yorke Esquire, and by force of the same Witchcraft felloniously the said Thomas Lister had killed, . . . was arraigned.
>
> To this Indictment upon her Arraingement, shee pleaded not guiltie, and for the Triall of her life put her selfe upon GOD and her Countrey.
>
> Thomas Potts, *The Wonderfull Discoverie*

At the York Assizes on 27 July 1612, Jennet Preston of Gisburn was found guilty of the capital offence of murder by witchcraft and sentenced to death. Her execution took place publicly on the Knavesmire. (A small stone carved with the name *Tyburn* marks the position of the original gallows, which stood on the grounds of what is now York Racecourse.)[1] According to Potts, she had lived near her victim, Master Thomas Lister, for many years. (To prevent confusion, Master Thomas Lister will be referred to as Lister senior from this point to differentiate him from his son, who bore the same name.) Regarding the relationship between witch and victim, Potts emphasizes that Jennet was very much in Lister senior's favour and benefited greatly

Fig 4.1. A seventeenth-century English kitchen maid holding a basket of produce. Engraving by W. Hollar, 1640

from being so, for she 'Had free accesse to his house, kind respect and entertainment; nothing denied her she stood in need of'.[2] Indeed, Jennet Preston was 'for many yeares well thought of and esteemed by Master Lister'.[3] The court clerk offers no real explanation as to why Jennet would be motivated to murder the man from whom she was profiting. We know that accusations of witchcraft typically arose because of some perceived wrongdoing, and in fact, the guilty conscience of the accuser was often a contributing factor when it came to prosecuting alleged witches. In the seventeenth century, the trend was that when a guilt-ridden individual fell ill, they would often convince themselves that the person *they* once wronged (in whatever manner and however long ago) had used *maleficium* to cause their illness as a form of vengeance.[4]

The Listers were a highly privileged family who traced their lineage back to the Mercian Royal Family. The Westby Listers were a prominent landowning family in the Gisburn area. (Listers owned land near the Yorkshire/Lancashire border in the White Moor area, which adjoins Blacko Hillside (part of the Pendle Forest). They also held some land in Colne.)[5] The Gisburn Parish Church Records show that Lister senior of Gisburn was buried on 8 February 1607 and had died while away from home in Bracewell. He was approximately thirty-eight years old. Furthermore, the 1607 *Bracewell Marriage Register* shows that his eldest son, Thomas, had been wed around the same time. The date of the wedding was likely sometime between Thursday, 1 February 1607 and Wednesday, the 7th. (The next record entry date is 8 February 1607.) Following his father's death, Thomas Lister inherited Westby Hall. He was only around sixteen years old at the time.[6] (We will refer to him as Lister junior from this point to avoid confusing him with his father.)

Evidence against Jennet Preston was provide
himself, and his testimony was corroborated b
Robinson. They gave the impression that Lister se
instantaneous, for he 'cryed very often in his great paines, to them that came to visit him during his sicknesse'.[7] On his deathbed, he became increasingly obsessed with the idea that Jennet was lurking somewhere in the house, and terrified that she might flee, he urged his visitors to find her: 'for Gods sake shut the doores, and take her, shee cannot escape away'.[8] His (rather dramatic) dying words were even about her: 'Jennet Preston lyes heavie upon me, Prestons wife lyes heavie upon me; helpe me, helpe me'![9] Potts concludes his account of Lister senior's demise by adding that, at some point before his burial, Jennet Preston had been brought to the body of Lister senior, and when she touched the corpse, it 'bled fresh bloud presently, in the presence of all that were there present'.[10]

The reader is informed that many other witnesses were examined, but because Potts does not include any other witness testimonials, we cannot confirm that this is true, and in fact, the following grammatically nonsensical sentence seems to contradict the claim: 'Anne Robinson and *others* [my emphasis] were *both* [my emphasis] examined, who upon their Oathes declared against her'.[11] This clumsy sentence was perhaps a poor attempt to exaggerate the weight of evidence against Jennet by replacing the name *Thomas Lister* with the word *others*. After all, we know that *The Arraignement* was most likely commissioned as a method of damage limitation to protect Judge Altham's reputation. In the introduction to *The Arraignement*, Potts even admits that animosity had grown towards Lister junior and 'others' because of the prosecution:

> You that were husband to this Jennet Preston; her friends and kinsfolkes, who have not beene sparing to devise so scandalous a slander out of the malice of your hearts, as that shee was maliciously prosecuted by Master Lister and others; Her life unjustly taken away by practise; and that (even at the Gallowes where shee died impenitent and void of all feare or grace) she died an Innocent woman, because she would confesse nothing.[12]

Clearly, Jennet's relatives were protesting that there had been a gross miscarriage of justice. Towards the end of the account, Potts unashamedly makes the bold claim that Jennet's grieving husband had gone on to attend the Lancashire Witch Trials and after hearing new evidence against his wife, provided by nine-year-old Jennet Device (which will be discussed later in the book), 'went away: being fully satisfied his wife had justice, and was worthie of death'.[13] This little lie was supposed to silence the doubters.

One glaring issue with Lister junior's testimony (which surely no juror could have failed to notice) is that he waited five years before seeking justice for the murder of his father. What possible explanation could there be for such an extensive time-lapse, when not only had Lister senior informed his son that it was Jennet Preston who was bewitching him, but in addition, members of the household had seen physical proof that Jennet was Lister senior's murderer. The belief that a murdered body would bleed when touched by the murderer was long established by the seventeenth century, and as Potts put it 'hath ever beene held a great argument to induce a Jurie to hold him guiltie that shall be accused of Murther, and have seldome, or never, fayled in the Tryall'.[14] This belief was endorsed by King James I himself, who in *Daemonologie* declared:

> For as in a secret murther, if the deade carcase be at any time thereafter handled by the murtherer, it wil gush out of bloud, as if the blud wer crying to the heaven for revenge of the murtherer, God having appoynted that secret super-naturall signe, for tryall of that secrete unnaturall crime.[15]

Even witchcraft sceptic Reginald Scot believed in the reality of the bleeding of the corpse, reasoning that the phenomenon was part of natural magic – the result of occult properties within our bodies.[16]

Another issue, which sets alarm bells ringing, is that Potts expects the reader to deem it plausible that even though he had proof that Jennet had just murdered his father, Lister junior remained on friendly terms with her:

> The favour and goodnesse of this Gentleman Master Lister now living, at his first entrance after the death of his Father extended towards her, and the reliefe she had at all times, with many other favours that succeeded from time to time, are so palpable and evident to all men as no man can denie them.[17]

Unwittingly, as Potts tries to portray Lister junior as a gentleman of the kindest and most generous nature, he destroys the credibility of Lister's testimony at the same time.

When we put the evidence together, we must surely conclude that at the time of his father's death and for a considerable period after, Lister junior did not believe Jennet Preston had murdered him. This means that the testimony regarding the bleeding of the corpse must have been fabricated. It was, perhaps, a lie based upon a half-truth, for the inclusion of the word 'relief' suggests the continuation of financial assistance, which in turn suggests that Jennet had found employment at Westby Hall. Therefore, it is possible that she had 'access to the house' because she was a servant, and maybe she had helped to clean and prepare the body for burial. Further evidence for this conclusion comes from the fact that Lister junior, with the help of his father-in-law, JP Thomas Heyber, had already sent Jennet to stand trial for practising witchcraft, at the York Assizes in April 1612, yet no mention was made here of her having used witchcraft to kill Lister senior. Instead, Jennet was indicted for using diabolical magic to kill a child.

Potts is not particularly forthcoming with the details of the first trial. We only learn three things: the presiding judge was Lord Bromley, the child in question was 'a Child of one Dodg-sonnes', and by the 'favour and merci-full consideration of the Jurie', she was acquitted.[18] Regarding the verdict of not guilty, by stating that Jennet was only acquitted because the jury had been merciful, Potts was implying that there *had* been sufficient evidence that Jennet was guilty of the crime, or at least enough evidence to prove she was a witch, but that the jury had chosen to set her free. In other words, she was only free because of their Christian compassion. It is impossible not to see this extreme interpretation of events as political spin. And although Potts is desperately trying to 'satisfie the World, how dangerous and malitious a Witch this Jennet Preston was, How unfit to live',[19] the reality of the first trial was that the prosecution had failed to persuade the jury of any such notion.

We are now left with the question of whether it seems plausible that in the short period immediately after the first trial and before the second, Lister junior came to believe that Jennet had bewitched and murdered his father. However, because there is no mention of the unearthing of new evidence (which would have helped to prove that this had been the case), and taking everything else into consideration, it seems that this was unlikely. Gaining justice for the murder of Lister senior, it would appear, was not the purpose of the second trial at all.

For some reason, Lister wanted to see Jennet hang. And if he was going to succeed in his macabre endeavour, he needed more convincing evidence of her having practised witchcraft to levy against her. He also needed this rather urgently, having less than three months to come up with the goods to ensure Jennet Preston would be tried again at the July Assizes. And so, to conclude, it is reasonable to assume that Lister junior fabricated testimony to bring Jennet to trial again, that he probably never really believed she was responsible for the death of his father, or that his father's death had been anything other than natural. Nevertheless, he was prepared to go to extremes and exploit his own father's death in order to see Jennet hang. The question remains, of course, as to why.

§

Through spirit communication, we have been given insight into the Jennet Preston trials. Our guide has made us aware that the new master of Westby Hall wore his entitlement like a crown. Lister junior had always been of a jealous and spiteful nature, even as a young child. Regarding his relationship with Jennet Preston, our spirit guide has helped us understand that he *never* liked her and grew to despise her. 'Too nice was she for my liking,' was his opinion of the woman. He did not trust her motives, believing that she pretended to be good-natured to exploit his parents' generosity. He was incredibly resentful of the bond which existed between Jennet and both of his parents, for he did not consider a woman of a lowly position worthy of their company. She was from a moderate home, and her husband – a man involved with woodwork – was far beneath the likes of the Listers. He also believed that she knew too much about him and his family and was adamant, even as a child, that what he did and what he said were nothing to do with her, for she was not family, even though she was often treated as such.

Jennet Preston was a great friend of Lister senior's wife, Mrs Jane Lister. She had been in service to Jane for many years which is how their friendship had come to form. Jennet had known Lister junior since he was a baby. She would inform his mother when he misbehaved, and this is how his resentment of her began. Jennet saw him for what he really was – a spoiled bully and a lying fool.

Following the death of his father, Lister junior began instigating some changes, one of which was to have Jennet removed from her position of employment at Westby Hall. Naturally, his mother was most aggrieved by the situation. Although she had lost her position, Jennet continued to visit Mrs Lister until her death, for she had recognized that Jane was not in good health and wanted to continue to care for her during the last stage of her life. Lister viewed her visitations as open defiance of his authority, and it made him hate her even more. Mrs Lister died around one year after her husband. We are informed that she would have defended Jennet against any accusations of witchcraft had they been levied when she was alive.

Jennet went on to assist other families with midwifery and childcare. This put her in a vulnerable position, for should the child in her care happen to fall ill, there was always the chance that the superstitious finger of blame would be pointed directly at the carer. But that being said, it was Lister junior himself who started the rumour that Jennet Preston was a witch. After stepping into his father's shoes, he had chosen to explain away his sudden misfortune, in the form of the loss of cattle and goods, as being the result of witchcraft. And who better to blame than the woman whom he neither liked nor trusted, for surely the removal from her place of employment had been motivation enough to cause Lister junior harm. Unfortunately for him, the first witch trial did not bring about his desired outcome; Jennet Preston was still alive. This infuriated the young man who was used to getting his own way. But fortunately for him (and unfortunately for Jennet Preston), his good friend across the border would help to guarantee success the second time around.

The Justice of the Peace

> In the end Roger Nowell Esquire, one of his Majesties Justices in these partes, a very religious honest Gentleman, painefull in the service of his Countrey: whose fame for this great service to his Countrey, shall live after him, tooke upon him to enter into the particular examination of these suspected persons: and to the honour of God, and the great comfort of all his Countrey, made such a discovery of them in order, as the like have not been heard of.
>
> Thomas Potts, *The Wonderfull Discoverie*

The protestant Nowell family had prospered greatly during the reign of Queen Elizabeth I. Relatives of note included Alexander Nowell, the dean of Saint Paul's, Lawrence Nowell, the dean of Lichfield, and Robert Nowell, a prominent lawyer. The latter held the post of Queen's Attorney of the Court of Wards.[1] Sir Roger Nowell was a justice of the peace for the county of Lancashire (then known as Lancaster). He had also served as High Sheriff in 1610, which until 1612 was probably his most impressive achievement. The monarch chose the bearer of this title in their position as the Duchy of Lancaster, and the potential expense to the incumbent of becoming High Sheriff was one of the reasons the role was for a single year only. High Sheriffs were tasked with choosing gentlemen suitable to form the grand jury at the assizes.

Roger Nowell is believed to have been born in 1551, making him around sixty years old in 1612. He inherited the estate of Read Hall from his father around 1591 and lived there with his wife, Katherine. The couple had ten children. Katherine died in 1620, and Roger died three years later. He was buried at Whalley churchyard on 31 January 1623.[2] His name pops up in the Clitheroe Court Roll in connection with land disputes and surrenders, and according to local author John A Clayton:

> In the years after the 1612 trials he was constantly at odds with his son, Roger, over his Read and Simonstone holdings. In fact Roger junior took his father to court in a bid to prove that he did not owe suite [labour in lieu of payment] to him in respect of Nowell senior's manorial rights. We have, then, at least a flavour of the man who instigated the Pendle Witch trials.'[3]

It is true that Roger Nowell was not a sentimental man. From our communication with his spirit, we know he had a cold nature. He was quiet, self-assured, and calculating. Physically, he resembled King Charles I, with his long-pointed face and petite frame. At the time of the trials, he had salt and pepper wavy hair which sat just above his shoulders. He liked to dress in fine, elegant clothes. He liked to be addressed as Sir. He enjoyed the sport of falconry because it allowed him to survey the land.

Author James R. McVicker succinctly summarizes the role of the JP: 'In seventeenth century England, county government largely devolved upon the justices of the peace. They were a body of trained peace-magistrates who through the detection, apprehension and prosecution of criminals functioned as the agency of police control.'[4] JPs were nominated by the Judges of Assize and named by the King. Nominees were sought amongst the landed gentry, for 'It was part of a country gentleman's education to read law for two or three years at the Inns of Court in London.'[5] Knowledge of the law was not the only requirement. In addition, JPs were officially required to be men of good and lawful character who owned land or tenements to the value of £20 a year, for it was believed that men of such means would not be tempted by bribery or extortion. JPs were bound by law to attend the assizes 'and to report to them [the judges] on the state of the King's peace and the enforcement of the laws of the realm.'[6] The position was usually for life, although one could be removed for misconduct or failure to carry out duties.

During the first half of the century, the JPs were the responsibility of the King's Judges, Privy Council, and the court of the Star Chamber who 'summarily removed cases from the justices' jurisdiction, quashed their proceedings for mistakes of law, and peremptorily ordered them to proceed in matters wherein they were inactive.'[7] In 1665, the Lord Chancellor threatened to proceed against many inactive JPs. It turns out that by the latter half of the century, many men were enjoying the political prestige which came with the title, even though they had not taken the required oath of office, following their commission. This meant that they never actively served.[8] Roger Nowell was not one of these men. He was ambitious and zealous, and furthermore, he enjoyed his work and believed in what he did. The subjects of the justices' jurisdiction included:

> All felonies, poisonings, enchantments, sorceries, magic acts, trespasses, forestallings, regratings, engrossings and extortions; persons who ride armed or lie in wait to maim or kill anyone; the enforcement of

the laws as to innkeepers, abuses of weights and measures, or acting wrongfully in the sale of victuals; the misbehaviour of sheriffs, bailiffs, stewards, constables and jailers in their offices; and all other crimes and offences of which such justices might or ought lawfully to inquire.[9]

Fig 4.2. A procession of seventeenth-century magistrates on horseback accompanied by guards. Engraving by F. Chauveau, between 1613 and 1676

We have learned from our spirit guide that up until March 1612, it was petty thieves and drunkards who occupied most of Nowell's time. JPs originally had the power to try capital offences, but by the seventeenth century, although it was still the responsibility of the JP to investigate accusations of felonious activity, the jurisdiction for such offences was reserved for the assizes. The role of the JP underwent a gradual change in this respect; their criminal jurisdiction moved from felony cases to misdemeanours, such as 'minor breaches of the peace, petty theft, receiving stolen goods, bastardy, disorderly drunkenness, vagabondage, recusancy, and non-conformity'.[10] (McVicker highlights that theft of goods exceeding the value of more than twelve pence was a felony, and petty thieves who continued to steal could be hanged.[11])

When investigating allegations of any type of crime, the JP's main aim was to extract a confession:

> The proceedings in these examinations were of an inquisitorial character. They were secret and were intended only for the use of the prosecution and the court. The prisoner on the one hand, and his accuser on the other, were examined apart. The defendant was not permitted to be present at nor to be represented by counsel in the examination of his accusers, and in fact he was to be kept in ignorance of the testimony against him up to the moment of trial.[12]

And so, even though JPs in Nowell's time had less judicial authority, they still had a great deal of power over the alleged criminal simply because they prepared the 'secret' indictments against them; it was this information which the judge and jury would rely upon at the assizes to decide whether they were guilty or innocent. Considering that those accused of felonies were given no legal representation at court nor any time to prepare a defence, for the testimony against them was to remain secret until the day of the trial, it is easy to see how a JP could abuse his position of power, manipulating testimony in order to obtain *his* desired outcome, be that a verdict of innocence or guilt. Witnesses did not even have to be present in court to give evidence. More often than not, witness testimony was read aloud in court by the prosecuting JP who would always declare that the written testimony 'agreed verbatim' with their verbal testimony recorded at the time of their interview (meaning that it was word-for-word.) But when the witness was not there to confirm this, where was the proof?

When trying to determine what motivated a man like Roger Nowell, we were given the following insight from our spirit guide:

> Nowell and those men like him (those with status) were all at risk, too, for they were often in danger of losing their status. Wealth and influence had been sought by mankind for generations; however, many who succeeded in obtaining both became fully aware that power was an illusion. Once you got more, you had even more to lose, and someone was always conspiring to take your position. Those who coveted power in society were prepared to take great risks to get it and had to be prepared to take even greater risks to hold on to it. Like the poor folk, the wealthy also did what they needed to do to survive. But to them, survival meant maintaining the level of privilege they had grown accustomed to.

Nowell's Ode to a Black Dog

Sir Roger Nowell feels no remorse for the part he played in the Pendle Witch Trials. 'None,' was his direct answer to the question. We learned from spirit communication that when the alleged bewitchment of pedlar John Law was brought to Nowell's attention, he was elated. Now he finally had something big to deal with and (along with it) an opportunity to acquire a new feather for his cap. On 30 March 1612, Alizon Device was marched to Read Hall to face questioning. Alizon impressed upon the medium that as she was seated in front of the magistrate, she was beside herself with fear, and her mind was spinning with confusion. Moving to stand over her, Nowell began his examination by simply asking Alizon whether she had cursed and lamed the pedlar named John Law. She gave a panicked response, blurting, 'Yes. I don't know!' When pressed for an answer again, she kept repeating the same words: 'I don't know, yes, I don't know, I don't know!' Nowell then demanded to know the names of other people who practised witchcraft, and on hearing the word witchcraft, she exclaimed that she did not do bad things. Nowell put it to her that her grandmother had encouraged her to become a witch and let the Devil appear to her. Alizon denied that this was true. Although she believed her grandmother *could* do some things that other people could not, 'She only tried to heal, not harm,' she told him.

Roger Nowell did believe in witchcraft. Specifically, he believed what the Church had taught him – that some people could conjure demonic spirits who, in turn, made those people do evil things. That being said, he did not necessarily believe that the men and women he sent to stand trial on charges of witchcraft were witches. He did, however, regard all peasants as authority-defying troublemakers who were unworthy of life. Nowell greatly desired to have more power over the people. He had no sympathy for Alizon Device or any of those whom he sent to Lancaster Castle. The poor were not worth his compassion. Ironically, even after 400 years of reflection, the former justice of the peace and upholder of the law does not see any problem with the fact that he fabricated evidence to secure convictions against those he sent to stand trial as alleged witches. He did so because he was determined to strengthen the likelihood of conviction.

The Witchcraft Act of 1604 was clear:

> That if any person or persons . . . shall use, practise, or exercise any invocation or conjuration of any evil and wicked spirit: or shall consult, covenant with, entertaine, imply, feed, or reward any evil and wicked spirit, to or for any intent or purpose . . . being of the said offences duly and lawfully Convicted and Attained, shall suffer paines of death as a Felon or Felons.[1]

Nowell sought evidence of Alizon having consulted with demons or familiar spirits. Abraham Law obliged Nowell by claiming his father confessed to seeing an evil black dog in the alehouse shortly before Alizon arrived there.

During his interview with Alizon, Nowell demanded that she tell him precisely how long she had been consulting with demons. Alizon denied that she had ever done so, but the magistrate did not desist. Instead, he informed her that there was no point denying the fact because many people had witnessed her in the company of a demonic black dog. He then tried his best to make her admit to conjuring the demon to lame the pedlar. Most taken aback by the accusation, Alizon immediately denied the charge. But then, almost as quickly, her survival

Fig 4.3. The Devil (or a demon) greets a gentleman and a judge. Woodcut, 1720

instinct kicked in, and in an attempt to absolve herself of blame, she pretended that she had seen a demon dog on the highway and that she saw it lame the pedlar. This lie allowed Nowell to position her one step closer to the gallows.

Black demonic dogs are a relatively common feature of British folklore. One of the earliest records of a vengeful, fiery-eyed, teeth-baring hellhound can be found in the eleventh and twelfth-century Peterborough version of *The Anglo-Saxon Chronicle*.[2] By writing that Alizon confessed to instructing such a creature to lame the pedlar, Nowell, as far as he was concerned, was showing sufficient proof that the pedlar's fall had been down to *maleficium*. (Just in case the jury might have been in any doubt.) The fact that she never confessed to doing so was irrelevant.

On the European Continent a few years prior, demonologist Jean Bodin had spread a rumour that the late Heinrich Cornelius Agrippa had associated with a demonic talking dog. Agrippa was a German physician, mathematician, soldier, theologian, pious Christian, and author of magical texts such as *The Three Books of Occult Philosophy*. In his lifetime, Agrippa was not afraid to attack all fields of supposed human knowledge, including religion, medicine, and occult philosophy. He set himself the challenge of reforming all forms of magic, including kabbalah, alchemy, and hermetic philosophy. Bodin dismissed the man's vast intellectual ambitions and achievements and chose to portray Agrippa as a mere necromancer. (His vast body of work was simply a necromancer's manual.) His demonization of Agrippa gained momentum with the help of the circulation of a rumour that a familiar spirit, or perhaps the Devil himself in the shape of a dog, told Agrippa news of faraway events. It was also rumoured that when Agrippa died around 1535, the demonic black dog threw itself into the river. Another version of the story was that Agrippa released the demonic dog upon his death. A former student of Agrippa, Johann Wier, eventually had enough of these defaming rumours and deemed it necessary to write the truth of the matter, which was that Bodin and his followers had turned Agrippa's beloved pet poodle into something diabolical:

> Having mentioned the book ascribed to Agrippa, in the interest of truth, I will no longer allow a statement that I have read . . . to be wrapped in silence – namely, that the Devil, in the form of a dog, had been a companion to Agrippa right up until his last breath, and that he then vanished somehow or other. It never ceases to amaze me that men of such repute sometimes speak, think and write so foolishly on the basis of an idle rumour that had circulated. The dog was black, of moderate stature, and was named Monsieur in French (which means Master); and if anyone knew him well, I did, since I often walked him on a rope leash when I was studying under Agrippa. He was truly a normal male dog.[3]

Closer to home at the end of the sixteenth century, there were rumours that a demonic dog, a witch, and the Devil were wreaking havoc on a wealthy family in Lancashire. This family just so happened to be related to Sir Roger Nowell. The demonic possession of seven people (most of whom were children) living at Cleworth Hall, near Tyldesley, was the largest group possession in England during the early modern period. (Presumably, it would have caused quite a stir.) Two Puritan ministers who had attempted to help the afflicted, George More and John Darrell, produced pamphlets about the household in which children, believed to be in the grip of some demonic force, would exclaim things such as: 'looke wher a greate blacke dog is, with a firebrand in his mouth.'[4] In 1599, another (somewhat sceptical) minister had charged both men with having conducted exorcisms of fraudulent possessions upon the children of Nicholas and Anne Starkey, their servants, and their guests, thereby imitating Catholic practices.[5] These pamphlets were similar to your average witch trial pamphlet in the sense that they were an attempt to clear the authors of any wrongdoing.

According to More's pamphlet, years before the supposed possessions began, the owners of the Cleworth Estate believed the deaths of their first four children had been caused by a curse which had been levied upon their family by some of Anne's papist relatives. (Nicholas Starkey was the nephew of Sir Roger Nowell, and it was actually some of Starkey's 'kindred' who had first posed this theory of death by papist witchcraft.)[6] The couple went on to have more children, and all was well with their health for a while. But in 1594, the curse struck again:

> [Their daughter Anne] was taken with a dumpishe [depressed] heavie countenance, and with a certain fearfull starting and pulling together of her bodie. About a weeke after, John Starkey the sonne was taken as he was going to schole and was compelled to shout vehementlie, not being able to stay him selfe. After this they waxed worse and worse, falling into often strange and extreame fittes.[7]

Starkey paid £200 for the services of physicians, but the children did not improve. And so, desperate to help his family, he resorted to contacting a 'Seminarie priest, who could do no good because . . . he had not then his bookes'.[8] The pamphlet does not state that the priest had been asked to perform an exorcism, but this is implied; Starkey must have considered that his children had been possessed by some demonic entity.

Starkey eventually came to employ the services of a man named Edmund Hartley. (Whom More describes as a *witch* who used 'popish charmes and hearbes'.)[9] Whatever his diagnosis was and whatever his methods of treatment were, the children recovered during his care. However, eighteen months later, when Hartley talked about stopping his regular visits to Cleworth, John Starkey started to display strange symptoms again. Eager to prevent a relapse and keep Hartley in the family's service, Starkey offered to pay Hartley forty shillings a year 'for his assistance in time of need'.[10] More states that Hartley accepted the offer but coveted more.

More then goes on to claim that the two men went on to travel together to visit Starkey's father at Huntroyde Hall, near Padiham. Following a bad night's sleep at the property, Hartley became obsessed with the idea that another man was trying to use witchcraft to kill him, and Starkey was persuaded to assist him in carrying out a form of ceremonial magic which would allow Hartley to bewitch this man:

> He went into a little wood not farre off from the house where he made a Circle the compas of a yard and halfe, with many crosses and partitions, which being finished he came back to call M. Starkie, telling him what he had done, and desired him to goe and tread out his circle, for he said he might not doe it him selfe. This being also dispatched, well quoth hee, now I shall trouble him that troubled me, and be meete with him that sought my death.[11]

(The art of using magic circles was typically associated with the scholarly magician. King James's *Daemonologie* even states that magicians conjured the Devil by creating magic circles.[12]) Having witnessed and participated in this act of ceremonial magic, Starkey's opinion of the man (who was now actually failing to treat his children) began to change, and so he secretly looked to a famous man for help – none other than the astrologer to Queen Elizabeth I: John Dee. (Whom More describes as being a *doctor*.)[13] (The leading character in Christopher Marlowe's *Doctor Faustus* is thought to have been based on John Dee. In the play the doctor invokes a demon from inside a circle and makes a fatal pact with the Devil to increase his powers.) Dee advised Starkey to find the assistance of preachers and join them in prayer and fasting.[14] Under Dee's advice, things then went from bad to worse in the household:

> But then they began their accustomed fittes: first Iohn Starkie about the 4 of Januarie 1596 as he was reading of a booke, something gave him such a thumpe in the necke, that he was suddenly striken down with a most horrible skrike, and said that Satan had broken his necke, lying there pitifullie tormented for the space of two hours. . . . At night on the same day being in bed, he leapt out on a suddaine with such a terrible outcry, that amazed them all, being tossed and tumbled a long time, being exceeding fierce and strong like a mad man, or rather like a madd dogge, that I may so speake, snatching at and biring [biting] euerie bodie that laide hold on him, not sparing in that fit his owne mother.[15]

As more members of the household began to have violent fits, Starkey convinced himself that Edmund Hartley had been responsible for the possessions from the very beginning. Hartley soon found himself being prosecuted under the Elizabethan Witchcraft Act for the bewitchment of the Starkey children and several other people. He was found guilty.

Because his victims were still living, his punishment under Elizabethan law was to be imprisonment. Reading between the lines, it seems that Starkey considered this sentence too lenient and so chose to introduce new evidence to the court – evidence of his former employee having practised ceremonial magic. It was only at this stage that Starkey decided to recount the tale of the creation of a magic circle at Huntroyde Hall, and because of this confession of conjuration, Hartley now faced the death penalty. (Even though Starkey himself had participated in the crime, he was not looked upon with suspicion.) Hartley was found guilty and hung – twice. During the first attempt the rope broke, and he had to endure the horrific ordeal a second time. It is said that Hartley had originally denied the charges against him and cried out that the Devil had promised him that no halter would hang him.[16]

It seems impossible to consider that Roger Nowell would not have been acutely aware of the diabolical events at Cleworth Hall. Whether he was sceptical about the claims or not, we can see that the trial had taught the magistrate one very important lesson: to ensure a witch is condemned, you must provide evidence of their association with demons.

Fig 4.4. A magician stands inside a magic circle and conjures a demon. Woodcut, c.1720

John Law

Truth be known, John Law was never totally convinced that he had been cursed. When walking with his wares on 18 March, he had started to feel unwell long before he even met with Alizon Device. By the time their paths did cross, he was already in an agitated state, now consumed with pain in his chest. All he wanted was to get to Colne to rest. This, it turns out, had been the real reason why he was dismissive of Alizon and had no time for her.

Following their hostile encounter, John has shown us that his next memory is of opening his eyes and seeing the bottom half of two pairs of legs standing in front of him, garbed in grey woollen stockings. We know now that a little while before, John had fallen face down onto the ground and briefly lost consciousness. As his awareness returned, he became aware of an aching pain in the left side of his face and left arm. He was also bleeding from his forehead. Alizon Device has already informed us that she had watched as two men came to assist the pedlar, and our spirit guide has made us aware that these men, who slowly helped him to sit upright, were locals named Skerrat/Sherrat and Todd. Soon after, a local woman named Margaret also came trotting by, curious to know what on earth had happened, and, while still in some distress, John's immediate response had been to blame Alizon Device. The pedlar had meant that it was her fault he fell because she had *riled* him. But unfortunately for Alizon, her family's bad reputation meant that John's words were soon interpreted to mean something far more sinister – Alizon Device, granddaughter of Elizabeth Sowthernes, had cursed the pedlar.

Fig 4.5. A seventeenth century pin seller holding his wares. Etching from The Cryes of the City of London Drawne after the Life. After M. Laroon, 1688

For the first couple of days after the incident, John was unaware of the hysteria which had begun to spiral around him, and it came as a great shock when he eventually realized people thought he had been cursed. After remembering that he had seen Alizon's face at the door of the alehouse, for a brief moment, he had started to worry that they might be right. But then, almost as quickly, he recalled how he had been feeling unwell before arguing with Alizon, and this was the main reason why he was unconvinced that the dire situation he was in at present was down to witchcraft. Unfortunately, by this stage, nobody was really interested in John's rational thoughts on the matter, and things got way out of John's control. When Abraham Law arrived, people were practically queuing up to tell him that his father had been bewitched, and Abe believed their allegations wholeheartedly. With his blood boiling, assisted by some other angry locals, he sought out Miss Device (a young woman whom he had never met) and dragged her to the constable, demanding justice for his poor father.

The next thing John knew, Sir Roger Nowell was at his bedside, having arrived to take his testimony. Nowell informed the pedlar that he had already extracted a confession of guilt from Alizon Device and was intent on prosecuting her. Now here was a man in a position of authority telling John that he was bewitched, and, more to the point, he had proof. What was he supposed to make of that? John has made us aware that Nowell coerced him into believing that, because of the curse he was under, he would never be well enough to work again, and the thought of not being able to earn a living frightened John more than witchcraft ever could. How was he to survive if he could not provide for himself? Clearly, Nowell wanted John to stand as a witness against Alizon in court, and because John initially had not wanted to do this, the magistrate attempted to instil fear into the pedlar to change his mind. He also dangled a rather appealing carrot, promising that if John went along with his plan, he would benefit financially; John would be provided with a source of income, but this would only happen if he went to court.

John Law did decide to stand as a witness against Alizon. We learn from *The Wonderfull Discoverie* that in court, Judge Bromley entreated that 'some present course should be taken for his [John's] reliefe and maintenance' and that 'Lord Gerard, Sir Richard Houghton, and others' promised to fulfil the request.[1] When we asked John whether he received any money, he answered, 'Yes, two shillings.' He did not elaborate upon how often this payment was received or who paid it.

John (a man of few words in life) told us that his wife (Abe's mother) died many years before he did and that he had lived alone and been a pedlar for many years. He resided in Wycoller in March 1612, approximately four miles east of Colne. When we asked him if he originally hailed from Scotland (having discovered that many pedlars came from the north of Great Britain), he answered, 'Not I.'

By the time of Alizon's trial on 19 August, the reality was that John *had* greatly recovered his health, making him more convinced than ever that he was never cursed in the first place. But nonetheless, guided by his son, he had decided to stick to his agreement with Nowell and intended to play the part of a bewitched man. But when in court, the moment he saw young Alizon, now almost unrecognizable, deep down in his heart, he *knew* she was innocent of the charge against her. And as she desperately pleaded for her life, he felt compelled to try and help her by crying out that he forgave her. But this offer of forgiveness would not save her. John Law lived for only a few more years after the trial, and those last years were tormented with guilt.

Familiars

> Regard not them that have familiar spirits, neither seek after wizards, to be defiled by them: I am the Lord your God.
>
> Leviticus 19:31, KJV

One common characteristic of early modern English witches is their association with familiars: demonic beings in the form of animals which assist the witch in carrying out diabolical acts. The origin of the idea of familiars is unclear, but Hutton highlights that there is an apparent lack of familiars in English witch trial records from the medieval era, which could suggest that it was not a long-held English belief but something which emerged during the Tudor era.[1] Hutton also highlights that the early satanic-witch trials in the western Alps 'contained the idea that witches were assigned a personal devil as a helper after swearing allegiance to the supreme one, or even made the original pact with such a minor demon; and these too could take the shape of beasts'.[2] And so it would appear to be the case that although the English were relatively slow to adopt the continental concept of the satanic-witch in its entirety, by the 1600s, the continental idea of witches being assisted by the Devil's helpers had been incorporated into the English concept of the anti-social witch.

Generally, in early seventeenth-century England, consorting with devilish abetters was still not regarded to be evidence of the witch having made a compact with Satan. Instead, at the time of writing *The Wonderfull Discoverie*, familiars were typically regarded to be an example of 'the meanes whereby they [anti-social witches] worke their mischiefe [*maleficium*]'.[3] From the pamphlet, we learn that during Nowell's examinations of the alleged witches, many had confessed to having allowed their familiar spirit to harm their neighbours. Potts is very clear that witches controlled their familiars: 'the Spirit [familiar] could never hurt, till they [witches] gave consent'.[4] And yet, the written testimony had not always been clear about precisely who controlled whom. For example, in the testimony of Elizabeth Device, Nowell had written that her familiar encouraged her to practise harmful magic.[5] We also read that Elizabeth Sowthernes' familiar became aggressive towards her when she refused to practise *maleficium*.[6]

What sets the Pendle Witch Trials apart from other witch trials of the period is the fact that many of the witches allegedly also confessed to making explicit pacts with the Devil – selling their souls to him in return for diabolical favours. Here was the first evidence of an oral compact with the Devil made on English soil. Witches in Lancashire were not merely using diabolical magic and familiar spirits to harm their neighbours; they had turned away from God and were part of the satanic conspiracy of witches to overthrow Christendom.

That being said, it is important to note that at the Lancashire Witch Trials, no one was actually prosecuted as a satanic-witch. The indictments were for *maleficium*, meaning that the Lancashire Witches were tried as anti-social witches, as was the norm in English witch trials. It seems likely that Judge Bromley was unsure about how a grand jury would react to the inclusion of this evidence of Christian heresy. Consequently, there was a lack of confidence in arraigning the alleged witches for having made compacts with the Devil. This part of the 1604 Witchcraft Act was, after all, controversial in England at this stage. After the trial, however, Potts greatly exaggerated these types of claims because this was exactly the kind of sensationalism which would attract readers. The result is that it is often unclear whether the demonic beings mentioned in the pamphlet were familiars or the Devil himself. In a sense, when Potts wrote about them, he made them one and the same.

Below is a record of those alleged witches who consorted with familiar spirts, according to *The Wonderfull Discoverie*. But before you read on, it is important to point out that during communication with the spirits of the trials, we asked the Device family what they could tell us about the concept of the familiar. Alizon Device responded that they simply did not believe in them.

Elizabeth Sowthernes

Familiar name: TIBB. Who took the form of a boy, a black cat, a brown dog, and a spotted bitch.
Length of time practising witchcraft: fifty years.
Date of covenant with the Devil: approximately 1592.

Anne Whittle

Familiar name: FANCIE. Who took the form of a she spirit, a Christian man, a man, a brown dog, and a bear.
Length of time practising witchcraft: about fourteen years.
Date of covenant with the Devil: around 1602, or 1606.

Alizon Device

Familiar name: not stated. Who took the form of a black dog.
Length of time practising witchcraft: not stated.
Date of covenant with the Devil: approximately 1610.

Elizabeth Device

Familiar name: BALL. Who took the form of a brown dog.
Length of time practising witchcraft: three or four years.
Date of covenant with the Devil: not stated.

James Device

Familiar name: DANDY. Who took the form of a black dog and possibly a brown dog.
Length of time practising witchcraft: about three years.
Date of covenant with the Devil: approximately 1610.

Margaret Pearson

Familiar name: not stated. Who took the form of a cloven-footed man.
Length of time practising witchcraft: not stated.
Date of covenant with the Devil: it is not alleged that Margaret had made a pact with the Devil.

5

Witches, Whores, & Simpletons

A Man's World

PHI. What can be the cause that there are twentie women given to that craft [witchcraft], where ther is one man?

EPI. The reason is easie, for as that sexe is frailer then man is, so it is easier to be intrapped in these grosse snares of the Devill, as was over well proved to be true, by the Serpent's deceiving of Eva at the beginning, which makes him the homelier with that sexe sinsine.

King James VI, *Daemonologie*

It is estimated that around eighty per cent of those accused of witchcraft in Europe were women. King James's explanation as to why there were such a disproportionate number of female witches compared to males was simply that Scripture, and in particular, the story about the first woman, Eve, who, with some encouragement from the Devil in the form of a snake, had persuaded the first man, Adam, to disobey God, proved that women were the wicked temptresses of men, and were more likely to be tempted by the Devil. In many respects, in the

Christian world, Eve's pivotal role in Original Sin is the cornerstone upon which misogyny (or the justification for misogyny) was built. According to Christian doctrine, this first human sin, from which all other sins have necessarily followed, is the reason why God has punished men and women ever since by making them mortal beings.

One slight problem with James's argument is that nowhere in the Hebrew Genesis story does it state that the talking serpent in the Garden of Eden was the Devil. According to many modern biblical scholars (who try to study the Bible without presuppositions), this conclusion seems to have been drawn by the ancient interpreters (an anonymous group of scholars from around 300BC–200BC) who were not happy to take the story at face value and accept that the creature in the garden was just a regular snake which happened to have the ability to talk. Author James L. Krugel points out that the ancient interpreters often assumed that Scripture contained hidden meaning; although God might have literally said one thing, He really meant something else. And so rather than translating Scripture directly, it became their job to postulate about what the true meaning might have been.[1] (After much deliberation, the chatty snake was concluded to be the Devil in disguise.)

Krugel also points out that the phrase 'the fall of man' does not appear in the Hebrew Genesis story, nor is it written that the garden had been a sin-free place before Adam and Eve ate forbidden fruit. (There is no mention that the fruit in question was an apple, either.) Fascinatingly, modern biblical scholars now consider that all of the elements which form the concept of Original Sin – a concept now synonymous with Christian dogma – were imagined by the ancient interpreters of Scripture as an explanation for human mortality.[2] What is certain is that this longstanding misogynistic interpretation of an obscure tale has been and continues to be incredibly harmful to women. It was common in the past to insult a woman by calling her a whore or a witch, and it still is today.

European women had very little power in the seventeenth century. Before marriage, women were under the control of their fathers, and the moment they wed, things could become a lot worse, for legally, under the law of coverture, a married woman had no independent status apart from her husband. Just like all her money and possessions, she became her husband's property as soon as the marriage contract was made. And because a wife did not exist as an individual, she was vulnerable to abuse and exploitation. It was not until the year 1878 that a law was passed which allowed British women to seek separation from abusive husbands, and it was legal for a man to beat his wife in the 1600s.

Domestic abuse in the form of physical chastisement was regarded as socially acceptable, even a necessary duty and obligation. (In fact, those men who did not chastise their wives were seen as abnormal and often ridiculed.) Women were a source of immorality who needed to be corrected by men if they began to resist their natural subordinate position. Common law permitted the physical disciplining of wives, servants, and apprentices.[3] If they died as a result, no one in authority batted an eyelid unless someone claimed that the perpetrator had used excessive force without provocation. For example, in 1737, John Totterdale was hanged for murdering his wife, Mary Totterdale. It was reported that he had dragged his sleeping wife out of bed, thrown her down the stairs and then beat her to death. Witnesses claimed that there had been no provocation on the wife's part, and prior to her death, the victim had told a neighbour that her husband was often violent towards her.[4]

If a woman killed her abusive husband in self-defence, it was legally regarded as revenge or a planned and deliberate attack. She was guilty of trying to usurp God's power of vengeance, and the law punished women more severely than men for the crime of murder. The Treason Act of 1351 proclaimed that if a subordinate should kill their superior (for example, if a servant killed their master) because it was a crime against the natural order of things, this was a crime against the state. Consequently, if a woman, in her subordinate role of wife, should be found guilty of murdering her husband, she would not be hanged as punishment. Instead, she would be drawn and burnt at the stake, as was the sentence fit for those who committed treason.[5]

Women who showed signs of getting above their station by scolding their husbands, expressing opinions, or arguing with neighbours, were often made to perform an act of public penance or punishment. The scold's bridle has to be one of the most infamous torture instruments associated with nagging wives. This barbaric iron device was essentially a human muzzle. Different versions existed, but many included a flat iron plate (or bit) which was designed to sit inside the mouth over the tongue, thus rendering speech impossible. (Some of these plates also contained metal spikes to pierce the tongue.) As well as being used on 'shrewish women', in Scotland, the scold's bridle was also used to torture those accused of practising witchcraft; Scottish law permitted torture as a means by which to extract a confession, and those accused of using witchcraft to kill King James VI in 1590 were subjected to suffer such cruelty. One of the alleged witches, an elderly woman named Agnes Sampson, was forced to wear a scold's bridle with tongue and cheek spikes. She was also chained to a wall, denied sleep for several days, and had a rope tightened around her head so that her flesh was stripped from her skull. Is it any wonder that she eventually confessed to attempting to murder the King?[6]

When we consider *why* the majority of those accused of witchcraft were women, as well as looking at scriptural influences, we must, once again, acknowledge the powerful influence of the demonological texts. Such texts took existing misogynistic ideas about women to a whole new level. For example, the *Malleus Maleficarum* was aggressively misogynistic. About women, Kramer had written:

> What else is a woman but a foe to friendship, an inescapable punishment, a necessary evil, a natural temptation, a desirable calamity, a domestic danger, a delectable detriment, an evil of nature painted in her fair colours! Therefore if it be a sin to divorce her when she ought to be kept, it is indeed a necessary torture; for either we commit adultery by divorcing her, or we must endure her daily strife.[7]

The text was designed to convince the reader that witches were almost exclusively female. In part, Kramer achieved this by arguing that women were predisposed to witchcraft because of their innate physical and intellectual limitations, as was proven by Scripture, Ancient Greek philosophers, and physicians. Furthermore, it was the female tendency to gossip which allowed witchcraft to spread: 'they [women] have slippery tongues, and are unable to conceal from the fellow-women, those things which by evil arts they know; and since they are weak, they find an easy and secret manner of vindicating themselves by witchcraft'.[8] Now, women talking to other women could even be viewed with suspicion, and by Kramer's logic, the only way to ensure that witchcraft was eradicated from the world was to eradicate all of the women! However, as women were a 'necessary evil' for men to endure, the next best thing was for men to carry out the odd campaign of witch-purging in order to prevent the destruction of Christendom. (This was his justification for the witch trials.)

A more recent theory regarding the appearance of female-centred witch trials centres around the labour shortage which began as a consequence of the Black Death in the fourteenth century. Plague had ravaged Europe, killing almost half of the population in some areas, and the unexpected result was that those labourers who had survived were now able to demand higher wages. (To the dismay of their employers.) Author Sylvia Federici sees the rise of the witch trials in Europe as being pivotal to the transition from feudalism into a capitalist society. Although seventeenth-century women were in a weak position of power, Federici highlights that European guild records demonstrate that the scales of equality were at one time more equally balanced between men and women when it came to paid labour:

> In England, seventy out of eighty-five guilds included women amongst their members. Some guilds including silk making, were dominated by them. . . . By the 14th century, women were also becoming school teachers as well as doctors and surgeons, and were beginning to compete with university-trained men, gaining at times a high reputation.[9]

Federici poses the theory that following the Black Death, accusations of witchcraft were used by ambitious men to destroy these successful women. Their main incentive was that prosecuting working-women led to their property being confiscated and transferred into the hands of the Church and other male-dominated guilds. Although it is, of course, not the case that women did not work at all from this point, by the seventeenth century, women were often paid less than men for the same work and were barred from entering into many professions and higher education entirely. They were also stereotyped as unpaid domestic labourers. (Or, in other words, 'housewives'.)[10]

Even now, in the twenty-first century, women are generally paid less than men for the same work and are often deemed incapable of carrying out some heavily male-dominated roles. In addition, the idea that women can have careers and do not have to have children or husbands is still a fairly novel one. And so, if Federici is correct, then it appears that the Witchcraft Acts were not only detrimental to the lives of the women accused of being witches between the sixteenth and eighteenth centuries. These antiquated laws continue to be detrimental to the lives of all European women alive today.

Elizabeth Sowthernes

I pray you give me leave . . . before I proceed to the Indictment, Arraignement, and Tryall of such as were Prisoners in the Castle, to lay open the life and death of this damnable and malicious Witch, of so long continuance (old Demdike) of whom our whole businesse hath such dependence, that without the particular Declaration and Record of her Evidence, with the circumstaunces, wee shall never bring any thing to good perfection: for from this Sincke of villanie and mischiefe, have all the rest proceeded; as you shall have them in order.

Thomas Potts, *The Wonderfull Discoverie*

In his fictitious story about the Pendle Witches, or 'the principall authors and actors in this late woefull and lamentable Tragedie, wherein so much Blood was spilt',[1] Potts makes Elizabeth Sowthernes (Demdike) the diabolical ringleader who encouraged her family and her neighbour Anne Whittle to become satanic-witches. According to Potts, she was 'a very old woman, about the age of Foure-score years, and had been a Witch for fiftie yeares'.[2] (We must remember that he never actually met her.) When Nowell interviewed Elizabeth's granddaughter Alizon Device, she protested that her grandmother was *not* a witch: 'Granny tried to help people,' she said. Alizon was then forced to give examples of the help she had given. She told him that her

Fig 5.1. A beggar woman with two crutches. Etching with engraving by J. Callot, c.1622

grandmother was once asked to 'amend' (heal) a sick cow. Elizabeth had agreed to try, but unfortunately, the cow died. To convince the jury that Demdike had practised *maleficium* on this occasion, Nowell added the following sentence to Alizon's testimony: 'And this Examinate verily thinketh, that her sayd Graund-mother did bewitch the Cow to death.'[3] In truth, Alizon had never thought or said that.

On 2 April 1612, Nowell arrested and interviewed Elizabeth Sowthernes, Anne Whittle (Chattox), and her daughter Anne Redferne on suspicion of practising witchcraft. Interviews took place at Ashlar House in Fence. Had she survived long enough to stand trial, it is most likely that Elizabeth Sowthernes would have been prosecuted for using witchcraft to murder the daughter of a local miller called Richard Baldwyn. According to Alizon's testimony, she once heard her granny tell the miller that she would pray for him and his family 'both still and loude'.[4] Nowell could turn such a confession into proof that Elizabeth Sowthernes had cursed Baldwyn's family and caused the child's death. (It was unfortunate for Nowell that Elizabeth died before she could be tried.)

Elizabeth Sowthernes has made it clear that she died in a cell (the Well Tower) at Lancaster Castle only a couple of weeks after arriving there. Even before her interview with Nowell took place, she had not been in the best of physical health. She had poor vision, pain in her right leg and left hip, and needed a stick to get around. In the cell, she had to crawl on her hands and knees in the dark. She suffered immensely. The Well Tower is still standing to this day; it is a damp, vaulted underground dungeon, void of any natural light. (You can still see the iron ring in the centre of the floor to which the prisoners would have been chained.) At least nineteen people would have been crammed into a space no more than twenty feet by twelve feet. Imprisoned in the castle's most unsanitary cell, starving and numb to the bone with cold, Elizabeth's already compromised health quickly deteriorated, and she died of pneumonia. She still visits the place in which she died and was unceremoniously buried. She still has a great deal of anger about the unjust circumstances of her death. Elizabeth makes the case that her family were merely living life in the same way many poor people had to. She might not have been saintly, she said, but she never committed the heinous crime of murder.

The nickname she had been given later in life was Old Dimdike, not Old Demdike. As her eyesight began to fail her, she could not see the once familiar landmarks in and around the Pendle Forest, and so, when walking unaccompanied, with her stick in hand, she had taken to using the watercourses as a method to get around; following the flow of water kept her heading in the right direction. The locals had grown accustomed to seeing her following these routes which is how the nickname came about; she was a dim-sighted old woman who was frequently seen walking alongside the dikes. She knew that people called her Old Dimdike. She did not like it because she felt they were ridiculing her. Potts tweaked the spelling of her nickname to convince the reader that her neighbours understood her to be a demonic creature. As a result, many today surmise that her nickname meant something like 'demon woman'. But this theory is, as Elizabeth wants it to be known, '*Rubbish, rubbish, rubbish!*'

At Ashlar House, Elizabeth recognized the severity of her situation as soon as she understood the nature of the questions she was being asked. Instinctively she knew that she would not come out of it alive, and she could not quite believe how after many years of friendship and rivalry between her and Anne Whittle, it had come to this for them both. By 1612 Elizabeth's mental, as well as physical, health was starting to deteriorate. She was showing some signs of senility, such as bouts of paranoia and confusion. Her poor eyesight exacerbated the problem. Nowell, taking full advantage of her age, tried to confuse her on purpose, putting words in her mouth.

According to her own testimony, around the year 1598:

> Upon a Sabboth day in the morning, this Examinate having a litle Child upon her knee, and she being in a slumber, the sayd Spirit [Tibb] appeared unto her in the likenes of a browne Dogg, forcing himselfe to her knee, to get blood under her left Arme: and she being without any apparrell saving her Smocke, the said Devill did get blood under her left arme. And this Examinate awaking, sayd, Jesus save my Child; but had no power, nor could not say Jesus save her selfe: whereupon the Browne Dogge vanished out of this Examinats sight: after which, this Examinate was almost starke madd for the space of eight weekes.[5]

Nowell had pressed Elizabeth to confess to having encounters with demonic dogs or the Devil. From communication with Elizabeth, we know that something like the incident above *had* happened but only in a dream. When alive, however, Elizabeth vehemently believed this bad dream had been a physical reality. Alizon, who was only a young child at the time (less than ten years old), believed what her grandmother was saying was true – the Devil had come to harm her family. (It seems reasonable to assume that it was Alizon who had first informed Nowell of this event as he pressed *her* to confess to more demonic encounters.)

Because Elizabeth Device made the decision to communicate with the Spiritualist medium, we can now make some sense of the scenario. We have learned that around the time of her having this nightmare, Elizabeth Sowthernes had suffered a mental breakdown which had been brought about by grief. This revelation immediately makes sense of the claim that she was mad for eight weeks – she had been unable to function normally due to trauma – and it was at this time that she first started to display symptoms of paranoia. Elizabeth had dreamt that a ferocious dog tried to attack her and kill her grandson, whom she tried desperately to protect. The reality was that her grandson had recently died, she had been unable to save him, and she was feeling utter despair at the loss of the child. (Clayton, when searching for records of the Device family, found that a boy child named Henry Denis was baptized in St Mary's Church in Newchurch in Pendle in 1593 and buried in 1599.)[6] Nowell informed Elizabeth that this confession was proof of her being a witch; she had allowed a familiar to suckle from her body and kill the child. Elizabeth refuted the accusation; she was no witch and had called out to Jesus to save them both from the Devil.

Elizabeth Sowthernes was a Christian and therefore believed in God and the Devil. But it also transpires that she believed in spirits in the same way many people who follow the religion of Spiritualism do today: she believed that our loved ones do not simply cease existing when their physical bodies die but continue as spiritual beings. She believed in spirits because she had seen and communicated with them. Her family and some of the locals were aware of her mediumistic ability. In the seventeenth century, because the Church believed in the reality of demons and (on top of that) taught that all non-authorized Christians who communicated with the spiritual realm were communicating with demonic beings, this ability made her vulnerable.

In *The Wonderfull Discoverie*, Potts writes, 'about twentie yeares past, as she was comming homeward from begging, there met her this Examinate neere unto a Stonepit in Gouldshey, in the sayd Forrest of Pendle, a Spirit or Devill in the shape of a Boy . . . his name was Tibb'.[7] Two confessions have been conflated here. Elizabeth had admitted to seeing a spirit child while on her travels, but this spirit child was not called Tibb. Before she and Anne Whittle became foes, way back in the past, the two women had met on occasion to pray for help from spirit guides, and Tibb was the name they attributed to one of those guides – a spirit which they considered to be a helper, teacher, and protector. Elizabeth never admitted to having attempted to conjure demons or the Devil – because she didn't. But Nowell wrote her testimony as though she had done so, often inserting the word Devil or familiar alongside the word she had used, which was spirit.

Anne Whittle & Anne Redferne

Alizon Device has explained that just about every family in Pendle thought they were better than their neighbours, and they all looked down on each other. The Sowthernes/Device family were no exception, for they believed themselves to be better than the Whittle/Redfernes. In turn, the Whittle/Redfernes considered themselves to be better than the Sowthernes/Devices, and both families had encouraged rumours that their rivals were thieves and witches.

Alizon Device grew up half believing that Chattox was a thief and a witch, and when interviewed by Nowell, in an attempt to protect her own family, she had told him that it was Chattox who did bad things to people, not them. Alizon informed Nowell that her family home had been broken into about eleven years ago and 'the most part of their linnen clothes, and halfe a peck of cut oat-meale, and a quantitie of meale . . . worth twentie shillings or above' were stolen.[1] One Sunday after, Alizon had seen Anne Whittle's daughter (we do not know if this was Anne Redferne or a different daughter) wearing a 'band and a coife' which Alizon thought to be two of the stolen items.[2]

According to Alizon's testimony, her father, John Device, fearing Anne Whittle might harm either himself or his goods, had struck a deal with her: John would make annual payments to Anne, in the form of a measure of ground cereal, in return for her promise not to cause harm during the year in which payment was received. (The implication here is that Anne Whittle used the threat of witchcraft to extort her neighbours.) It is written that John had broken their agreement during the last year of his life and on his deathbed had said Anne Whittle 'did bewitch him to death, because the said meale was not paid the last yeare'.[3] When we asked our spirit guide if they could shed any light on what had really happened between John and Anne, the impression we gained was that Anne Whittle had helped John Device with a health complaint some years before his death, and John had paid Anne for her services with a measure of cereal. Full of gratitude for her help in improving his condition, John had continued to give her food on occasion, when he could afford to do so. (Interestingly, author Joyce Froome uncovered evidence that nineteenth-century cunning folk were often paid annual retainers by their clients in springtime for services such as keeping witchcraft away from their farms.[4])

While imprisoned in Lancaster Castle, Alizon felt an unimaginable amount of guilt, blaming herself for how things had turned out. If she had not met with the pedlar, none of this would be happening, and if she had not opened her mouth and spoken of her grandmother and Anne Whittle, they would not have been imprisoned. But what Alizon could not have known at the time was that Anne Whittle would not be indicted for any of the accusations levied by her. Instead, she was prosecuted for using witchcraft to murder Robert Nutter of Greenhead. And this was because of testimony provided by someone called James Robinson, who was also examined by Nowell on 2 April.

About eighteen years ago, 'he [James Robinson] dwelled with one Robert Nutter the elder, of Pendle'.[5] During the summertime, Robert Nutter's grandson who was also called Robert Nutter, fell ill and held witches responsible:

Fig 5.2. A beggar woman with one stick holds out her hand. Etching with engraving by J. Callot, c.1622

> He [grandson Robert] verily thought that the said Anne Whittle, alias Chatox, and the said Redfernes wife [Anne Redferne], had bewitched him: and the said Robert Nutter shortly after, being to goe with his then Master, called Sir Richard Shattleworth, into Wales, this Examinate heard him say before his then going, unto the said Thomas Redferne [Anne Redferne's husband], that if ever he came againe he would get his Father to put the said Redferne out of his house, or he himselfe would pull it downe; to whom the said Redferne replyed, saying; when you come back againe you will be in a better minde: but he never came back againe, but died before Candlemass in Cheshire, as he was coming homeward.[6]

Potts suggests that this threat of eviction had been Anne Whittle's motive for murder.[7] But the real reason for the confrontation between tenant Thomas Redferne and the son of the property owner is revealed by Anne Whittle in her own voluntary confession: Robert Nutter had attempted to sexually assault Thomas's wife:

> Robert Nutter did desire her Daughter one Redfearns wife, to have his pleasure of her, being then in Redfearns house: but the sayd Redfearns wife denyed the sayd Robert; whereupon the sayd Robert seeming to be greatly displeased therewith, in great anger tooke His horse, and went away, saying in a great rage, that if ever the Ground came to him, shee should never dwell upon his land.[8]

Like her mother, Anne Redferne was also indicted for the murder of Robert Nutter (the man who had attempted to rape her). But by 'the favour and mercifull consideration of the Jurie, the Evidence being not very pregnant against her, she was acquited, and found Not guiltie'.[9] It seems likely that the lack of evidence of her having a familiar spirit saw Anne Redferne being acquitted of the crime. There was also no indication that Anne Redferne had made a pact with the Devil. These omissions were a significant oversight on Nowell's part; he had not proved Anne Redferne had practised *maleficium*. Perhaps this oversight was because he had spent too much time concocting testimony to condemn her mother. Nowell lied that Anne Whittle confessed to using her own familiar spirit, Fancie, to bewitch Robert Nutter:

> Whereupon this Examinate called Fancie to her; who came to her in the likenesse of a Man in a parcell of Ground called, The Laund; asking this Examinate, what shee would have him doe? And this Examinate bade him goe revenge her of the sayd Robert Nutter. After which time, the sayd Robert Nutter lived about a quarter of a yeare, and then dyed.[10]

What is particularly heartbreaking about Anne Redferne's trial is that on hearing the verdict of not guilty, she must have believed that her ordeal was over and that she would soon be free. But her freedom never came, for the following day, she was made to stand trial for a second time, hastily accused of using witchcraft to murder Robert Nutter's father, Christopher. She was found guilty of this crime. The main evidence came from the testimony of the now deceased Elizabeth Sowthernes, which (apparently) had also been supplied on 2 April. (Nowell must have had a very busy day.) According to this rapidly fabricated testimony, half a year before Robert Nutter died, Tibb 'in the shape of a black Cat' had informed Elizabeth that both Chattox and her daughter Anne were making pictures of clay of Christopher Nutter (Robert's father), Robert Nutter, and Mary Nutter (Robert's wife).[11]

The testimony of Robert Nutter's sister Margaret Crooke was also read aloud in court. Margaret had recalled that Anne and her brother fell out eighteen years ago 'about Whitsontide'[12] and that 'he did a hundred times at the least say, That the said Anne Redferne and her associates had bewitched him to death'.[13] This much about Robert we know already, but Margaret also added that her father, Christopher Nutter, 'about Maudlintide next after following fell sicke, and so languished, until Michaelmas then next after, and then died: during which time of his sicknesse, hee did sundry times say, That hee was bewitched; but named no bodie that should doe the same'.[14] This testimony clearly indicates that Margaret's father had *not* named Anne Redferne as his murderer. Furthermore, earlier testimony, supplied by Margaret's brother, John, which had been read aloud during Anne's first trial, gave the impression that Christopher Nutter did not believe his tenants were witches. On 2 April, John Nutter (described as a yeoman from Higham Booth) had recalled to Nowell that he heard Robert Nutter say to his father:

> Father, I am sure I am bewitched by the Chattox, Anne Chattox, and Anne Redferne her daughter, I pray you cause them to bee layed in Lancaster Castle: whereunto this Examinates Father [Christopher Nutter] answered, Thou art a foolish Ladde, it is not so, it is thy miscarriage. Then this Examinates Brother weeping, said; nay, I am sure that I am bewitched by them, and if ever I come againe (for hee was readie to goe to Sir Richard Shuttleworths, then his Master) I

will procure them to bee laid where they shall be glad to bite Lice in two with their teeth.[15]

At the end of the account of Anne Redferne's second trial, Potts asserts: 'All men that knew her affirmed, shee was more dangerous then her Mother, for shee made all or most of the Pictures of Clay, that were made or found at any time.'[16] As we will go on to see, these 'pictures of clay' were deemed by Nowell and King James I to be some sort of effigies which, when crumbled, could cause harm to an individual. This lie about Anne Redferne was likely added to the pamphlet because, on reflection, Potts knew that the evidence in the second trial of Anne Redferne had also not been particularly 'pregnant'.

Ironically, although she had been found innocent of bewitching Robert Nutter, our spirit guide informed us that Anne Redferne *had* wished a curse upon Robert Nutter when he tried to sexually assault her almost twenty years earlier. She had done so as a method of self-defence to frighten him away, and her quick thinking paid off. Robert became immediately afraid of her, fled her home, and never attempted to assault her again. There is an indication that, at this time, some people already suspected that her family were witches, so the curse played on Robert's mind. This revelation explains why he was so insistent, to just about anyone who would listen, that he had been cursed! It also transpires that when his father heard his son's accusation, he called him a foolish lad, not because he presumed his son was lying about the two Annes, but because he was naive enough to believe in curses. Christopher Nutter had been a very strong-willed man with no fear of such rubbish! Christopher has confirmed that he did not believe in witchcraft one iota and never believed a witch was responsible for his demise. (Whether

Robert Nutter ever confessed to his father that he had attempted to rape one of his female tenants is still a mystery.)

More than anything else, Anne Redferne wishes to communicate the following message to us: all the pettiness and quarrels of this life are not worth it. This she now knows. Life on Earth is short and should be spent in a much better way.

§

Potts describes Anne Whittle as being approximately eighty years old. According to him, she was:

> [A] withered, spent and decreped creature, her sight almost gone: A dangerous Witch, of very long continuence; alwayes opposite to old Demdike: For whom the one favoured, the other hated deadly. . . . In her Witchcraft, always more ready to doe mischief to mens goods, then themselves. Her lippes ever chattering and walking: but no man knew what.[17]

We know from our communications with Anne Whittle that she was a strong 'no-nonsense' character with a loud voice. She was a small-statured woman like Elizabeth Sowthernes but a little stockier and more robust. During her lifetime, despite being a woman in a patriarchal world, she had not been afraid to speak her mind and tell people what she really thought of them. In fact, up until her imprisonment in Lancaster Castle, she was not afraid of anything. Through our spirit communications, we learned that gaoler Thomas Couell, JP

James Anderton of Clayton, and Lancaster Mayor William Sandes interviewed/interrogated Anne Whittle when she was imprisoned in Lancaster Castle to learn more about *how* the witches bewitched people and to make her confess to more crimes. These men were most fascinated to discover whether Anne made poisons, and they pressed her on this issue, for they were certain witches were people who made diabolical potions. During this interview, Anne Whittle attempted to put the blame for the death of Robert Nutter of Greenhead onto the now-deceased Demdike and someone referred to as 'Widdow Lomshawe, (late of Burneley) now deceased'.[18] This was Anne's attempt to regain her freedom, and we must understand that to get the men to go away, she *had* to confess to knowing about some kind of diabolical activity. The interview in Lancaster Castle was far more frightening to Anne than the interview with Nowell at Ashlar House had been; torture was officially illegal, but gaolers were allowed to harm prisoners, and the threat of violence often proved a sound technique for getting prisoners to confess.

Potts writes that while imprisoned in Lancaster Castle, Anne Whittle confessed to carrying out all manner of diabolical crimes. But the truth is that, even under duress, Anne had done no such thing. According to Potts, she had confessed to converting to devil-worship under the influence of Demdike and said that the pair ate a diabolical feast together to celebrate.[19] But this confession was born from Potts' imagination. It suited his narrative of painting Elizabeth Sowthernes as the most powerful witch in Lancashire and Anne Whittle as her subordinate. It was composed with a copy of *Daemonologie* in hand.

When she was alive, Anne believed that she had the ability to help the sick, and she would do so – as long as they paid her for her medicine. It was true, she said, that she and Elizabeth Sowthernes were rivals, but their rivalry came about because they both tried to make money by helping people and animals who were sick or injured. During her lifetime, Anne had been quite sure that her medicine was more

Fig 5.3. St Mary's Church, Newchurch in Pendle

powerful than Old Dimdike's and that she was more skilled than her in the things she could do. There is no way she would have thought of herself as being second in skill or importance to Elizabeth.

Anne had made and sold what she referred to as 'smell-bags'. These were different mixtures of dried herbs and plants wrapped in small pieces of cloth. Anne thought that the healing properties of plants lay in their smell. (It is possible that Anne believed in miasma theory: that 'bad air' or bad smells from things such as rotting organic waste caused people to become sick.) Anne's smell-bags could be used in two ways, either dry or wet, depending on the health complaint. For example, someone with a cough would be advised to sleep with a dry smell-bag on their pillow and inhale the aroma, and someone with a headache would be advised to wet a smell-bag and place it on their head. Anne also sold smell-bags designed to keep insects away from the home and instructed people to keep them in their beds. In the seventeenth century, we know that the poorer sort slept on mattresses and pillows stuffed with natural materials which would harbour all kinds of bugs. Human fleas and lice were commonplace, and a dirty straw bed, warmed by several bodies, was the perfect breeding ground for disease. Solutions to infestations were sought out during the era.

At one point in *The Wonderfull Discoverie*, Potts writes that James Device had confessed that Anne once took some skulls from Newchurch Cemetery:

> And further saith [James Device], That twelve years agoe, the said Anne Chattox at a Buriall at the new Church in Pendle, did take three scalpes [skulls] of people, which had been buried, and then cast out of a grave, as she the said Chattox told this Examinate; and took eight teeth out of the said Scalpes, whereof she kept foure to her selfe, and gave other foure to the said Demdike, this Examinates Grand-mother: which foure teeth now shewed to this Examinate, are the foure teeth that the said Chattox gave to his Grand-mother, as aforesaid; which said teeth have ever since been kept, until now

> found by the said Henry Hargreives and this Examinate, at the West-End of this Examinates Grand-mothers house, and there buried in the earth, and a Picture of Clay there likewise found by them, about halfe a yard over in the earth, where the said teeth lay, which said picture so found, was almost withered away, and was the Picture of Anne, Anthony Nutters daughter; as this Examinates Grand-mother told him.[20]

The 1604 Witchcraft Act stated that it was a capital offence to use any part of a corpse as part of witchcraft, sorcery, charm, or enchantment. Anne wants it to be known that the teeth 'uncovered' by the constable in the Device family home (which inspired this tale) were family members' teeth. There was a superstitious belief that teeth brought good luck, so when teeth fell out, they were often kept in people's homes to stave off adversity.

Anne Whittle still has a great deal of anger about how she came to die and has been unable to find real peace. She stresses that nothing she had ever done in her life justified the evil cruelty she was subjected to as an elderly woman. She grows weary of hearing people casually state that the Pendle Witches should be pardoned. 'Talked about, talked about, but never put right,' she complains. She wants the world to know the truth and for her name to be cleared. This is the least we could do for her.

Elizabeth Device

Advantageously for Roger Nowell, both the Sowthernes/Device and Whittle/Redferne families had bad reputations, making it easier for him to use them to advance his career. Both families had sometimes bullied and scared their neighbours to get what they wanted – or *needed* in order to survive – more is the point. They were not well-liked as a result, and Nowell had gambled that there would be few who would openly question his motivation for sending them to Lancaster Castle. Nowell had been most eager to examine Alizon Device, recognizing that witch trials often drew the attention of the King. After Alizon gave him reason to arrest her grandmother and Anne Whittle, Nowell's ambition quickly grew; if he played his cards right, this could be the trial that made his career – as long as the right verdicts were reached, that is.

Our spirit guide has made us aware that Nowell's life got better as he arrested more and more people on suspicion of practising witchcraft; people looked up to him because he was seen to have control over the bad and the evil. JP Nicholas Bannester had been quick to get in on the action by helping and encouraging Nowell to conduct further interviews. Thanks to the spirit of Bannester's wife (who unexpectedly came to communicate with us), we learned that Bannester had seen a chance to 'clean up the place'. Peasants' lives meant nothing to Bannester. He saw an opportunity to send as many troublemakers as possible to

Fig 5.4. A beggar woman with three young children.
Etching with engraving by J. Callot, c.1622

the gallows: what better way was there to be rid of the local disturbers of the peace than by making them out to be witches. (Like Potts and Nowell, Bannester was also asked if he feels any remorse for the part he played in the trials. But unlike them, he declined to answer.)

The next obvious targets on Nowell's list were Elizabeth and James Device. But despite the fact that the Device family had a bad reputation – in the sense that they were deemed to be untrustworthy people – Nowell actually struggled to find any accusations of witchcraft to levy against them. Potts' pamphlet states that Alizon Device, Elizabeth Sowthernes, Anne Whittle, and Anne Redferne were sent to Lancaster Castle around 2 April.[1] Elizabeth and James Device were examined by Nowell some twenty-five days later, and this gap of almost four weeks can be seen as an indication that the four women had not made any accusations of Elizabeth or James being involved with witchcraft, for if they had done so, Nowell would have arrested them immediately. Sadly for the mother and son, Nowell eventually did find reason enough to arrest them.

The testimonies of Elizabeth Sowthernes and Alizon Device both refer to a disagreement between the Device family members and local miller Richard Baldwyn:

Testimony of Elizabeth Sowthernes:

> And upon her examination, she [Elizabeth Sowthernes] further confesseth, and saith. That a little before Christmas last, this Examinates Daughter [Elizabeth Device] having been to helpe Richard Baldwyns Folkes at the Mill: This Examinates Daughter did bid her this Examinate goe to the said Baldwyns house, and aske him some

thing for helping of his Folkes at the Mill, (as aforesaid:) and in this Examinates going to the said Baldwyns house, and neere to the said house, she mette with the said Richard Baldwyn; Which Baldwyn sayd to this Examinate and the said Alizon Device (who at that time ledde this Examinate, being blinde) get out of my ground Whores and Witches, I will burne the one of you, and hang the other. To whom this Examinate answered: I care not for thee, hang thy selfe.[2]

Testimony of Alizon Device:

And further this Examinate sayth, that Richard Baldwin of Weethead within the Forrest of Pendle, about 2. Yeeres agoe, fell out with this Examinates Graund-mother, and so would not let her come upon his Land: and about foure or five dayes then next after, her said Graund-mother did request this Examinate to lead her foorth about ten of the clocke in the night: which this Examinate accordingly did, and she stayed foorth then about an houre, and this Examinates sister fetched her in againe. And this Examinate heard the next morning, that a woman Child of the sayd Richard Baldwins was fallen sicke; and as this Examinate did then heare, the sayd Child did languish afterwards by the space of a yeare, or thereaboutes, and dyed: And this Examinate verily thinketh, that her said Graund-mother did bewitch the sayd child to death.

And further, this Examinate sayth, that she heard her sayd Graund-mother say presently after her falling out with the sayd Baldwin, shee would pray for the sayd Baldwin both still and loud: and this Examinate heard her cursse the sayd Baldwin sundry times.[3]

In general, millers did not have the best reputations. An anecdote in *The Annals of Colne* shows that, in 1596, the inhabitants of Colne and Marsden complained that 'the Towneleys and their miller, Stephen Hargreaves, exact and take excessive and undue toll at the Colne Water Corn Mill'.[4] Proceedings were instituted in the Duchy Court, where it was explained that in recompense for the grinding of their corn, the locals who were under suit and soak (meaning those who were obliged to have their corn ground at the Townley mill as part of their tenancy agreements, and in addition were also obliged to contribute to the repair of the mill) were in the habit of bestowing on the miller 'some small benevolence in meall, of meare goodwill, some more, and some lesse, as was thought good to them'.[5] They went on to allege that the Townleys often pretended that they had received less corn than had been brought to them, either on horseback or in 'winne or cartte'. The Townleys denied this and argued that they were entitled to 'one mette out of every thirty mettes brought, for mulcture and toll'.[6] (Mulcture was the portion of the ground grain millers were entitled to in lieu of a money payment.)

There is very little on record about Richard Baldwyn's character or his mill, but the spirits of the Pendle Witches have helped us to find the cause of the Device/Baldwyn conflict: Elizabeth Device had found occasional cleaning work at the mill. (More often than not, she was paid to sweep the floor.) On one occasion, Richard Baldwyn had heard that to try and earn extra money, Elizabeth was providing sexual favours for the workmen (possibly even his own son), and he instantly dismissed her for it. A little while later, most aggrieved to learn that Baldwyn had not paid her daughter the money owed for her cleaning work, Elizabeth Sowthernes set off for Baldwyn's home, accompanied by Alizon. But on seeing their approach, he had barred them from entering through his gate, shouting that the Device family were whores, witches, and simpletons and were not welcome on his land.

When her husband, John Device, died circa 1600, life had become very hard for Elizabeth Device and her children. The family had lost their main breadwinner. (The same scenario, we are informed, had also happened to her mother, Elizabeth, who also became a widow with children to care for.) In the seventeenth century, families without a male head of household were vulnerable: easily exploited and abused. There was also a stigma attached to matriarchal households, for they went against the natural order of things, and households headed by more elderly women were stigmatized even more, for there was a common fear that post-menopausal women gained magical power. Elizabeth had always been of a placid nature, but following the death of her husband, she became depressed, anxious, and more prone to anger, for life was now an uphill struggle. She struggled to find enough food and money to keep her children alive, and her mind knew little peace. (Even when she obtained food, she constantly worried about where the next meal would come from.) Over time, Elizabeth's demeanour hardened as she tried to provide for her family in whatever way she could. On occasion, she had even resorted to prostitution.

John Device was unwell, with a series of different health problems, for a long period of time before his eventual death. This meant that he was less able to work and provide for his family. As a result, in order to feed her children, Elizabeth secretly began resorting to 'the most ancient mode of income' when John was still alive. Doing so was not without consequence, for she became pregnant, and although she tried to hide her growing belly, her husband eventually realized that she was with child and knew the baby could not be his own. This led to a great argument between the couple. A baby girl was born shortly after John died, and although she carried his surname, the truth is that Jennet Device was not the daughter of John Device. The birth of her youngest daughter caused Elizabeth Device greater anxiety still, for she now had another mouth to feed.

Moving forward to the year 1612, in order to be able to arrest her, Roger Nowell was searching for evidence of the widow Elizabeth Device having been involved in any criminal activity. Looking back over his records, he found a potential bastardy case which had never amounted to anything at the time. But, with a little digging, he discovered that the proposed fathers of the bastard child had since died, and with a little embellishment, their deaths could easily be turned into evidence of her having practised witchcraft. Elizabeth was interviewed by Nowell and Bannester on 27 April 'at the house of James Wilsey' (Ashlar House, in Fence.)[7] According to *The Wonderfull Discoverie*, she confessed to using witchcraft to murder two men called John Robinson (alias Swyer) and James Robinson because they scolded her for having an illegitimate child.[8] The only truth here is that Elizabeth Device knew that one of these men was Jennet's biological father, but she did not know which one. And that, in the past, she had approached and argued with both of them to encourage them to provide for Jennet – but had not benefitted from doing so.

Nowell wrote that Elizabeth had used 'pictures of clay' to kill her victims. At the end of Elizabeth Sowthernes' trial notes, Potts inserted the following fabricated confession to explain how these objects were made and used:

And further this Examinate confesseth, and sayth, that the speediest way to take a mans life away by Witchcraft, is to make a Picture of Clay, like unto the shape of the person whom they meane to kill, and dry it thorowly: and when they would have them to be ill in any one place more then an other; then take a Thorne or Pinne, and pricke it in that part of the Picture you would so have be ill: and when you would have any part of the Body to consume away, then take that part of the Picture, and burne it. And when they would have the whole body to consume away, then take the remnant of the sayd Picture, and burne it: and so thereupon by the meanes, the body shall die.[9]

Fig 5.5. The Devil (or a demon) hands out effigies to four witches. Woodcut, 1720

When Nowell had Constable Hargreives search the Device family home for evidence of witchcraft, a tiny amount of misshapen, dried-out clay had been discovered. When Nowell told Elizabeth that a crumbled clay effigy had been uncovered in her home, she responded that this item must have been one of her daughter Jennet's toys. Elizabeth Device informed us that much like many children today enjoy playing with modelling clay, in the seventeenth century, many children also used clay to make what the Device family referred to as 'clay dolls'. (There was a lot of clay in the area, some fields even bear the name Marl Field.) During long winter evenings, many parents of the poorest children also took pleasure in making funny-shaped little people and animals to entertain their child for a few hours or days. Inevitably, sooner or later, they would begin to dry and crumble. This so-called diabolical picture of clay was nothing more than the remains of an innocent child's toy.

Potts is particularly cruel in the way he describes Elizabeth Device:

> This odious Witch was branded with a preposterous marke in Nature, even from her birth, which was her left eye, standing lower than the other; the one looking downe, the other looking up, so strangely deformed, as the best that were present in that Honorable assembly, and great Audience, did affirme, they had not often seene the like.[10]

> Barbarous and inhumane Monster, beyond example; so farre from sensible understanding of thy own miserie, as to bring thy owne naturall children into mischiefe and bondage; and thy selfe to be a witnesse upon the Gallowes, to see thy owne children by thy devilish instructions hatcht up in Villanie and Witchcraft, to suffer with thee, even in the beginning of their time, a shamefull and untimely Death.[11]

There was a common perception that witches had physical disabilities; superstitions abounded that 'unnatural deformities' were caused by the Devil. By making out that the audience at court could hardly bring themselves to look upon the face of Elizabeth Device – her being such a grotesque creature – Potts was intentionally playing to this stereotype. While it was true that Elizabeth did have a facial abnormality, it was a very minor and common abnormality; she simply had a turned eye. At the time of her trial, she also had significant swelling and bruising to her face. So, by convincing the reader that her 'unusual appearance' was further proof that she had consorted with demons, Potts was also deflecting from the reality of her having sustained physical injuries during her imprisonment at Lancaster Castle.

The Good Friday Meeting

The Following extract is reproduced from *The Wonderfull Discoverie of Witches in the Countie of Lancaster*:

Heere this worthy Justice M. *Nowell*, out of these particular Examinations, or rather Accusations, finding matter to proceed; and having now before him old Demdike, old Chattox, Alizon Device and Redferne both old and young, *Reos confitentes, et Accusantes Inuicem*. About the second of Aprill last past, committed and sent them away to the Castle at Lancaster, there to remaine untill the coming of the Kinges Majesties Justices of Assise, then to receive their tryall.

But heere they had not stayed a weeke, when their Children and Friendes being abroad at libertie, laboured a speciall meeting at *Malking Tower* in the Forrest of *Pendle*, upon Good-fryday, within a weeke after they were committed, of all the most dangerous, wicked, and damnable Witches in the Country farre and neere. Upon Good-fryday they met, according to solemne appoyntment, solemnized this great Feastivall day according to their former order, with great cheare, merry company, and much conference.

In the end, in this great Assemblie, it was decreed M. *Couell* [the gaoler] by reason of his Office, shall be slaine before the next Assises: The Castle of *Lancaster* to be blowen up, and ayde and assistance to be sent to kill M. Lister, with his old Enemie and wicked Neighbour *Jennet Preston*; with some other such like practices; as upon their Arraignement and Tryall, are particularly set foorth, and given in evidence against them.

This was no secret, but some notice of it came to M. *Nowell*, and by his great paines taken in the Examination of *Jennet Device*, al their practices are now made knowen. Their purpose to kill M. *Couell*, and blow up the Castle, is prevented. All their Murders, Witchcraftes, Inchauntments, Charmes, and Sorceries, are discovered; and even in the middest of their Consultations, they are all confounded, and arrested by Gods Justice: brough before M. *Nowell*, and M. *Bauester* [Bannester], upon their voluntary confessions, Examinations, and other Evidence accused, and so by them committed to the Castle: So as now both old and young, have taken up their lodgings with M. *Couell*, until the next Assises, expecting their Tryall and deliveraunce, according to the Lawes provided for such like.

In the meane time, M. *Nowell* having knowledge by this discovery of their meeting at *Malking Tower*, and their resolution to execute mischief, takes great paines to apprehend such as were at libertie, and prepared Evidence against all such as were in question for Witches.[1]

James Device

Our spirit guide has made it clear that James Device had a learning disability. During his lifetime, he gave such little thought to the consequences of his actions that many of his neighbours regarded him to be intellectually weak. When Richard Baldwyn barked the derogatory word *simpleton* in the direction of Alizon and her grandmother, he was referring to James Device. The miller had long since refused to allow James anywhere near his property, considering him to be a liability.

Potts records James's occupation as a labourer.[1] He was the eldest child of Elizabeth and John Device and their only surviving son. As he grew into adulthood, his mother became frustrated with James because he was not bringing enough money home. But the reality was that his disability prevented him from understanding and fulfilling family responsibilities. Alice Nutter informed us that James was a notorious fibber and that he frequently told fibs to Alizon. This was the main source of tension between the siblings. He often convinced himself that the lies he told, as he sat warming his big stockinged feet over the hearth, were true, and Alizon, being of a credulous nature, had often believed him. As we shall see, the lies James went on to tell Roger Nowell would result in gaoler Thomas Couell ensuring that he suffered immensely under his charge. The balding, sweat-stained, well-built turn-key showed utter contempt towards this young man. Consequently, by the time of his trial, James was near to death and had to be physically held up to hear his arraignment. This startling image stuck in Potts' mind, and he felt the need to offer a defensive explanation for his shocking appearance:

> This wicked and miserable Wretch, whether by practise, or meanes, to bring himself to some untimely death, and thereby to avoide his Tryall by his Countrey, and just judgement of the Law; or ashamed to bee openly charged with so many devillish practices, and so much innocent bloud as hee had spilt; or by reason of his Imprisonment so long time before his Tryall (which was with more favour, commiseration, and reliefe then hee deserved) I know not: But being brought forth to the Barre, to receive his Triall before this worthie Judge, and so Honourable and Worshipfull an Assembly of Justices for this service, was so insensible, weake and unable in all thinges, as he could neither speake, heare, or stand, but was holden up when hee was brought to the place of his Arraignement, to receive his triall.[2]

While searching for a reason to arrest James during the summer of 1612, Nowell had managed to find a farmer from Barley called John Robinson who professed that the young man had stolen one of his sheep sometime ago and that he was most happy to see James be punished for it. (We do not know why John Robinson had not sought justice sooner.) In addition, Master Towneley of Carre Hall declared that he knew James and Elizabeth Device were thieves. Around two years prior, his wife 'charging this Examinate [James] and his said mother, to have stolne some turues [turf] of hers, badde him packe the doores: and withall as he went forth of the doore, the said Mistriss Towneley gave him a knock between the shoulders'.[3] This second accusation of theft had more gravitas because Mistress Towneley had since passed away from ill health. Nowell easily turned her death into an act of witchcraft, writing that James met with 'a thing like unto a black dog' two days after the quarrel who convinced him to make and slowly crumble a picture of clay of Mistress Towneley as revenge for her ill-treatment.[4]

Fig 5.6. A male vinegar seller with his donkey. Etching from The Cryes of the City of London Drawne after the Life. After M. Laroon, 1688

We have learned that James had found occasional work at Carre Hall, helping to maintain the piggery. We also know that he could be incredibly rude, which could be another explanation as to why Mistress Towneley had thumped him in the back and bid him to leave her home. James was someone who would think nothing of being disrespectful to people. He would even conduct the ultimate insult of showing his bare backside to those whom he believed deserved it! James's questionable behaviour played a big part in the formation of the family's bad reputation. But he was unaware of the harm he was causing.

Nowell's interview with James led to the arrest of five other local people. He had named those who had visited the family home since his sister and grandmother were arrested, and Nowell searched for as much dirt as possible on the named associates of the Device household. According to Potts, James claimed the following people had recently visited Malkin Tower:

> The wife of Hugh Hargreives of Barley; the wife of Christopher Bulcock [Jane Bulcock] of the Mosse end, and John her sonne; the mother of Myles Nutter [Alice Nutter]; Elizabeth, the wife of Christopher Hargreives, of Thurniholme; Christopher Howgate, and Elizabeth his wife; Alice Graye of Coulne, and one Mould-heeles wife, of the same [Katherine Hewit].[5]

Potts' pamphlet informs us that Christopher Howgate was Jennet Device's uncle.[6] Elizabeth Sowthernes has confirmed that Christopher is her son. (It is not difficult to see why he would have gone to the Device household around the time of the arrest of his mother.) Nowell could not find anyone willing to accuse Mrs Hargreives or Christopher and Elizabeth Howgate of participating in criminal activity. This, it transpires, is why they were not examined or incarcerated. Sadly, it was a different story for the other locals on James's list, thanks to his penchant for telling a tall tale. The magistrate's main objective was to link those named to recent deaths or ill health in the community. James Device was instrumental in making this happen. His particular learning difficulty meant that he could not see that he was putting his family and neighbours in harm's way. James was not really aware of other people's suffering; he lacked empathy.

Some individuals today, just like James, need extra support to understand spoken information and explain themselves. In the seventeenth century, Roger Nowell actively sought to exploit this young man's vulnerability and used him as a pawn. (There would be no mention of his mental capacity in court.) He was someone whom Nowell could get to say almost anything he wanted. During his interview with Nowell, the magistrate told James Device that he had been arrested for being a thief and a witch and tricked him into believing that his life would be spared if he told him everything he knew about the other local witches. Even though he did not really know much about witches, James, gullibly believing that he would be set free if he did what Nowell wanted, was most eager to please him.

It was not long before Lister junior and JP Thomas Heyber came to hear about the arrests in Pendle and the greater renown Nowell was already receiving. Heyber had just failed to get a witch-hanging under his belt, but now a new opportunity to do so had presented itself. After learning that the associates of the Device family were being rounded up, Heyber and Lister junior wanted Nowell to add Jennet Preston to the list. By placing Jennet Preston at Malkin Tower, they could build a stronger case against her, and they felt confident they would achieve the outcomes they desired. From their perspective, it was the right place, the right time.

When we asked Lister junior why he wanted Jennet to hang, his response was a nonchalant, 'Why her? Why not her.' Lister junior hated Jennet Preston, and he wanted her dead. (No further explanation is deemed necessary by Lister junior.) He seems to have believed that the privilege he was born with gave him the right to decide who was worthy of life. His father-in-law, Thomas Heyber, has been a little more forthcoming with information, expressing that at the time of Jennet's first trial, he thought the successful prosecution of a witch would bring him greater renown. Prestige was also his primary motive for prosecuting Jennet Preston on the second occasion, and because she had been formally accused of practising witchcraft, Jennet was now a prime suspect for whatever crime they invented.

Nowell decided that this would be an advantageous move for him too, not merely because it would be good to be owed a favour by Lister junior, but because he was also looking to place more people at Malkin Tower. And so the men conspired to exploit James's vulnerability to help secure a conviction against Jennet Preston. Under Nowell's order, James travelled to Gisburn with Constable Henry Hargreives and identified Jennet as having been in his family home.[7] Nowell had made him feel as though he was incredibly important and specially chosen to assist in the arrest of this odious witch. Having the type of power to arrest people had appealed to James greatly, and, with his chest puffed out, he had happily marched to Gisburn to capture a witch. Nevertheless, his enthusiasm aside, the reality was that Jennet Preston had never been to Malkin Tower, James had no clue who she was, and when they arrived in Gisburn, she had to be pointed out to him.

The idea of the Good Friday meeting was born out of James's own testimony. Those named as having visited Malkin Tower over the past few weeks would all be accused by Nowell of being part of a witches' sabbath. It turns out that James *had* once stolen a sheep from John Robinson, and although this occurred long before Good Friday 1612, Nowell (as we know) was not afraid to put a spin on the truth. With a degree of artistic licence, he manipulated the timeline, using this former crime as further evidence of the recent diabolical meeting of witches at Malkin Tower:

> Upon Shear-Thursday last, in the evening, he this Examinate stole a Wether from John Robinson of Barley, and brought it to his Grand-mothers house, old Demdike, and there killed it: and upon the day following, being Good-Friday about twelve of the clocke in the day time, there dined in this Examinates mothers house a number of persons, whereof three were men, with this Examinate, and the rest women.[8]

The implication was that on a day when they should have been mourning the crucifixion of the Lord Jesus Christ, the local witches were communing and dining with the Devil. Potts later added that 'the Devill did but labour to assemble them together' to labour the point.[9]

As well as being successful in getting James to name people who had recently visited his family home, Nowell was also successful in getting James to say *why* they had been there. He repeated what he had heard them discussing: they were eager to hear more about the demonic dog that lamed the pedlar, he said. Nowell then asked if they had referred to this demonic creature by name. James thought about this question for a minute and said they did not know its name because Alizon was not there to tell them the answer. With a little manipulation, this became the first of a list of three reasons Nowell created for why the diabolical meeting (or sabbath) had taken place:

> The first [reason] was, for the naming of the Spirit which Alizon Device, now prisoner at Lancaster, had, but did not name him, because she was not there.[10]

Nowell changed James's words to make it appear as though the witches had planned to participate in a communal act of ceremonial magic.

The third reason for the meeting was added to ensure that Jennet Preston would hang:

> And the third Cause [reason] was, for that there was a woman dwelling in Gisborne Parish, who came into this Examinates said Grandmothers house, who there came and craved assistance of the rest of them that were then there, for the killing of Master Lister of Westby [Lister junior], because (as shee then said) he had borne malice unto her, and had thought to have put her away at the last Assizes at Yorke, but could not.[11]

Nowell got James to agree that the witches conspired to help Jennet Preston kill Lister junior. He then wrote that James saw Jennet 'had a Spirit with her, like unto a White Foale, with a blacke spot in the forehead'.[12] Presumably, this spirit was supposed to be her familiar, a detail which would strengthen the case against her in Nowell's opinion.

Potts even notes that Nowell sent some of the testimony to York so that it could be read aloud during her second trial.[13]

The second reason for the meeting is the most well-known. It came about because James had informed Nowell that some neighbours visited Malkin Tower to discuss whether anything could be done to help get Alizon and Elizabeth Sowthernes back home. (It seems like this would have been the natural desire of someone like Christopher Howgate who wanted to save his mother and niece from the noose.) Nowell saw yet more opportunity in James's words. Could he get James to confess to overhearing his relatives and neighbours plotting to use witchcraft to set them free? He pressed James to tell him how they intended to help them. To answer this question, James, with his child-like mind, thought about how *he* would get his sister and grandmother out of prison – the solution came to him quickly – he would kill the gaoler and blow up the castle. Nowell could not believe his luck, for this far-fetched treasonous answer was better than anything he could have dreamt up himself:

> The second Cause [reason] was, for the deliverie of his said Grandmother; this Examinates said sister Alizon; the said Anne Chattox, and her daughter Redferne; killing the Gaoler at Lancaster; and before the next Assizes to blow up the Castle there, to the end the aforesaid persons might by that meanes make an escape and get away.[14]

When Nowell had everything he needed from James, he packed him off to Lancaster Castle along with his mother. James could not understand why this was happening; he had done everything Nowell asked. Gaoler Thomas Couell eagerly awaited the arrival of the miserable wretch who had dared to threaten his life. Taking his threats incredibly seriously, it was not long before he dragged James out of his cell, demanding to know how he intended to blow up the castle and how he was planning to murder him. James was terrified. All he could offer up now was a feeble, 'I don't know!'

Fig 5.7. Ashlar House, Fence

Fig 5.8. Samlesbury Hall, Preston

Alice Nutter

> The two degrees of persons which chiefly practise Witchcraft, are such, as are in great miserie and povertie, for such the Devill allures to follow him, by promising great riches, and worldly commoditie; Others, though rich, yet burne in a desperate desire of Revenge; Hee allures them by promises, to get their turne satisfied to their hearts contentment, as in the whole proceedings against old Chattox: the examinations of old Demdike; and her children, there was not one of them, but have declared the like, when the Devill first assaulted them.
>
> Thomas Potts, *The Wonderfull Discoverie*

Here we see how King James's *Daemonologie* directly influenced the Pendle Witch Trials, for the opinion above concerning who was more likely to be attracted to witchcraft was that of the reigning monarch. (Arguably, the leading authority on witches and witchcraft in England in the early seventeenth century.) King James had reasoned that the Devil drew people to witchcraft by tempting 'three passiones that are within our selves: Curiositie in great ingines [a desire for knowledge (particularly to know the future)]: thrist of [desire for] revenge, for some tortes deeply apprehended: or greedie appetite of geare, caused through great poverty'.[1] In the King's opinion, curiosity was the 'inticement of Magiciens or Necromanciers', not of witches. (Or, in other words, wealthy scholars.) Witches were

Fig 5.9. An old woman praying the Rosary. Etching possibly after J. Callot

people drawn to witchcraft to carry out acts of vengeance or to gain relief from poverty.[2]

For the most part, Potts had been able to satisfy himself that the witches at the Lancashire Assizes had been seeking revenge or riches, but Alice Nutter of the Forrest of Pendle was problematic, for she was neither poor nor vengeful: 'For it is certaine she was a rich woman; had a great estate, and children of good hope: in the common opinion of the world, of good temper, free from envy or malice'.[3] Potts acknowledged that to 'attempt [tempt] this woman in that sort, the Divel had small meanes'.[4] The clerk could only surmise that she might have been swayed by the other witches or else by some other 'unfortunate occasion'.[5] Because she did not fit the mould, Potts emphasizes that Judge Bromley devised a test of innocence, or 'an extraordinary meanes of Triall, to marke her out from the rest'.[6] The challenge for the prosecution was to find evidence which would convince the gentlemen of the jury that this respectable woman was a witch. We shall soon see that this 'remarkable test' was really carried out to ensure that Alice and as many of the other alleged witches as possible were found guilty and convicted.

Alice was arraigned on 19 August for the murder of Henry Mitton by witchcraft. The evidence against her came from the testimony of James Device, taken before Nowell and Bannester on 27 April.[7] James lied that he heard his grandmother say that she and his mother, together with 'the wife of Richard Nutter of the Rough-Lee, Alice Nutter the prisoner aforesaid . . . had killed one Henry Mitton, of the Rough-Lee aforesaid, by Witchcraft' for refusing to give his grandmother a penny.[8] Similarly, according to *The Wonderfull Discoverie*, James's mother confessed to Nowell that she and the two other women had 'joyned altogether' and bewitched Henry Mitton to death.[9] In reality, Elizabeth Device confessed to no such thing.

Of all those accused at the assizes, Alice Nutter receives the most public sympathy. (She even has her own memorial statue.) Many people regard her as the innocent party or the only real victim of the trials. Bizarrely, more than 400 years later, they still hold on to the Jacobean notion that witches were poor or vengeful (and real, of course). As a result, they are reluctant to accept the possibility that Alice Nutter was a witch and yet have been only too willing to accept that the remainder of the accused who were portrayed by Potts as jealous beggars, were guilty as charged.

Two defensive explanations for why Alice came to find herself on trial for witchcraft have been posed. The most persistent conspiracy theory is that Alice was a Catholic recusant, tried as a witch because of her adherence to the Catholic faith. The recusant theory probably grew out of the fact that two people with the same surname were hanged, drawn, and quartered for being Roman Catholic priests – John Nutter was hung in 1583, and his brother Robert in 1600.[10] (The family name of Nutter is one of the most ancient and abundant names in the Forest of Pendle and we do not know if these men were directly related to Alice's husband, Richard.) Intriguingly, we do have some evidence of the northern JPs being under pressure to prosecute non-conformists (those who refused to submit to authority) at the exact same time as Nowell began collecting evidence of acts of witchcraft in and around Pendle.

In March 1612, all Lancastrian justices of the peace received an order from London to report those who refused to take communion in church: 'The council ordered that on Easter Sunday (8 April) notice should be read from every pulpit in the county that non-communicants had twenty days in which to conform or be listed for prosecution.'[11] Arresting suspected witches who were also known to have Catholic sympathies was, arguably, all the better for the reputation of the JP, but the idea of hanging Alice Nutter as a witch simply because she was a Catholic does not hold much water, for half of Lancashire (including many JPs themselves) would have been hung as witches if this were the case.

Those found to be harbouring Catholic priests could be dealt with more severely, but more generally, recusants were punished by way of fines or loss of property (thus benefitting the crown's coffers), not by loss of life. After the Gunpowder Plot was foiled in 1605, it is thought that many of the Catholics involved fled to Lancashire, a county known to be a Catholic stronghold. In May 1606, to guarantee the loyalty of King James's subjects, the Popish Recusants Act was passed. Recusants were to be fined £60 or made to forfeit two-thirds of their land if they did not take communion at least once a year in their parishes.[12]

Another conspiracy theory which has grown in popularity is that Alice Nutter was killed because of a land dispute between herself and Roger Nowell. Clayton suggested in 2007 that this theory possibly grew out of the fact that Nowell was involved in various land disputes with the Whitakers of Simonstone.[13] Local author Gladys Whitaker had previously linked Alice to this surname (though not the same branch of the family). We know from *The Wonderfull Discoverie* that Alice had a husband called Richard whose father's name was Myles. (Alice and Richard had a son called Myles and other children who are not named.) The 1561 Clitheroe Court Rolls mention that a Miles Nutter, his wife, Elizabeth Nutter, and their son, Richard Nutter (presumed by Gladys Whitaker to be Alice's husband and in-laws), requested the surrender of half a farm property in Roughlee. Half of the farm which was being used by James Whittaker, his brother John, and some other people, was surrendered to Miles and Elizabeth Nutter for their use. It was also determined that upon their deaths, a quarter share was to go to ' "Alice Nutter, now wife of the said Richard Nutter for life, in the name of her dower." The remainder of the property was to go to Richard and his heirs.'[14] Gladys Whittaker states that at the time of their marriages, the wives of James and John Whitaker were also to receive 'one fourth part' of their husband's property for life. To her, this suggested that James and John Whitaker had been Alice's representatives at the time of her marriage and were therefore likely to be her brothers.[15] (This is a somewhat convoluted argument and maybe a bit of wishful thinking on the author's part due to her surname.) It was actually not that unusual for a relatively wealthy husband to leave a dower like this to provide for his wife in the event that she should become widowed. This was different from a *dowry* which was property a wife brought to her husband when married (although the term dower is often used to describe both circumstances). The truth is the conspiracy theory that Roger Nowell murdered Alice Nutter because of a land dispute has nothing in the way of physical evidence to back it up.

Part of the folklore surrounding Alice Nutter is that she lived at the late sixteenth-century Roughlee Old Hall. Given Potts' description of a wealthy woman from Roughlee, this was an obvious conclusion to jump to, and perhaps William Harrison Ainsworth's romantic novel *The Lancashire Witches* reinforced the belief. However, Gladys Whitaker's research into occupiers of the hall uncovered no evidence of her ever having lived there, and now the consensus amongst historians is that Alice Nutter lived in the hamlet of Crowtrees. Alice Nutter has informed us that she lived in the Thorneyholme area and that her home is still standing but has been extended over the years. Her husband had been a yeoman, and she had enjoyed cooking for him and her children. Alice describes herself as being a superstitious woman.

Much has been made of her silence during the trial, for Potts makes no mention of Alice attempting to defend herself, and some authors have taken this silence to be contrition. Alice's response to the medium's question of why she did not speak up for herself was that she was a clever enough woman for the time but lacked any power. On trial for her life, she described the courtroom as a place filled with anger; there was simply too much anger from all involved, and she understood that only God had the power to help her now. (Alice's words give the impression that by the time of her trial, the crowds in the courtroom were baying for blood.) We must remember that during the seventeenth century, there was no such thing as a fair trial for alleged felons, for they were not given any legal representation. The accused were presumed guilty (not innocent) and were expected to defend themselves (if given the opportunity to). On top of that, given that witches did not have to be physically present to harm their victims and that gossip was often seen as sufficient evidence of guilt, how then was Alice supposed to prove that she did not use witchcraft to murder Henry Mitton? How could anyone prove that they were *not* a witch?

When we asked if she knew her alleged murder victim, Alice responded that she knew him from church. When asked why she was accused of witchcraft, she responded that she had been in the wrong place at the wrong time. She has affirmed that what was said in court about there being a diabolical meeting of witches at Malkin Tower was untrue, but nevertheless, she had been to the Device family's home. Alice had known the Device family and had empathy for them. On Good Friday, she lit a candle next to a small wooden cross in her home and said a prayer for the women who had been taken to Lancaster Castle. Her feeling was that the Lord would help. The following day, she set off for Blacko with some food she had prepared for Elizabeth, James, and Jennet Device. According to Alice, since the arrests were made, people had been visiting the Device family home, bringing prepared food or whatever they could spare. We might liken the situation to how friends and neighbours visit the households of those who have been recently bereaved, taking food to try and help or bring comfort in some way. But, of course, local people were not just visiting to offer their condolences; they were also equally concerned and intrigued by tales of recent events and had gone to the Device family home to find out exactly what had been happening. Alice, who was naturally a very calm person, had gone to lend her ear. The household, she says, was distraught, and mother Elizabeth Device showed the most obvious signs of despair – a mixture of sorrow and anger. Alice recalls how sad it was seeing Elizabeth Sowthernes' chair sitting empty. It was a humble wooden structure; the seat and back were made from horizontal strips of rag, some coloured, some undyed.

During later life, Alice suffered from severe arthritis in her lower back and left foot, and Elizabeth Sowthernes made potions from the herb comfrey for Alice to help her condition. Alice would give Elizabeth prepared food, eggs, or money as payment. The relationship between the two women became stronger after Richard Nutter died, for he had not wanted his wife to associate with her. Things had gotten very heated when he had learned of their occasional meeting (after Alice had presented him with some of Elizabeth's medicine to help with his foot pain). Alice saw value in Elizabeth's medicine and learned a lot from her. She even copied some recipes. (Interestingly, comfrey is still used today to treat inflammatory conditions, so Elizabeth's recipe probably did have medicinal value.) We asked Alice if she knew Anne Whittle, and she answered that she did not have dealings with Anne Whittle because it was better to deal with one of them, not both. (This comment hints at the rivalry which existed between Demdike and Chattox.) Very sadly for Alice, because they knew that their mother interacted with the Devices, her own family did not give her much support around the time of the trials. Due to this association alone, they came to question whether their own mother was, in fact, a witch.

Fig 5.10. The Alice Nutter memorial statue, Roughlee

6

How to Hang a Witch

The Samlesbury Witches

When it came to condemning witches, King James had a couple of warnings for judges. The first was that 'to spare the life, and not strike when God bids strike, and so severelie punish in so odious a fault and treason against God, it is not only unlawful, but doubtlesse no lesse sinne in that Magistrate . . . comparable to the sin of Witch-craft itselfe'.[1] The second was that they 'ought indeede to beware whome they condemne: For it is a great crime (as Salomon sayeth,) To condemne the innocent, as to let the guiltie escape free'.[2] Admittedly, when it came to prosecuting witches, they were in a bit of a 'rock and hard place' scenario: on the one hand, being pressured into executing witches so as not to sin against God, and on the other hand, being warned to be a bit wary about executing witches so as not to sin against God! But it seems that the main point James was actually trying to make was that they 'ought to beware to condemne any, but such as they are sure are guiltie'.[3] Those in positions of judicial authority *must* have sufficient evidence of witchcraft to justify sending someone to their death.

The fact that witches did not have to be physically present to carry out a crime and could cause harm at a distance by nonphysical means made witchcraft different from all other crimes. Special provisions were therefore allowed in a court of law to establish guilt – all of which were regarded as sufficient proofs of witchcraft. Typically, when it came to prosecuting suspected witches, the prosecution was more interested in establishing the witch's motive (her desire for revenge or riches) than in establishing how the witch had carried out *maleficium*.[4] JPs were also directed to discover the following facts about accused felons, all of which could be used to decide whether they were innocent or guilty of the alleged crime:

> His parents, if they were wicked, and given to the same kind of fault. . . . His nature; if civill, or hastie, wittie and subtill, a quarreller, pilferer, or bloudie minded. . . . His trade, for if a man liveth idly or vagrant . . . it is a good cause to arrest him upon suspition, if there have been any felony committed. His companie; if Ruffians, suspected persons, or his being in companie with any [of] the offendors. His course of life . . . if a common Alehouse-haunter. . . . Whether he be of evil fame, or report.[5]

Although Judge Bromley was acutely aware that the lack of physical evidence in witch trials could be a stumbling block for jurors, he instructed them to ignore this thorny issue. In *The Wonderful Discoverie*, Potts asserts: 'Expect not, as this reverend and learned Judge saith, such apparent proofe against them, as against others, since all their workes, are the workes of darkenesse: and unless it please Almightie God to raise witnesses to accuse them, who is able to condemne them?'[6] Jurors were advised to give a great deal of credence to witness testimony. But a witness did not necessarily have to be someone who had seen the accused practising some form of witchcraft. They could simply be someone who had heard a rumour that the accused was a witch. In addition, when it came to witchcraft trials, an exception was made so that the jury could hear witness testimony from the types of people who, under normal circumstances, would not have been deemed credible, namely, other witches, known liars, and children. In *Daemonologie*, King James asserted:

> But in my opinion, since in a mater of treason against the Prince, barnes, or wives, or never diffamed persons, may of our law serve for sufficient witnesses and proofes. I thinke surely that by a far greater reason, such witnesses may be sufficient in matters of high treason against God: For who but Witches can be prooves, and so witnesses of the doings of Witches.[7]

King James's *Daemonologie* has the reputation of being a witch-hunter manual, much like the infamous *Malleus Maleficarum*, which was a deliberately frightening tale designed to terrify the reader into believing that witches are real and that they work for the Devil. But the King was trying to present a much more rational argument than had gone before, designed as much to ensure that the wrong people are not convicted, as the right people are. Unfortunately, his message of caution was lost on many of his subjects; many assumed they had been granted carte blanche to persecute suspected witches. Even after his death, this misconstrued message prevailed, and the self-appointed Witch-finder General, Matthew Hopkins, went on to create a living doing just that. (It is highly unlikely that the King would ever have foreseen that his words would enable a serial killer, but he was not known as 'the wisest fool in Christendom' for no reason!) Some modern historians have suggested that the King's belief in witchcraft started to waver as he became older, but this seems unlikely because, at heart, James was a king who was exceptionally nervous of conspiracy, and arguably with good reason too. His own father had been strangled, his mother was executed on the order of Queen Elizabeth I, there had been at least two attempts to kidnap James himself, and let's not forget the Gunpowder Plot. What really seems to have happened is that his belief in witches remained steadfast throughout his lifetime, but it became more apparent to the King that many of the accusations of witchcraft which resulted in convictions were fraudulent.

The following case, which was brought to James's attention in August 1605, reveals the true intent of the King. Now king of both Scotland and England, James became involved in a case of English witchcraft. At Exeter College Oxford, a wealthy man named Brian Gunter gained an audience with His Majesty, where he exclaimed that three witches had cursed his daughter Anne – she was suffering from convulsions and was even pulling pins from her nose. Rather than bringing the witches to justice (as Gunter had expected a king who had a reputation for being hellbent on persecuting witches would do), James ordered that the Archbishop of Canterbury examine Anne. It did not take the Archbishop long to determine that the accusations levied by her father were a lie, as Anne quickly confessed to putting the pins in her nose herself. Evidently, Gunter had been seeking revenge against these women and attempted to use the King, the law, and his own daughter to get it. Fortunately for the women, his plan backfired, and unfortunately for him, he was fined and imprisoned for three years.[8] Gunter had totally misread the new king of England but in doing so, had provided a clear demonstration to some of the cannier Englishmen in judicial authority that the exposure of false accusations of witchcraft was, in the King's eyes, as important a duty as the uncovering of witchcraft itself.

While it is true that ten individuals were condemned at the Lancashire Witch Trials in 1612, people often overlook the fact that seven individuals known as the Samlesbury Witches were acquitted. Potts writes about the trial of three of the seven alleged witches from Samlesbury. On the morning of 19 August, Judge Bromley presided over the trial of Jennet Bierley, Ellen Bierley, and Jane Southworth. The women were accused of using witchcraft 'upon one Grace Sowerbuts: so that meanes thereof her bodie wasted and consumed'.[9] The majority of testimony against these women came from their fourteen-year-old victim. We learn that Jennet was her grandmother, Ellen was her aunt and Henry Bierley's wife, and Jane was the widow of John Southworth. (Jane does not appear to have been a direct relation to either Grace or the other women.) Jane's late husband, John, was the son of Sir John Southworth of Samlesbury Hall, which, you may recall, was the home in which the pedlar's trunk had been hidden, and which harboured many a Catholic priest.

Grace testified that together with another woman called Old Doewife, the women 'did violently draw her by her haire of the head, and layd her on the toppe of a Hay-mowe, in the said Henry Bierleyes Barne'.[10] Not long after, Jennet appeared to Grace:

> In her own likenesse, and after that in the likenesse of a blacke Dogge, and as this Examinate did goe over a Style [stile], shee picked [pushed] her off: howbeit shee saith shee had no hurt then, but rose againe, and went to her Aunts in Osbaldeston, and returned backe againe to

> her Fathers house the same night, being fetched home by her father. And she saith, That in her way home-wards shee did then tell her Father, how shee had beene dealt withall both then and at sundry times before that.[11]

On Saturday, 2 April, Grace met again with Jennet at a place called Two Bridges. Similarly, she appeared first in her own likeness and then again in the shape of a black dog (but a black dog with two legs this time):

> Which Dogge went close by the left side of this Examinate, till they came to a Pitte of Water, and then the said Dogge spake, and persuaded this Examinate to drowne her selfe there, saying it was a faire and easie death: Whereupon this Examinate thought there came one to her in a white sheete, and carried her away from the said Pitte, upon the comming whereof the said blacke Dogge departed away; and shortly after the said white thing departed also.[12]

But that was not the end of it, for when she was only two or three fields distance away from the water, the black dog met her again and carried her into the barn of Hugh Walshman:

> [It] layed her upon the Barne-floore, and covered this Examinate with straw on her bodie, and Haye on her head, and the Dogge it selfe lay on toppe of the said straw . . . her speech and Senses were taken from her: and the first time shee knew where shee was, shee was layed upon a bedde in the said Walshmans house, which (as shee hath since beene told) was upon the Monday at night following.[13]

On Tuesday evening, when travelling home with her parents, Jennet and Ellen appeared again at Two Bridges, and Grace fell down and was unable to speak or walk until Friday. While she lay in her father's house, the two women appeared to her yet again but did nothing, and this was the last time she saw them.[14]

Grace also testified that sometime before these events, she, along with the three women on trial, had gone to Thomas Walshman's house. During the night, Jennet took 'a little child' from Walshman's bedchamber and 'thrust a naile into the navell of the said child: and afterwards did take a pen and put it in at the said place, and did suck there a good space [time], and afterwards laid the child in bed againe'.[15] The child languished and died soon after. After the burial of the child, Grace, Jennet, and Ellen went to the church and took the body of the child to Jennet's house 'and having it there did boile some thereof in a Pot, and some did broile on the coales, of both which the said Jennet and Ellen did eate'.[16] After which they did 'seethe the bones . . . and with the Fat that came out of the said bones, they said they would anoint themselves, that thereby they might sometimes change themselves into other shapes'.[17]

Grace also claimed that six months before her interview, she, along with the three women 'did meete at a place called Red banck, upon the North side of the water of Ribble, every Thursday and Sonday at night by the space of a fortnight . . . [where] there came unto them . . . foure black things, going upright, and yet not like men in the face'.[18] The black things carried the women over the water to Red Bank, where some strange meat appeared. Although the other women ate it, Grace refused. Then, after dancing with 'the said black things [they] did pull downe the said three Women, and did abuse their bodies'.[19]

Potts informs the reader that after hearing this cornucopia of accusations, many in attendance at court were of the opinion that these witches were more worthy to die than any of the other witches. But then the accused pleaded to the judge:

> [Ask Grace Sowerbuts] who set her on, or by whose meanes this accusation came against them. Immediately the countenance of this Grace Sowerbuts changed. . . . In the end his Lordship examined the Girle, who could not for her life make any direct answere, but strangely amazed, told him, shee was put to a Master to learne, but he told her nothing of this.[20]

Upon hearing this news that Grace had been schooled by a Catholic priest, Judge Bromley then went on to state, 'That if a Priest or Jesuit had a hand in one end of it, there would appeare to be knaverie, and practise in the other end of it'.[21] After which 'some that were present told his Lordship the truth, and the Prisoners informed him how shee went to learne with one Thompson a Seminarie Priest, who had instructed and taught her this accusation against them, because they were once obstinate Papists, and now came to Church'.[22]

As a result of this counter-accusation, Bromley commanded two more northern JPs, William Leigh and Edward Chisnal, to question Grace. She quickly admitted to these men that Master Thompson '[who] she taketh to be Master Christopher Southworth, to whom shee was sent to learne her prayers, did perswade, counsell, and advise her, to deale as formerly hath beene said against her Grandmother, Aunt and Southworths wife'.[23] Judge Bromley must have been highly pleased with himself, not only had he exposed a fraudulent accusation of witchcraft, he had also discovered a Jesuit priest and foiled a Catholic plot to boot. Surely this work would impress the King.

In court, the finger of blame was pointed at the Catholic priest. But we must also consider the possibility that much of the false testimony was the creation of Grace herself and the JP who brought the Samlesbury women to trial. Magistrate Robert Houlden, from Holden Hall in Haslingden, happened to be the son-in-law of Nicholas Bannester. He was also a Catholic and was marked as a papist in the freeholders' list of 1600.[24] The outcome of the Samlesbury Witch Trials must have been a catastrophe for Houlden from a career perspective. Not only had he been outwitted by a fourteen-year-old girl, but the fact that he was a known papist must have made some Protestants question whether *he* was also behind this Catholic plot. Given that so many people seemed to have been aware of the Catholic conspiracy, we have to ask whether Houlden had even bothered to interview these three alleged witches before packing them off to Lancaster. Perhaps he had been only too willing to believe Grace, blinded by the belief that this uncovering of witches would be the making of his career. After all, Roger Nowell and his father-in-law were already receiving much admiration in neighbouring Pendle. But Houlden's hopes of adoration were dashed, as these women, along with the four other men and women he brought to trial, were all acquitted.

If we read between the lines, we can view Grace as a teenager who, at first, had lied to avoid getting into trouble with her parents. Going back to Grace's first statement, perhaps rather than violently pulling her hair and laying her on top of the haystack in her uncle's barn, the truth was that her relatives had pulled her hair violently to drag her off it. Had Grace been attempting to hide from an angry aunt? Was she sleeping when she should have been working? Or was she in a compromising position when she was discovered? When grandmother Jennet knocked her off the stile, maybe it was because she was abruptly sending her home because of her bad behaviour, and maybe while walking home, Grace became fearful that her aunt and grandmother would tell her father about what she had been doing. Was she trying to convince him of her side of events before they had their say? When Grace added that her granny could shape-shift, her tale turned into one of witchcraft, not just domestic violence. It is not difficult to see how she might have been tempted to protect herself by making up outlandish stories inspired by recent gossip coming out of Pendle. (We will go on to see that in 1633 a local Pendle boy used the same kind of lie to explain why he was home late one evening. He had been distracted by two greyhounds that shape-shifted into a witch and a boy.)

Grace was interviewed more than once by Houlden, and it is impossible to decipher what was said when. But this initial event seems to have occurred only a short time before 4 April, for we are told that on this date, she was tormented again by Jennet in the form of a black dog who bid her to kill herself. Maybe the Catholic priest decided to encourage Grace's lies, either as revenge for their conversion to Protestantism or to save his own skin, fearing that the new converts might be tempted to reveal his whereabouts to the authorities. Even Potts finds the timing of Grace's examination suspicious: 'Saterday the fourth of this instant Aprill . . . Which was about the very day the Witches of the Forrest of Pendle were sent to Lancaster. Now was the time for the Seminarie to instruct, accuse, and call into question these poor women.'[25] By this date, there would have been widespread gossip about the arrests of the Pendle Witches, and the similarities in the accusations levied against the Samlesbury and Pendle Witches cannot be coincidental. Here we have again the appearance of a demonic dog, an individual who was rendered unable to move or speak, and even a sabbath or two. It is worth noting that Grace even states she was bewitched near to a bridge, which is also very similar to the story of the bewitching of John Law, given that we now know the incident happened near Carry Bridge in Colne.

Through our communications with the spirit world, we have been able to glean some of the truth behind the Samlesbury Witch Trials. The crux of the matter is that Grace and Christopher Southworth did not want to be rid of Ellen, Jennet, and Jane out of vengeance on account of their alleged conversion to the Protestant faith but because the three women had become aware of their secret: the supposedly celibate Catholic priest had been paying fourteen-year-old Grace to have a sexual relationship with him. They had been discovered together in a barn where Southworth kept his horse.

§

Potts attempts to construct a rational argument to demonstrate why the witchcraft accusations levied against these three Samlesbury women were easy to disprove. But his argument is frankly as ridiculous as the accusations themselves. For example, he says:

> Shee [Grace] describes the foure Blacke things to goe upright, but not like Men in the face. The Seminarie mistakes the face for the feete: For

> Chattox and all her fellow Witches agree, the Devill is cloven-footed: but Fancie had a very good face, and was a very proper Man.[26]

The first problem with his argument is that the other witches do not claim that the Devil appeared to them as a good-looking hooved man. (In addition, what about the fact that Anne had also described seeing the Devil in the form of a bear? Had this been a false confession?)The second problem is that Potts was arguing that a person's opinion of what the Devil looked like could be used to determine if they were a witch. When it came down to deciding what was true during the seventeenth century, the Bible was the typical point of reference. But there is very scant information regarding the Devil's appearance in Scripture. The most we really get is 'Your enemy the devil prowls around like a roaring lion looking for someone to devour' (Peter 5:8). (Which arguably did not mean that he was thought to be a literal lion.) It is also written that, at times, he may appear like an angel of light (Corinthians 11:14). As we have already established, nowhere in Genesis is it stated that the Devil was a talking snake; this was the assumption of the ancient interpreters. And, more to the point, nowhere is it written that the Devil had hooves. This now familiar image of Satan lacks any scriptural foundation, and, as a result, many witchcraft sceptics (and believers) would have disagreed with Potts' argument wholeheartedly.

Katherine Hewit & Alice Gray

Katherine Hewit was indicted for using witchcraft to murder a child named Anne Foulds.[1] According to *The Wonderfull Discoverie*, she was also known by the alias Mould-Heeles, and for hundreds of years, people have speculated about what this strange name might have meant. What many people have failed to notice is that on other occasions in the text Potts writes that it was Katherine's husband who was known as Mould-Heeles.[2] The only other detail we learn about him is that he was a clothier from Colne, which suggests that he made and/or sold cloth.[3] When we asked for clarity over which of the Hewits was referred to by this nickname, we learned that it was actually both of them; the name was connected with their place of work. It seems that the shop where they worked was called Mould & Heeles at the time or had previously been a shop called Mould & Heeles (these being two surnames). Either way, the two names had become synonymous with the property and amalgamated into one word by the common folk, who would declare something along the lines of, 'I'm off to mouldheeles,' when setting off to buy wares from the Hewits.

In addition to selling lengths of cloth, the couple also sold readymade garments and soft furnishings which Katherine made. She was an accomplished seamstress and milliner, and her fine clothes were bought by the middling and wealthier sort. Many locals who were not wealthy enough to buy readymade garments would purchase lengths of cloth and cut and sew their own clothes. By 1612, the Device family did not even have enough money to buy material, but Alizon Device would visit the Hewits' shop quite often to see whether Katherine had any offcuts of fabric she could spare. (The Device family often had to resort to wearing shoes made out of rags.) Katherine had liked Alizon, and after she heard rumour of her arrest (her living near Colne Field), she visited Alizon's mother at her home to find out what had happened.

Alice Gray was also indicted for using witchcraft to kill Anne Foulds. (Her name mistakenly appears on the list of the witches from Samlesbury, but she was from Colne.[4]) According to Potts' pamphlet, the evidence against Alice and Katherine had been supplied by both James and Elizabeth Device.[5] Potts begins his account of Katherine's trial by asking the following question: 'Who but Witches can be proofes, and so witnesses of the doings of Witches? since all their Meetings, Conspiracies, Practises, and Murthers, are the workes of Darkenesse.'[6] The reader was being reminded that gossip repeated by witches about other witches was to be regarded as sufficient proof of witchcraft, for this (as was established previously) was the opinion of the reigning monarch himself.[7] Perhaps we should assume Potts felt the need to make this reminder because he was aware that the evidence against the two women had been somewhat thin on the ground. After all, there is no mention of the women making pictures of clay, associating with familiars, or making pacts with the Devil.

Katherine Hewit was found guilty and hung, and Alice Gray was acquitted. Given that the testimony against the two women must have been very similar, it is odd that one was condemned and the other acquitted. (We will examine the most likely explanation for this later.) We would presume that as they were accused of conspiring to murder the same child, Katherine and Alice must have known each other well. But this was not the case. They knew *of* each other because they both worked and lived in the same town, but they seldom had any contact. They described their relationship to us by using the metaphor of being like ships that pass in the night. Alice Gray ran an alehouse known as The Nags Head (she sold ale and beer), and Katherine would often go to her premises to fetch a jug of beer for her husband, which he would

Fig 6.1. A dingy tavern with backgammon players and an amorous couple observing a pregnant woman as she drinks. Mezzotint by J. Stolker

drink as he worked. Out of the two women, due to occupation alone, it was more likely that Alice would have been accused of being a witch because alewives generally did not have good reputations. The common perception was that they were immoral persons who encouraged men to drink themselves into a stupor.

The earliest depictions of professional female brewsters are found in ballads and pamphlets which accuse these women of lying and cheating to make greater profits. The most common allegation was that they watered down the strong beer with weaker beer and added unsavoury ingredients to the mix, such as chicken manure! John Skelton, the famed English poet and tutor to Henry VIII, wrote a long, satirical, raucous poem about an alewife called Elynour Rummyng. In *The Tunning of Elynour Rummyng*, Elynour is described as 'well worne' with a hooked nose and skin bristled with hair. She walks with a stoop and dresses in old garb. The somewhat misogynistic author goes on to describe her usual clientele:

But to make up my tale,
She breweth noppy ale,
And maketh therof port sale
To travellers, to tynkers,
To sweters, to swynkers,
And all good ale drynkers,
That wyll nothynge spare,
But drynke tyll they stare,
And Brynge themselfe bare.
With, "Now away the Mare,
And let us slay care,
As wyse as a hare![8]

It is possible that male brewsters, who slowly began to take over the industry, encouraged derogatory rhymes and rumours to circulate about female competitors in their vicinity. What we know for sure is that men and women were encouraged to have a fearful dislike of female alehouse proprietors, and it does not take a huge stretch of the imagination to see how the stereotype of the untrustworthy, immoral alewife could lead to rumours that the one in your local town might also be a witch. As a result, alewives were prime suspects when adversity came your way. We learned from Alice that 'People thought she lived like a witch and so must have been a witch.' She was an easy target for Roger Nowell and Nicholas Bannester during their mission to clean up the place. They successfully manipulated James and had him place her at Malkin Tower, even though she had never been there. He also agreed with the magistrates when they suggested she had confessed (while in his company) to having killed young Anne. Going one step further, James sealed Katherine's fate by adding that she had helped Alice to carry out the heinous crime. James had known that Alizon and Katherine were associated through cloth. As it became more widely known that Katherine consorted with Alizon, disaproving locals were more inclined to believe that the seamstress was a witch.

We asked the two women whether they were ever accused of having familiar spirits. They gave a response which indicated that, unlike those in charge of dishing out justice, they believed that the idea of familiars and other sufficient proofs of witchcraft were utter nonsense: 'Who didn't have animals around them or make things believing that they would help them or gain from them?' they asked. It seems a perfectly reasonable question. (You say familiar, I say Pet. You say charm, I say prayer.) About their life experience, they emphasize that during the seventeenth century life was only about survival, and you simply had to manage the best you could with whatever life you had. They have moved on in the spirit world but sometimes reflect on their lives and revisit the places they knew. Katherine maintains a great sadness for how her life ended, saying of the judges and magistrates, 'They were wicked, not I. There was no reasoning, no justice, no chance.' Katherine wants it to be known that at the moment of her death, there was total darkness. But then the black slowly changed into the colour purple before the light returned once again, and this time it was brighter than ever before.

Sufficient Proofs of Witchcraft

On average, across Europe, a magistrate might prosecute a witch only once during their entire career, meaning that magistrates were not typically seasoned witch-hunters. Many were not even sure about what a witch was, what they were supposed to do, or how they were supposed to find them. As a result, they often struggled to decide whether an alleged witch was guilty or innocent. Most of the early modern witch-hunters relied on the Bible and/or the texts by the continental demonologists to prepare evidence for the courts. But the Pendle Witch Trials are unusual in that they relied on the King's own book, *Daemonologie*, instead. In an attempt to ensure that one hundred per cent of the people he sent to stand trial for witchcraft were condemned, Nowell had made the canny move of using the words and wisdom of James I to hang them. After all, who amongst his contemporaries would dare argue against the authority of the absolute monarch?

The testimony of the Pendle Witches was filled with examples of their having participated in activities which King James regarded to be sufficient proofs of witchcraft. And when Potts came to write *The Wonderfull Discoverie*, he weaved even more details from *Daemonologie* into their confessions. The small selection of examples which follow illustrate how alike the King's text and the testimony in the pamphlet often were:

Example 1 – On Pictures of Clay

Daemonologie:

To some others at these times hee [the Devil] teacheth how to make Pictures of waxe or clay: That by the rosting thereof, the persones that they beare the name of, may be continuallie melted or dryed away by continuall sicknesse.[1]

The Wonderfull Discoverie:

Elizabeth Sowthernes' testimony against Anne Whittle and Anne Redferne:

The said Elizabeth Southernes saith upon her Examination, that about halfe a yeare before Robert Nutter died . . . this Examinate went to the house of Thomas Redfearne. . . . And there within three yards of the East end of the said house, shee saw the said Anne Whittle, alias Chattox, and Anne Redferne wife of the said Thomas Redferne, and daughter of the said Anne Whittle . . . the one on the one side of the Ditch, and the other on the other: and two Pictures of Clay or Marle lying by them: and the third Picture the said Anne Whittle, alias Chattox was making: and the said Anne Redferne her said Daughter, wrought her Clay or Marle to make the third Picture withall. And this Examinate passing by them, the said Spirit, called Tibb . . . said; they are making three pictures . . . of Christopher Nutter, Robert Nutter, and Marie, wife of the said Robert Nutter.[2]

James Device's testimony against Elizabeth Device:

And he, this Examinate also saith, That about three yeares ago, this Examinate being in his Grand-mothers house, with his said mother; there came a thing in shape of a browne dogge, which his mother called Ball, who spake to this Examinates mother, in the sight and hearing of this Examinate, and bad her make a Picture of Clay like unto John Robinson, alias Swyer, and drie it hard, and then crumble it by little and little; and as the said Picture should crumble or mull away, so should the said Jo. Robinson alias Swyer his body decay and weare away. And within two or three days after, the Picture shall so all be wasted, and mulled away; so then the said John Robinson should die presently. . . . And the next day, this Examinate saw his said mother take Clay at the West-end of her said house, and make a picture of it after the said Robinson, and brought into her house, and dried it some two dayes: and about two dayes after the drying thereof, this Examinates said mother fell on crumbling the said Picture of Clay, every day some, for some three weekes together; and within two dayes after all was crumbled or mulled away, the said John Robinson died.[3]

James Device's voluntary confession:

And within two or three daies after, this Examinate went to the Carre-Hall, and upon some speeches betwixt Mistress Towneley and this Examinate; Shee charging this Examinate and his said mother, to have stolne some turues [turf] of hers, badde him pack the doores: and withall as he went forth of the doore, the said Mistress Towneley gave him a knock betweene the shoulders: and about a day or two after that, there appeared unto this Examinate in his way, a thing like unto a black dog . . . who bad this Examinate make a Picture of Clay, like unto the said Mistris Towneley: and that this Examinate with the helpe of his Spirit . . . would kill or destroy the said Mistress Towneley. . . . And the next morning after, this examinate tooke Clay, and made a Picture of the said Mrs Towneley and dried it the same night by the fire: and within a day after, hee, this Examinate began to crumble the said Picture, every day some, for the space of a weeke: and within two daies after all was crumbled away: the said Mistris Towneley died.[4]

Example 2 – On Magical Feasts

Daemonologie:

I say, that they [witches] can suddenly cause be brought unto them, all kindes of daintie disshes, by their familiar spirit.[5]

The Wonderfull Discoverie:

Anne Whittle's testimony against Elizabeth Sowthernes:

And at the same time she saith, there was victuals, *viz.* Flesh, Butter, Cheese, Bread, and Drinke, And after their eating, the Devill called Fancie, and the other Spirit calling himselfe Tibbe carried the remnant away.[6]

Example 3 – On the Devil's Appearance

Daemonologie:

For as to the formes, to some of the baser sorte of them [witches] he [the Devil] oblishes him self to appeare at their calling upon him, by such a proper name which he shewes unto them, either in likenes of a dog, a Catte, an Ape, or such-like other beast . . . to some he will be a continuall attender, in form of a Page.[7]

The Wonderfull Discoverie:

Elizabeth Sowthernes' voluntary confession:

The said Elizabeth Sowtherns confesseth, and sayth; That about twentie yeares past, as she was comming homeward from begging, there met her this Examinate neere unto a stonepit in Gouldshey, in the said Forest of Pendle, a Spirit or Devill in the shape of a Boy, the one halfe of his Coate blacke, and the other browne, who bade this Examinate stay, saying to her, that if she would give him her Soule, she should have any thing that she would request. Whereupon this Examinat demanded his name? and the spirit answered, his name was Tibb.[8]

(See chapter four: Familiars, for further examples of the Devil appearing in the form of cats, dogs, and other animals.)

John & Jane Bulcock, Margaret Pearson, & Isabel Robey

In August 1612, Roger Nowell also prosecuted John Bulcock and his mother, Jane. We learn from *The Wonderfull Discoverie* that John lived with his mother and father, Christopher Bulcock, at a place called 'Mosse-end' in the Forest of Pendle. The mother and son were indicted for using witchcraft to waste and consume the body of a woman called Jennet Deane, causing her to become 'madde'.[1] At the Malkin Tower feast, James had allegedly heard the two confess 'That they had bewitched, at the new-field Edge in Yorkeshire, a woman called Jennet, wife of John Deyne, besides, her Reason; and the said Womans name so bewitched, he did not heare them speake of'.[2] The testimony about the bewitchment of Jennet Deane appears very odd when we read that James both heard and did not hear the Bulcocks say whom they had bewitched.

Potts writes that in court, the Bulcocks, who had apparently previously confessed to the crime and to attending the Good Friday meeting when interviewed by Nowell, now denied the accusations:

> [They were] crying out in a very violent and outrageous manner, even to the gallowes, where they died impenitent for any thing we know, because they died silent in the particulars. These of all others were the most desperate wretches (void of all feare or grace) in all this Packe; Their offences not much inferior to Murther.[3]

Potts was attempting to convince the reader that their executions had been justified; their angry demeanour and lack of remorse supposedly proved that they were witches. Their defiance was *not* to be interpreted as an indication that they had been falsely accused, were fighting for their lives, and were prepared to go down kicking and screaming. (However, only the guilty can show remorse.) Confusingly, in *The Wonderfull Discoverie*, it is written that the Bulcocks were acquitted, but we know that this was not the case thanks to an apologetic note added by the publisher, Barnes, who took full responsibility for the print errors in the pamphlet, explaining that the odd mistake occurred because the work was done 'in such great haste, at the end of a Tearme'.[4] (Maybe Potts had been struggling to keep to a deadline.)

The Bulcocks had been an easy target for Nowell because they were a poor family who knew the Device family well, and, like them, they also had a reputation for theft. Jane and John Bulcock told us that they *had* stolen from their neighbours but that their only motivation for doing so was hunger. They are still angry about the circumstances of their deaths. In their words, they were, 'Set up.' There was nothing else to it.

§

During the summer of 1612, Nicholas Bannester had busied himself assisting Roger Nowell with the examinations of several Pendle folk. He was anticipating that he would gain some recognition for his efforts, but, rather last minute, he decided to bring his own witch to the party to be certain of the fact. He chose a prime suspect – Margaret Pearson, wife of Edward Pearson of Padiham.

We learn from Potts' pamphlet that Margaret had already stood trial twice before: firstly, for murder by witchcraft and, secondly, for bewitching a neighbour. On this third occasion, Margaret was accused of using witchcraft to harm goods.[5] According to *The Wonderfull Discoverie*, she was 'little inferiour in her wicked and malicious course of life to any that hath gone before'.[6] During her third trial, testimony was supplied by her neighbour Jennet Booth. Bannester examined Jennet on 9 August, which was little more than a week before the Lancaster Assizes were due to commence. Jennet Booth had confessed that while recently carding wool in the home of Margaret and her husband, John, she had asked Margaret (known as Margerie) for some milk for her child. While Margaret poured some milk into a pan, Jennet re-kindled the fire. When the milk was finally boiled, Jennet removed the pan from the fire and noticed:

> Under the bottome of the same, there came a Toade, or a thing very like a Toade, and to this Examinates thinking came out of the fire, together with the said Pan, and under the bottome of the same, and that the said Margerie did carrie the said Toade out of the said house in a paire of tonges; But what shee the said Margerie did therewith, this Examinate knoweth not.[7]

What the jurors were supposed to make of this tale is not clear. Was it alleged that Margaret had summoned a demon from the fire? Was this toad-like creature supposed to be a familiar? Was the toad there to bewitch the milk? Was it just a toad which had found an unfortunate hiding place? Was it even a toad or just a toad-shaped lump? Having failed to drum up any better evidence against Margaret, Bannester decided to strengthen the case against Margaret Pearson by adding some of his own totally fabricated testimony:

> The said Anne Chattox being examined saith, That the wife of one Pearson of Paddiham, is a very evill Woman, and confessed to this Examinate, that shee is a Witch, and hath a Spirit which came to her the first time in the likenesse of a Man, and cloven footed, and that shee the said Pearsons wife hath done very much harm to one Dodgesons goods, who came in at a loop-hole into the said Dodgesons Stable, and shee and her Spirit together did sit upon his Horse or Mare, untill the said Horse or mare died. And likewise, that shee the said Pearsons wife did confesse unto her this Examinate, that shee bewitched unto death one Childers wife, and her Daughter, and that shee the said Pearsons wife is as ill as shee.[8]

There is no indication of when Anne Whittle made this confession or to whom she made it, making it all the more obvious that the confession had never occurred. Unfortunately for Margaret, Bannester's tactic of pretending she had associated with one of the Pendle Witches made the jury conclude she was guilty of harming a horse via the arts of witchcraft. As a result, she was to be subjected to the following punishment for her crime:

> The Judgement of the Court against you, is, You shall stand upon the Pillarie in open Market, at Clitheroe, Paddiham, Whalley, and Lancaster, foure Market dayes, with a Paper upon your head, in great Letters, declaring your offence, and there you shall confesse your

> offence, and after to remaine in Prison for one yeare without Baile, and after to be bound with good Sureties, to be of good behaviour.[9]

Margaret Pearson was to be made an example. Her very public punishment would be a warning to those tempted to practise witchcraft. When we asked Margaret if she would like to tell us anything about her trial, she said she wants it to be known that she had, 'Done nothing.'

§

Isabel Robey, from the Windle area, was prosecuted by JP Sir Thomas Gerard. She appears to have been arraigned for using witchcraft to make her neighbour ill, although this is never explicitly stated by Potts. On 12 July 1612, Gerard had examined Peter Chaddock of Windle. Peter confessed that before he was married, he heard a rumour that 'Isabel Robey was not pleased that hee should marrie his now wife: whereupon this Examinate called the said Isabel Witch, and said that hee did not care for her. Then within two days next after this Examinate was sore pained in his bones'.[10] From testimony supplied by Margaret Lyon, we learn that Chaddock's wife was the god-daughter of Isabel.[11]

Peter Chaddock then recalled that Isabel and his wife had once had an argument and that on the same day, 'this Examinate with his said wife working in the Hay, a paine and a starknesse fell into the necke of this Examinat which grieved him very sore'.[12] It appears as though Peter was often quick to conclude that his ailments were caused by witchcraft, and he sought out cunning folk to undo the curses that were frequently levied upon him. On this occasion, he 'sent to [for] one James a Glover, which then dwelt in Windle, and desired him to pray for him, and within foure or five dayes next after this Examinate did mend very well'.[13] Before James had arrived, Peter complained that he had a great heat in his body and could not quench his thirst, no matter how much he tried. When James the glover/cunning man arrived, he agreed that this peculiarity was a result of witchcraft. As remedy, he instructed Peter to 'take that drinke, and in the name of the Father, the Sonne, and the Holy Ghost, drinke it, saying; The Devill and Witches are not able to prevaile against God and his Word'.[14] Peter did what James commanded and was cured of his affliction, remaining in good health until twelve months before the witch trials when he became 'sore pained with great warch in his bones, and all his limmes'.[15] As usual, he was adamant that Isabel Robey was the cause of his pain.

Potts includes a snippet of testimony supplied by Jane Wilkinson of Windle. Perhaps it was a guilty conscience which led her to believe that Isabel had caused her to become so sick that she could not walk; prior to her illness, the two had argued over Jane's refusal to give her some milk.[16] From our communications with the alleged witches, we have gleaned that Isabel was a poor and 'uncouth' woman who was bullied and pushed around a lot during her life. She worked as a scullery maid and was the lowest-ranking female servant. She carried out the menial household chores which many other servants did not want to do. In her lifetime, she was accused of anything and everything, including thievery and witchcraft.

The magistrate who prosecuted her, Sir Thomas Gerard, 1st Baronet, was one of the men who had offered to provide some form of relief to the bewitched pedlar John Law. Gerard's family seat was The Brynne near Ashton-in-Makerfield. We can say that out of all of those who came to prosecute witches at the Lancashire Witch Trials of 1612, it

Fig 6.2. A beggar woman with a stick holds out a bowl. Etching possibly after J. Callcot

was Gerard who had the greatest fear of losing his position of power, and with good reason. His father had been a Catholic recusant, implicated in the Babington Plot no less – the grand conspiracy to remove Protestant Queen Elizabeth I from her throne and replace her with the Catholic Queen Mary of Scots. His youngest brother, John

Gerard, was a Jesuit priest who had been imprisoned in the Tower of London in 1606, accused of conspiring with the 'gunpowder plotters' to blow up Parliament in the previous year. (He managed to avoid execution by escaping and fleeing the country.) The family (perhaps understandably) were under surveillance, and when Thomas Gerard eventually inherited his knighthood and family estates from his father, he knew that he would have to try harder than most to hold on to his status. His first move had been to conform to the Protestant Church. His second move was to buy the honour of a baronetcy from King James in 1611. The cost was the grand sum of £1000.[17]

Magistrates with Catholic sympathies were in a difficult position. We know that in 1612 Parliament was pushing JPs to report all who refused to take communion. (In other words, papists.) But a truly God-fearing Catholic JP would have been reluctant to prosecute fellow Catholics. And so, in one respect, witches can be seen as the ideal scapegoat in this situation. The witch was a type of nonconformist, and by prosecuting Isabel Robey, Gerard could be seen to be doing what the King had asked without actually doing it. (No doubt Gerard had offered to provide for John Law, not out of the goodness of his heart, but because it would do wonders for his reputation.)

The Search for Malkin Tower

In 2011, while undertaking routine maintenance work in the village of Barley, a team of utility workers stumbled upon a ruined seventeenth-century cottage hidden beneath a grassy mound. The ruin was in remarkable condition; it even contained a nineteenth-century range, tin bath, and bedstead. But it was the discovery of a sealed room with a mummified cat bricked into a wall which saw it being quickly dubbed 'the witch's cottage', and people began to speculate that the infamous Malkin Tower had finally been found. However, despite the national interest that this news story generated, because this building sits outside the Forest of Pendle boundary, near Lower Black Moss Reservoir, it is unlikely that this property was Malkin Tower. And in addition, the consensus of the archaeologists involved in excavating the house was that the cottage was more likely to have been owned by a weaver than a witch.[1] Nevertheless, this did not deter the tourists, and due to damage caused by winter weather, but also because of damage caused by modern-day witch-hunters, the cottage was re-covered in order to preserve it in early 2012.

The location of the infamous Malkin Tower is one of the biggest mysteries of the Pendle Witch story. Purportedly the home of Elizabeth Sowthernes and the Device family, this property also served as the meeting place for the diabolical sabbath held on Good Friday 1612, which, according to Nowell and Potts, was attended by more than twenty odious witches. This claim, made in *The Wonderfull Discoverie*, along with its grandiose sounding name, has made it *the* most sought out property of all those mentioned in the witch trial testimony.

Fig 6.3. Witches dine with four demons.
Woodcut, 1720

Upon Blacko hillside, situated to the north-east of the Pendle Forest, there sits a property which currently bears the title Malkin Tower Farm, and, naturally, this site attracts much attention, even though the present property (according to the best knowledge of the current owners) was built by Richard Townley in the eighteenth century.[2] (Unfortunately, the property deeds only date to the nineteenth century.) Author John A. Clayton believes the east end of the property to be the oldest part, onto which a barn was later added.[3] According to Clayton's theory, a tenant named John Hargreaves built another barn onto the western end of the first extension in 1860. Clayton's idea about the build date of the western barn came from consideration of the census records and from a carved stone in one of the barn walls which bears the date 1860 and the initials JH.[4] However, it might be the case that this part of the property was renovated by someone with the initials JH in 1860 because an OS map from 1848 shows that the western barn was in situ more than ten years earlier.[5] A photograph from around 1900 also shows that a small two-storey building once adjoined the frontage of the first barn extension.[6]

As you drive through Pendle, you cannot help but notice the thirty-foot-high round tower which sits on the ridge of Blacko Hill. Its rough stone exterior and widely spaced battlements give it the appearance of a medieval fortress, and it is easy to imagine that such a place would be fit for a meeting of the Devil's army. But the reality is that Blacko

Fig 6.4. Stansfield Tower, Blacko

Tower (officially called the Stansfield Tower) was built around 1890 by a successful local greengrocer called Jonathan Stansfield, not the Devil incarnate. The tower is a folly: essentially an elaborate viewing platform. Back in the 1960s, authors Edgar Peel and Pat Southern observed that 'Blacko Tower has no connection with witches, despite the fact that from 1891, the date it was built, the deeds of Malkin Tower Farm begin to refer to "Malkin Tower, otherwise Blacko Tower" – a careless error, which once made has been copied since.'[7] However, the authors made an error themselves here by assuming that Malkin Tower Farm became mistakenly known as Blacko Tower because of its proximity to the folly, when in fact, the 1848 OS map (surveyed in 1844) shows that around forty-five years before the folly was constructed, Malkin Tower Farm was called Blacko Tower.

The 1841 census also shows that when sixty-year-old John Hargreaves lived in the property, it was called Blacko Tower. Moving forward to the 1851 census, yeoman William Sutcliffe is now residing at 'Maulkin Tower', and he is still living at the property with his family ten years later, written then as 'Mawking Tower'. By 1880 the property was owned by John Holt. (Perhaps, therefore, it is John Holt's initials which are carved into the western barn extension.) The deeds to Clough Farm in Barrowford show that John owned 'Maltkiln Tower otherwise known as Blacko Tower'.[8] This additional evidence further demonstrates that the property had undergone a name change, and if we are to be guided by all of this information, this appears to have occurred sometime between 1844 (after the land was surveyed for the 1848 OS map) and 30 March 1851 (the date of the 1851 census in England).

Clayton recently discovered new evidence that 'Businessman, John Swinglehurst, owned Mawkin Tower Farm in 1803. . . . The property was described in the Rate Return for that year as a Farm House and Shop. . . . The shop was a two-storied extension built on the front elevation of the farm cottage and used for handloom weaving.'[9] This last piece of evidence sounds very much like the present property (prior to the removal of the front extension after 1900). So, as a final twist, we now know that the eighteenth-century property was called Malkin Tower Farm at the dawn of the nineteenth century, was renamed Blacko Tower before 1841 and then renamed Malkin Tower Farm, once again, by the middle of the century!

Such is the interest in the location of the infamous Malkin Tower that in 2018 an international team of archaeologists descended upon Pendle and began a dig in a field belonging to Malkin Tower Farm to find evidence of older buildings. Geophysical exploration during the previous year showed promising evidence of two other buildings which led to the excavation of two archaeological trenches. The first was dug near the back of the present farmhouse and revealed that one of the two buildings was a timber cruck framed construction (possibly medieval) which showed no sign of human habitation. The second trench created more excitement. At the time of the dig, the early discovery of a hearth left head archaeologist Dr Charles Orser, of Ontario's Western University, in little doubt that he had uncovered a tumbled house.[10] The house was situated near the eastern field boundary, close to the area of boundary wall which contains a drystone feature often referred to as the gable end or Malkin gable.

Orser's team observed that the tumbled property seemed to have been used as a dumping ground for a considerable amount of time, with the majority of the debris being made up of post-medieval ceramic fragments – around two thousand were discovered in total. A detailed analysis of 400 of those fragments has since shown that the majority were parts of vessels, primarily storage jars, milk pans, cups, mugs, bowls, and shallow dishes. Arguably, the most important revelation has been that most of the identified wares were in production between the mid-to-late seventeenth century and nineteenth century and that none of the wares analysed dated before 1640. As a result, it was decided that this could not have been the site of Malkin Tower. Archaeology student Madeleine Connolly concluded:

> The recorded production dates for the identified ware types suggest that the excavated portion of the site is too late to be Malkin Tower. . . . The majority of these wares were produced primarily during the late 17th and early 18th centuries. The Pendle Hill Witches were executed in 1612, nearly half a century earlier than production for most wares began. Red Border wares are the only exception, having been in production since the late 16th century . . . ; however, the Border ware forms identified at Malkin Tower assemblage did not begin to be produced in the Red Border Ware until much later.[11]

It is highly probable that some of the stone from this tumbled house was incorporated into the present Malkin Tower Farm. It is also reasonable to assume that some stone was used to construct the gable feature in the drystone wall. As fancy as it is, this feature seems most likely to have been built to block the gateway between fields which once provided access to the now-tumbled house.

So far, archaeological investigation has failed to uncover the remains of a seventeenth-century property on Malkin Tower Farm land, but we do know that the names Malkenyerd and Mawkynyarde appear in the Clitheroe Court Rolls as early as the sixteenth century for the year 1508/09 and 1564. (Yard, typically described the enclosed land around a house or building.) Unfortunately, the only indication of location given is that Mawkynyarde lay 'in the north end of Colne'.[12] According to Peel and Southern, Dr Laycock, who used to lecture on the Pendle Witches, saw evidence that an 1828 survey (made by George Hennet for the construction of Teesdale's Map of Lancashire) showed three fields called Malkin Fields, belonging to Saddlers Farm in Newchurch. But when the authors subsequently studied the property's seventeenth-century deeds (including a field map), they were disappointed to learn that although field names are listed, none bore the name Malkin. Instead, there was a field named Kiln Field, and the authors speculated that this field name might have inspired folklore.[13] Another area which has received much more recent attention is a ruined eighteenth-century farmstead called Mancknowles Ing in Barley. In 2012, Clayton made a case for the farmstead having been named after John Mancknowles who owned the land around 1567. He considered that the locals might have shortened the name of the area to Malking.[14] Believing that there was an indication of a pre-existing structure, this site was eventually surveyed by the same team who conducted the geophysical survey of Malkin Tower Farm land in 2017. But while the results showed old field boundaries, there was no clear evidence of previous structures on the site.

On some occasions in the past, the word malkin was used to describe a slattern (untidy) woman. As a result, some authors have suggested that the name Malkin Tower was perhaps a colloquial, derogatory nickname given to the property on account of the inhabitants. (There is little evidence to support this theory.) Our investigation into the present Malkin Tower Farm has shown that, in the past, Malkin was written as Maulkin, Malt kiln, and several other variants. (Even Potts cannot make his mind up on the correct spelling.) This means we should be a little cautious here and perhaps only consider that the seventeenth-century name of the Device abode sounded 'something like' Malkin Tower.

The 1841 census lists the following properties which still stand upon Blacko Hillside today: Spout House, Burnt House, Hollin Hall, Blacko Hillside, and a property called Blacko, which was the home of

Fig 6.5. A derelict property near Carry Bridge, Colne

a cattle dealer named Nowell. (This was probably the farm now called Blacko Foot Farm.) There is also a property called Drivers; the exact location of this house is unknown at present. It is worth noting that the older properties in and around the Pendle Forest appear to be named either after topography or after the surname of an owner. For example, we see that the properties which surround Malkin Tower Farm follow this pattern: Blacko Hillside is situated upon Blacko Hillside, Blacko Foot Farm is at the foot (or bottom) of Blacko Hill, Hollin Hall was probably surrounded by a holly hedge. (*Hollin* in Old English). Spout House was near a spring. There were people living in the area in the eighteenth century who bore the surname Drivers which is the most likely explanation of how the Driver property got its name. An exploration of the Clitheroe Court Rolls and parish records has not revealed any surnames which sound similar to Malkin, so it is unlikely that the home of the Device family was named after a local family. But, intriguingly, the nineteenth-century deeds of the present Malkin Tower Farm show that a hollowed area of land just north of the excavation site was known as Mawkin Hole.[15] Could the Devices' home have been named after this feature?

There might be a slight chance that you have heard someone use the archaic phrase 'a gaping maw' in conversation. The word *maw* describes this natural feature perfectly well when we understand that it was an old word used to describe the throat or mouth. Those peering over the edge of Mawkin Hole were peering into the mouth of the land. Clayton noted that the field 'immediately to the east of Malkin Tower Farm' is marked as 'Mawkin Hole Field, on a Clitheroe Estate map'.[16] We also have evidence from the sale of White Moor Farm in Whitemoor in 1852 that there was a field called Mokin Hole Pasture and another called Mokin Hole Plantation somewhere nearby.[17] Interestingly, *mow* can also mean mouth, which might explain the interchange between mawkin and mokin, and all of these findings seem to be little clues that a seventeenth-century property could have existed near Mawkin Hole. But unfortunately, there is a spanner in the shape of a map from 1580 to throw into the works here.

The map in question, known as the 1580 Whitemoor Map, was drawn as evidence in a suit between the Tenants of Foulridge and the Tenants of Barnoldswick regarding rights to cut turves and pasture their cattle upon Whitemoor. It is not the most user-friendly map, but it has been painstakingly interpreted over many years by local-history enthusiasts who have noted that, on this document, the large hollow feature is not marked as Mawkin Hole, but as Haynslack.[18] Frustratingly, as this map was constructed only thirty-two years before the Pendle Witch Trials, we could take this finding to indicate that the name Mawkin Hole was attributed to the land feature much later on. But there is also the possibility that the feature was known by more than one name in the 1500s. This is not a crazy idea, for, after all, the nineteenth-century folly on top of the hill in Blacko is simultaneously known as Blacko Tower and Stansfield Tower. In addition, the names Mawkin and Haynslack do seem to describe the same thing, for *slack* (from the Norwegian *slakke*), like *maw* and *mow*, can mean a hollow or a dip. And *hay* (possibly from the Icelandic *hagi* or *haw*) meant a hedge, a fence, or an enclosed field or yard. (This natural feature may have been used to house animals.)

So far, we have considered several possibilities for why the abode of the Device family was known as Malkin, but what about the second part of the name? Many historic properties in the Lancashire area include the word tower in their title because they were fortified buildings at one time, built primarily for defence. For example, Hoghton Tower was built in the 1100s (and was home to the Gerard family at the time of the Pendle Witch Trials). And Gawthorpe Hall was originally one of the Peel towers – small fortified buildings built along the English and Scottish borders and in the north of England. The only contemporary description we have of Malkin Tower comes from the year 1633 when Reverend Richard James, Fellow of Oxford, visited the area: 'Malkin's Tower, a little cottage, where reporte makes caitive witches meete to swear their homage to ye devil'.[19] Assuming that the reverend was looking at the right property, we can conclude from his account that Malkin Tower was a much humbler structure than its name suggests, certainly not a fortified house.

Given the unlikelihood that one of the poorest families in the Pendle Forest would be occupying a fortified home (usually reserved for the gentry), we might consider the possibility that the property name was the result of its proximity to a tower-like structure. In 1925, Alfred Watkins published *The Old Straight Track* in support of the controversial topic of ley lines. In this book, Watkins discusses various ancient trackways and the mounds, moats, beacons, and mark stones which sit alongside them. He postulated that many hilltops have names which 'indicate use as fire beacon points . . . such as Black Hill'.[20] (In this case, black meaning to burn.) Watkins argued that such beacons were used as warning signals during the medieval era, but their initial purpose was to guide and direct. Is it plausible that a beacon tower was lit on Blacko Hill? Is that how the hill got its name? There is (as previously mentioned) a farm called Burnt House, in Blacko. And this property could have given some weight to the beacon theory if it had not been for the fact that *burnt* is also an archaic term for a small stream or brook and that a stream runs beneath the farm.[21]

Although there is a lack of physical evidence to support the beacon theory, this investigation has highlighted one important fact: there is a lot of running water on Blacko Hillside. Did Malkin Tower take the latter part of its name from its proximity to a tall structure related to a watermill? In truth, the mill theory is not new, and local historians have noted that the 1580 map shows a point marked as Black Dyke Mill on the ridge of Blacko Hill.[22] Sadly, their subsequent investigation failed to uncover any physical evidence of an old mill, and it might be the case that because much of the handwritten map is illegible, it really says Black Dyke Gill. Admergill is close by, and the map also marks Oxgill and Twirling Gill. The map is primarily concerned with marking the water course upon Blacko Hill and Whitemore, and *gill* in this context probably meant a streambed on a precipitous hillside.

If the appellation did not relate to a fortified building, a beacon, or a tall mill-related structure, there is always another possibility: 'to tower' can simply mean to be relatively high, and arguably, a property situated on top of Blacko Hillside (or any other hill) could be considered relatively high in relation to the properties below it. Perhaps tower simply referred to the position the property held in the land, being in the highest position and towering over the other buildings.

§

My research into Malkin Tower began before I commenced writing this book. Like many other people, I was keen to discover its location. At that time, I admit that I had not considered the consequences of such a revelation. Later, during one communication with Elizabeth Sowthernes, she was asked if she would be happy for the location of her home to be written down, but her response was that she did not want the world to know exactly where she had lived because she had been disturbed enough. This was also the sentiment of the remainder of the Device family. They do not want the people of these times to know where the site of Malkin Tower is because they would not have any peace if they knew. Frankly put, they do not get much peace now, and if their home was exposed, it would be worse; it would cause them yet more pain. The fact that the excavated cottage in Barley had to be re-covered because of the negative impact tourists were having is evidence enough that the revelation of the true location of the Device family home would be extremely detrimental to Pendle, and the present inhabitants of the area, be they living or dead. The purpose of this book is to educate the living about the reality behind the legend – the barbaric injustice these poor souls experienced during their lifetime – and to prove that they were accused of doing things they could not possibly have done. It is not a tour guide for witch-hunters.

Elizabeth Sowthernes and the Device family are happy for people to visit Pendle for the right reason – to learn the truth about them. They do not want to be forgotten, but they want to be shown respect. They want it to be known that their spirits should be allowed to come and go as they please, to visit places they knew when they were alive without daily interference and disturbance from the droves of people who turn up to Pendle to summon up witches. They want this behaviour to stop. What the Device family would like to happen is for a memorial plaque or memorial stone to be placed in the general area in which they lived, with their names written upon it. This should be the focal point for those who want to respectfully learn about them. This memorial should also firmly emphasize that despite the things they were accused of in life, they were just ordinary people living in very hard times, in the same way many people had to. They want to be remembered in this way.

About their home, Elizabeth Sowthernes and the Device family are happy for it to be known that it was situated in Blacko. When asked what their home was like, Elizabeth described their house as a hovel but stressed that it was a clean hovel! It was a simple stone structure attached to the end of another building which they described as a black gable. Alizon confirmed that this was, 'Where I lived with my granny.' Their home was tiny, consisting of one room with a hearth and very little in the way of furniture. There was also a loft space above with a wooden floor. Clothes and blankets were piled upon a table in the loft space, and their beds were sacks filled with straw. Alizon, Jennet, and Elizabeth Device slept close together to keep warm, and James had his own mattress. In later life, Elizabeth Sowthernes slept downstairs.

During another communication, I had thought to ask what they understood the word malkin to mean when they lived in Pendle, and interestingly the reply was a hollow or a ditch. On another occasion, they were asked if they could explain what type of building or structure the tower was which their home was named after, and this answer was most enlightening. For hundreds of years, people have attempted to find the ruins of a tower in the Pendle Forest. But the truth is that, despite what has been written repeatedly, there was no tower. Because this part of the property title has remained constant, we have all assumed that this part of the property name must be correct when, in truth, it is a total fabrication.

The real name of the Devices' humble home, as spoken by the family in their own Lancashire dialect, was not Malkin Tower. It was Mockin Toft. The word *toft* was an old term used to describe a house, particularly a farmhouse with buildings attached, or in law, a place where a messuage has stood.[23] (Messuage was the legal term for a dwelling house with adjacent buildings and curtilage for the use of the household.) *Toft* could also mean a hillock or knoll. Mockin Toft was the name of the homestead in which their humble home was situated. It was Potts 'the storyteller' who thought to change the name from Toft to Tower for dramatic effect. An ominous tower filled with diabolical witches would be a terrifying image for the reader. It was conceivable that odious witches were plotting with the Devil to overthrow Christendom from such a place.

Jennet Device

Twenty-one years after the Pendle Witch Trials, there was a local resurgence in witch-hunting. On All Saints' Day in November 1633, Edmund Robinson, a mason who resided in the Pendle Forest, became concerned because his ten-year-old son, Edmund, had not arrived home. Some hours before, under his father's instruction, young Edmund had gone to drive some cows home, but neither the cows nor the boy had arrived. His father set out searching for him and heard the boy crying out in a pitiful manner, most afraid and confused. When Edmund took hold of the boy, he did not recognize his father. It took him fifteen minutes to come to his senses, after which time young Edmund Robinson was able to offer a curious explanation for what had happened. He told his father that when picking plums near Fence, he had seen two greyhounds which he tried to get to chase a hare, but they would not, so he beat them with a stick. One of the hounds then turned into one of his neighbours – a woman called Frances Dicconson – and the other turned into a boy. Frances then turned the boy into a horse and carried Edmund away to a house called Hoarstones, where sixty witches were eating a magical banquet. The terrified Edmund had managed to run away from the witches, but they had chased him for a long time. And, as if this ordeal wasn't enough, he had met a boy with cloven hooves and fought with him, which was why his clothes were dirty.

Instead of chastising the boy for creating such an elaborate lie to explain away his failure to bring the cows home, his father accepted that this story was the truth. But as we shall see, Edmund's father was not the sort of man who would let an opportunity pass him by. For a period of three months after, Mr Robinson took his son to a number of local churches, placed him high up on a stool in the middle of the congregation, and told the boy to point out the witches he had seen at the diabolical banquet. One sceptical church curate had referred to Edmund as 'the boy that discovers witches'.[1] News of witchcraft soon reached magistrate John Starkey, the son of Nicholas Starkey. It was he who, as a boy, had been under supposed demonic possession in the late 1500s which had resulted in the hanging of Edmund Hartley. In February 1634, nineteen people were put on trial for witchcraft. Seventeen of those people were found guilty.[2]

Although the jury had totally bought Edmund's story, the judges were surprisingly hesitant to condemn those who had been found guilty of practising witchcraft. This was because, now, more than ever before, they worried about the repercussions of hanging innocent people. At Leicester in 1616, a twelve-year-old boy had claimed he had been bewitched, the case had gone to trial, and nine women were hanged. One month later, King James I decided to interview the boy and quickly discovered that he had been lying.[3] As a consequence, the judges were soundly rebuked, and the message went out that those in positions of judicial authority ought to be very cautious about condemning witches, especially when relying on the testimony of a child to do so. The fear-filled judges presiding over the 1634 Pendle Witch Trial made the wise decision of referring the matter to the Privy Council and King Charles I, the new monarch, for their superior consideration.

Four of the accused were sent to Fleet Prison in London to face further examination, while the remainder were left imprisoned in Lancaster Castle. The King asked physician William Harvey to re-examine the four women, and his team of midwives and physicians set about searching for physical evidence of witchcraft upon their bodies in the form of witch or Devil's marks. Unable to find anything of a suspicious nature, the King then ordered that mini-witch-finder Edmund Robinson be re-interviewed. Like in the 1616 trial, it was quickly discovered that the boy had been lying. In this case, the lie had been created by the child to avoid a beating. Edmund was inspired by stories of diabolical meetings at 'Mocking Tower' and witches roaming through the land. Furthermore, it was also revealed that his father had been blackmailing local women, saying they would be accused of being witches unless they paid him.[4]

The 1634 trial highlights that the people of Pendle had not learned a thing from the executions of 1612, for women were still being labelled as witches left, right, and centre. And local magistrates were still viewing witch trials as an opportunity to make names for themselves. At least six of the people on Edmund's list were already suspected witches, and amongst the accused was none other than the now grown-up Jennet Device. Thanks to the lies of a boy around the same age as she had been when she gave evidence in court against her own family, Jennet had been found guilty of using the diabolical arts of witchcraft to murder a woman named Isabel Nutter. Back in 1612, Roger Nowell had gotten very lucky indeed, for he found not one but two malleable members of the Device family to help him make the 1612 witch trial more sensational than any that had gone before. On 18 August, young Jennet Device (who was around eleven years old, not nine) had been ushered into the crowded courtroom, placed high upon a table so all could see her, and there she did denounce her mother as a witch:

> Jennet Device, Daughter of Elizabeth Device, late Wife of John Device, of the Forrest of Pendle aforesaid Widdow, confesseth and saith, that her said Mother is a Witch, and that this shee knoweth to be true; for, that shee hath seene her Spirit sundrie times come unto her said Mother in her owne house, called Malking-Tower, in the likenesse of a Browne Dogge, which shee called Ball; and at one time amongst others, the said Ball did aske this Examinates Mother what she would have him to doe: and this Examinates Mother answered, that she would have the said Ball to help her kill John Robinson of Barley, alias Swyre: by helpe of which said Ball, the said Swyer was killed by witch-craft accordingly; and that this Examinates Mother hath continued a Witch for these three or four years last past.[5]

On seeing her youngest daughter brought to give false testimony against her, Elizabeth Device had gone into meltdown. Potts writes:

> Her Mother, according to her accustomed manner, outrageously cursing, cryed out against the child in such fearefull manner, as all the Court did not a little wonder at her, and so amazed the child, as with weeping teares shee cried out unto my Lord the Judge, and told him, shee was not able to speake in the presence of her Mother. . . . In the end, when no meanes would serve, his Lordship commanded the Prisoner to be taken away, and the Maide to bee set upon the Table in the presence of the whole Court, who delivered her evidence in that Honorable assembly, to the Gentlemen of the Jurie of life and death.[6]

In the days since her mother and brother were arrested, Jennet had been under the control of Roger Nowell. He was determined to make her understand that her relatives were witches, and he succeeded. Jennet believed everything Nowell told her. In court, she went on to speak the words which Nowell had put into her mouth, unaware that her mother, brother, and neighbours would be hung as a consequence. While she had understood that they were in prison because they were witches, she had not really grasped that they were on trial for their lives. During her interviews with Nowell, Jennet had not been shy to answer the magistrate's questions, even though she did not understand everything she was being asked. On one occasion, Nowell had asked whether she had seen her mother and brother interact with familiar spirits in the form of animals. The brown and black dogs she talked about – Dandy, who she went on under Nowell's instruction to say was her brother's familiar spirit, and Ball, who she later said was the familiar spirit of her mother – were Jennet's imaginary friends. In Jennet's young, naive mind, when Nowell asked about familiar spirits (a concept she had never heard of), she thought that he perhaps meant make-believe friends. (As a child, Alizon had also had pretend animal friends, and maybe she had encouraged the unhappy Jennet to imagine her own.) Still somewhat confused by the question, Jennet also informed Nowell that, at one time, a ginger cat had become a family pet and that they had other pets too, in the past.

Jennet has emphasized that as a child, she was aware that she was a burden. She was of a sour nature – her anger stemmed from the feeling that her mother did not want her. When she was a very young child, she had often travelled by her mother's side and sometimes heard her arguing with neighbours. Some of the things she heard confused her, and she became emotionally troubled; she didn't know who her father was. Jennet had been born into dire poverty and the dysfunctionality which came along with it. Extreme and prolonged periods of stress had triggered mental illness; her grandmother suffered from episodes of paranoia in which she saw enemies all around her. (She could even become suspicious of her own family.) Her mother suffered from depression and anxiety and could become incapacitated by worry. Her brother often did and said confusing things which made things worse. It is important to Jennet that we acknowledge that she did not have a father to turn to and that the feeling of being unwanted never left her, even as she grew into adulthood. She was often lonely.

When they passed to the spirit world, Alizon and Jennet Device carried an unimaginable amount of trauma with them. But fortunately, the spirit world is not like the physical realm, and they were met there with care. A spirit guide, who had been a Sister of Mercy during her lifetime on Earth, has worked diligently to help the two sisters recover from their traumatic life experience, and they have made progress. But even now, after all this time, they sometimes require support.

We have learned from spirit communication that following the 1612 trial, Jennet Device had been taken out of the Pendle area 'away from Pendle folk' and was fostered by a clergyman named John Myers. Between the age of fifteen and nineteen, thanks to this man's influence in the community, she found employment in a domestic role in a couple of houses, with cleaning being her main duty. Sadly, the emphasis is that life was not always kind to Jennet, and from the age of nineteen, she struggled to find work and shelter. She was not a particularly clever woman – not quick to learn or understand – and we know that, like her brother, James, she lied and made-up stories as a child and adult too. In childhood and adulthood, she was not emotionally or mentally stable.

Some authors have suggested that William Device, whose name was mentioned during the 1634 trial, was another brother of Jennet. But she informed us that he is her son and that she had miscarried another child. She did not know the name of William's father. She never married. She died in Lancaster Castle from sepsis caused by a tooth infection. Even though Jennet and the other prisoners from the 1634 trial had been acquitted, a list of prisoners drawn up by gaoler Thomas Couell shows that a witch named Jennet Device was still imprisoned in Lancaster Castle in August 1636. She featured under the heading 'Witches remaining in his Majesty's Jail'.[7] In order to be released, a prisoner first had to clear their debt, and it is likely that Jennet was unable to do this. Thankfully, her son William survived her and went on to have a 'sweetheart'.

In 1612, Roger Nowell used young Jennet to help him to hang her brother and mother. But this was not his only plan for her, and before the day was out on 18 August, Jennet's actions in court would prove to be the final nail in the coffins of a lot more innocent people. Using the testimony of a child would not usually be allowed under English law because children under the age of fourteen were not deemed credible witnesses. However, *Daemonologie* promoted the use of such testimony in witch trials on account of the lack of physical evidence of criminal activity. The King reasoned that it was impossible for children to be witches because they 'are not that capable of reason as to practise such thinges'.[8] By the King's reckoning, children made good witnesses in witch trials because their intellectual limitation was an assurance that they themselves could not be practising witches. But his acknowledgement that children are not best able to think, understand, or form logical judgements highlights what a nonsensical argument this was, for this was the very reason why they had been deemed noncredible witnesses in the first place.

Nowell used and exploited Jennet's young impressionable mind. She saw what he wanted her to see and thought what he wanted her to think. In Jennet's testimony, Nowell wrote that she had witnessed the Good Friday meeting at Malkin Tower. Her testimony states that around midday, 'about twentie persons' met in her grandmother's house and ate the mutton which had been killed by her brother, as well as beef and bacon.[9] Potts emphasizes that Judge Bromley himself was cautious about child witness testimony and put Jennet under the microscope:

> After these Examinations were openly read, his Lordship being very suspitious of the accusation of this yong wench Jennet Device, commanded one to take her away unto the upper Hall . . . Master Couel was commanded to set all his Prisoners by themselves, and betwixt every Witch another Prisoner, and some other strange women amongst them, so as no man could judge the one from the other: and these being set in order before the Court from the prisoners, then was the Wench Jennet Device commaunded to be brought into the Court: and being set before my Lord, he tooke great paines to examine her of every particular Point, What women were at Malking-Tower upon Good Friday? How she knew them? What were the names of any of them? And how she knew them to be such as she named?
>
> In the end being examined by my Lord, Whether she knew them that were there by their faces, if she saw them? she told my Lord she

> should: whereupon in the prescence of this great Audience, in open Court, she went and tooke Alice Nutter, this prisoner by the hand, and accused her to be one: and told her in what place shee sat at the Feast at Malking-Tower, at the great assembly of the Witches, and who sat next her: what conference they had, and all the rest of their proceedings at large, without any manner of contrarietie.[10]

This carefully staged identity parade was a stroke of genius on Bromley and Nowell's part. Here justice and entertainment were rolled into one. Jennet was ordered to take the hand of each person who had been to Malkin Tower, and she did so. When she took the hand of John Bulcock, Potts claimed that she even added that he had turned the spit which held the meat.[11] Finally, as she had been instructed to do by Nowell, she remembered to add that there was 'a woman that came out of Craven to the Great Feast . . . but shee could not finde her out amongst all those women'.[12] As a final test of credibility, Judge Bromley asked Jennet 'whether she knew a Johan a Style? She alledged, she knew no such woman to be there, neither did she ever heare her name'.[13] This had been the equivalent of asking a child today whether they knew a Joe Bloggs or John Doe – a hypothetical average person – and the audience would have understood this well. The only conclusion to be drawn was that 'This could be no forged or false Accusation, but the very Act of God to discover her [Jennet Preston]'[14] and all the other witches. God had raised up this young witness to condemn the wicked. It was an ingenious way to convince the jury that the accused really were witches. You did not need evidence of pictures of clay or of associations with familiars when your star witness had been provided by God Himself.

It seems likely that the one person Jennet did not identify as having gone to her home was Alice Gray. We know from our spirit guide that Alice had never been to Malkin Tower, and it appears as though Jennet did not know the woman and so was unable to pick her out from the crowd. This was the only reason why Alice was acquitted, and Katherine Hewit was condemned for allegedly committing the same crime.

Fig. 6.6. The Gatehouse, Lancaster Castle

A sixteenth-century proverb says those born with an ill name are already half-hanged. On the one hand, as a child, Jennet Device had been revered for the role she had played in the uncovering of a major satanic-witch plot, but on the other hand, she was a Device by name, and the fact that she was arrested under suspicion of witchcraft in 1634, demonstrates that local people were suspicious that she herself was a witch. It is impossible to imagine that the events of 1612 could not have caused considerable psychological harm to the already troubled Jennet, for her mother and brother were executed, in part, because of her actions at the trial. How would anyone, let alone a child, cope with that level of guilt? And how could anyone live with the stigma that must have come with being the daughter of Elizabeth Device, granddaughter to Elizabeth Sowthernes, and sister to Alizon and James Device – the most notorious witches in the whole of Lancaster County? But of course, we must remember that the real shame lies not with the child but with the men who manipulated her: willing to see a child orphaned and a family destroyed for their own gain.

The Decline of Witchcraft Prosecutions

One hundred years after the second wave of witch trials in Lancashire, there was a seismic shift in Great Britain; officially, witchcraft was no longer a reality. The Witchcraft Act of 1604 was eventually repealed in the eighteenth century during the reign of King George II. Parliament decreed that from 24 June 1735, 'no Prosecution, Suit, or Proceeding, shall be commenced or carried on against any Person or Persons for Witchcraft, Sorcery, Inchantment, or Conjuration, or for charging another with any Offence, in any Court whatsoever in Great Britain.'[1] Back in the sixteenth century, witchcraft sceptic Reginald Scot had faced immense criticism for arguing that witchcraft was a fraudulent activity – with some even branding him a heretic for doing so. But now, two centuries later, those in authority had come around to his way of thinking, and the Witchcraft Act was duly amended to show this new point of view:

> And for more effectual preventing and punishing of any Pretences to such Arts or Powers as are before mentioned, whereby ignorant Persons are frequently deluded and defrauded; be it further enacted by the Authority aforesaid, That if any Person shall . . . pretend to exercise or use any kind of Witchcraft, Sorcery, Inchantment, or Conjuration, or undertake to tell Fortunes, or pretend, from his or

> her Skill or knowledge in any occult or crafty science, to discover where or in what manner any Goods or Chattels, supposed to have been stolen or lost . . . shall, suffer Imprisonment by the Space of one whole Year.[2]

Evidence suggests that witchcraft prosecutions had begun to fall by the wayside before the law was repealed. For example, Macfarlane observed that in Essex (the English county where the greatest number of witch trials occurred), 'formal prosecutions of witchcraft ended over fifty years before the Witchcraft Act was repealed'.[3*] We would be wrong to assume that prosecutions ceased because people simply stopped believing in witchcraft. The failure, or lack of willingness, to prosecute witches was actually a direct result of the judges' growing fear of chastisement for wrongful condemnation. (Arguably, what judges cared about the most was safeguarding their careers.) The reduction in prosecutions boiled down, not to a reduction in superstitious beliefs necessarily, but to the fact that it became increasingly difficult in a court of law to prove that witchcraft had occurred. King James himself had discovered that many of the accusations of witchcraft which had led to the execution of men and women had been total fabrications, and this had made a mockery of the English judicial system.

Of course, from our position in time, we can see that at the heart of the problem lay the fact that the sufficient proofs of witchcraft developed by demonologists and the King himself were an absurdity. They proved nothing other than the fact that the Witchcraft Act was

---

* Reproduced with permission of the Licensor through PLSclear, © Alan Macfarlane, 2nd edn., 1999, *Witchcraft in Tudor and Stuart England: A Regional and Comparative Study*

a law which could be easily exploited by those with a grudge to bear or a feather to gain. Sadly, we would have to get through another seven monarchs and a Lord Protector before the make-believe idea of sufficient proofs of witchcraft was officially scrapped, meaning that many more innocent men and women would lose their lives before we got to this stage.

When King Charles I ascended to the throne in 1625, he was of the opinion that witness testimony should not be taken at face value in a court of law, and this marked the first significant change. Following the shambolic Lancashire Witch Trials of 1634, judges were warned by the new monarch that the accusations of children, witches, and ne'er-do-wells alone were not to be regarded as sufficient proof of witchcraft. In order to condemn a witch, magistrates now needed to find *physical* evidence of witchcraft. Many scholars mark this change as the beginning of the end for witch trials because it eventually came to be that if something could not be demonstrated physically, you could not use it as evidence in a court of law. And when it became almost impossible to get a conviction in the courts, it was inevitable that the statute would be repealed.[4] Unfortunately, this new insistence upon finding physical evidence of witchcraft added to the ordeal suffered by the accused in the meantime.

Under the reign of Charles I, the continental satanic-witch stereotype became more widely accepted in Britain. We can argue that one major reason for this was that it had become increasingly difficult to condemn the anti-social witch because of the lack of physical proof of *maleficium*. By the middle of the seventeenth century, those who were seriously intent on prosecuting witches had moved away from trying to prove that *maleficium* had occurred, focusing their attention instead on finding physical evidence of the alleged witch having made a pact with the Devil. Notestein observed that by the middle of the seventeenth century, Parliament was clear that 'There were to be no convictions except upon proof of express compact with the Devil, or upon evidence of the use of imps [familiars], which implied the same thing.'[5] Less than fifty years earlier, the English Jacobean Parliament had viewed the familiar as proof that the witch was being assisted by demons, but not proof necessarily that the witch had sold her soul to Satan. But by 1650, this was no longer the case, and we cannot underplay the role that the Pendle Witch Trials of 1612 had played in helping the satanic-witch conspiracy to gain credence in seventeenth-century England. We also cannot ignore the fact that Potts' pamphlet often implied that the familiar and the Devil were one and the same.

It has been suggested that the government's failure to prosecute witches under King Charles I led to an initial increase in fear of witches, for communities now felt that they had no protection against them. Anxiety about diabolism was particularly high during the 1640s, for England was in the midst of the Civil War, and there was a genuine fear that the Devil was wreaking havoc in the land. Many Puritans even thought that the world was ending and that King Charles himself was in league with the Devil. Although many magistrates were now reluctant to investigate accusations of witchcraft, accusations of witchcraft persisted nonetheless, and a few canny men took full advantage of the situation. Witch-hunters now travelled to towns and villages and encouraged those who had suffered at the hands of witches to come forward and name them.[6]

No witch-hunters are more infamous than the self-appointed Witchfinder General, Matthew Hopkins, and his associate John Stearne.

Masquerading as men of the law, they promised to get your local witch to trial – for a small fee. With the mob firmly behind them, it is estimated that between one hundred and three hundred people were executed as witches during their fourteen-month reign of terror. Thankfully their success was short-lived, and ironically, the actions of these men can be seen to have contributed to the eventual rejection of witchcraft in law, for it made those in authority question whether there really was any such thing as *physical* proof of witchcraft.

Hopkins and his merry band of torturers had set about attacking men and women (mostly women) with sharp instruments until they found Devil's marks. The idea of the Devil's mark had been dominant on the European Continent for a long time. Part of the Satanic-witch conspiracy was the belief that the Devil left his mark upon the body of a witch when she agreed to give her soul to him; if the witch-hunter could locate this mark, they had physical evidence of a diabolical pact before them. Beliefs about Devil's marks actually varied greatly, and there were many wild theories when it came to deciding how the mark was made. For example, some demonologists postulated that the Devil dragged his claws across the skin, while others believed that he licked a death skull pattern onto the flesh. What they did agree upon was that the mark (however it had been made) remained invisible to the naked eye but could be detected by pricking the body of the alleged witch. Witches would feel no pain in this area and/or would not produce blood from the place where Satan had laid his hand/tongue/claws. (It is widely understood that Hopkins often used a knife with a retractable blade to fool onlookers into believing that the innocent woman he had strapped to the table was aligned with the Devil.[7])

John Gaule, the vicar of Great Staughton, was totally opposed to the methodology of Hopkins and the amount of hero worship he was receiving. On hearing news that Hopkins and his witch-hunting team were intent on carrying out their barbaric work in his parish, Gaule set about openly preaching against him and delivered a series of sermons with the aim of discrediting the man's authority. He then went one step further and published a book entitled *Select Cases of Conscience Touching Witches and Witchcraft*. In this text, Gaule wrote that Hopkins had 'lucratory skill', meaning that Hopkins had devised the whole campaign as a money-making racket. He also highlighted that this man had no formal parliamentary approval or legal training and that he chose easy targets:

> Every old woman with a wrinkled face, a furr'd brow, a hairy lip, a gobber tooth, a squint eye, a squeaking voyce or a scolding tongue, having a rugged coate on her back, a skullcap on her head, a spindle in her hand, and a dog or cat by her side; is not only suspected but pronounced for a witch.[8]

The book came into the hands of a group of Norfolk gentlemen who carried considerable influence. Appalled by what they had read, in spring 1647, they went into open court in Norwich to present their objections to visiting Westminster judges. The men took great umbrage at the fact that Hopkins was using methods akin to illegal torture to extract confessions. These included walking the victim for hours until a confession was heard and denying them sleep for several days. The men also complained that there had been an inhumane and unmerciful trial by tying women's limbs together and heaving their bodies into the water.[9] Hopkins, in answer to this allegation, quoted *Daemonologie*, arguing that King James said it is a certain rule that witches deny their baptism when they make a pact with the Devil.[10] The idea behind this barbaric act was that a satanic-witch would be rejected by the water because they had rejected the water of baptism and would therefore float, whereas an innocent Christian would sink. Fortunately, the justification that a king who had been dead for twenty-two years had once approved of this procedure did not hold as a legal defence, and, furthermore, the practice of ordeal by swimming had been condemned by the Church as early as 1215.

Hopkins tried to save his reputation by lying about the amount of money he received for his endeavours, but the accounts were there to be witnessed by all. The records at Stowmarket alone show that his fees cost the town £23 plus his travelling expenses. Notestein observed, 'At such a rate for the discoveries [of witches] we can hardly doubt that the two men [Hopkins and Stearne] cleared from three hundred to a thousand pounds, not an untidy sum in that day, when a day's work brought six pence.'[11] The Witch-finder General was yet another example of someone who had exploited the Witchcraft Act for personal gain, and he had done so on a colossal scale.

In England, the reluctance to believe in the reality of the satanic-witch had meant that prior to the mid-seventeenth century, a JP who ordered a suspected witch's body to be searched was usually hoping to find a witch's mark: a visible, supernatural mark from which their familiar or the Devil could suckle. Witch marks proved that the accused was aided by demons. We would eventually get to the stage where if the 'unusual' marks on a woman's body could not be proven to be of a supernatural nature, they must then be assumed to be natural. This is the exact opposite of what had gone before, where natural marks such as moles, birthmarks, and scars were presumed to be supernatural if they were on the body of an alleged witch.

When physician William Harvey was asked by the King to physically examine four of the accused Lancashire women for witch-marks in 1634, he seems to have been searching for marks resembling teats. (Given that the familiar was supposed to suckle from the witch, there was a degree of logic in searching for extra nipples!) No teat-like marks were found on three of the women's bodies, but two teat-like marks were detected on the fourth woman's body. With further investigation, Harvey was able to provide a medical explanation for the presence of the first mark. He also concluded that the second, more unusual, mark could not, in his opinion, physically function as a teat and so must also be natural as opposed to supernatural.[12] (Interestingly, Harvey is regarded to have been a witchcraft sceptic, for it is often quoted that he once dissected a toad which was alleged to be a witch's familiar. He did so to demonstrate that there was no physical evidence to prove that the creature was supernatural.[13])

As one century rolled into another, we moved further away from a reality based on natural philosophy. The ancient contradictory postulations, regarded as the pinnacle of knowledge for such a long time, were slowly being challenged by scientific experimentation and technological advancement. By the 1600s, for example, Venetians in Murano had been able to produce glass with such clarity that Galileo was able to utilize it to construct a telescope which, in turn, advanced our understanding of the mechanics of the stars. Those men such as Galileo and Harvey who set off down the mechanical philosophy path were not necessarily doing so with the aim of discrediting our widely held beliefs, for mechanical philosophy was often stimulated by Neoplatonist and Hermetic ways of thinking. But, from our vantage point, we can see that the new emphasis on proving or disproving an idea by physical demonstration would unravel the union between science and magic. Traditional ideas concerning occult properties and sympathetic influences came to be rejected by many intellectuals and were eventually replaced with biology, chemistry, and natural laws. As people began to agree that many events had natural as opposed to supernatural causes, natural philosophy became regarded as a pseudoscience. But, as we are all aware, superstition did not totally disappear.

Empathy for the Witches

On 20 August 1612, Alizon Device, James Device, Elizabeth Device, Anne Whittle, Anne Redferne, Alice Nutter, Katherine Hewit, John Bulcock, Jane Bulcock, and Isabel Robey were taken from their underground prison cell (into which many had been incarcerated for five months), forced into horse-drawn carts and driven through the streets of Lancaster, before stopping at their final destination: Gallows Hill, on the outskirts of town. It would be impossible to successfully convey the terror they were experiencing at this time, each of them fully aware that they were about to die in a horrifically brutal, humiliating manner. The carts drew beneath the gallows, and nooses were fastened tight around their necks while men in authority shouted of God's justice. Some of them continued to protest their innocence. Some were praying for help from God. Alizon wept hysterically. The order was given for the horses to be led on, and as the carts were taken from under their feet, one by one, the Lancashire Witches began to suffer a slow and painful death, their bodies helplessly dangling from the rope, legs and feet kicking, desperately reaching out for ground that wasn't there.

The hanging noose was designed to slowly strangle its victim to death, not to break the neck. These witches were to suffer for their great crimes, and the crowd had gathered to watch them suffer. It took, on average, between ten and twenty minutes for a person to die in this way. When their bodies finally became still, the carts returned. Their now lifeless bodies were cut down, dumped into them and then buried unceremoniously in a mass unmarked grave nearby.

One of the saddest truths about the Lancashire Witch Trials is that had they occurred during the latter half of the seventeenth century rather than the beginning, there is a strong probability that the accused would have been acquitted. By this point in time, witness testimony provided by children was subjected to greater scrutiny, and King James's sufficient proofs of witchcraft were being widely rejected and discredited in court. It is probably just as true that if King James had bothered to interview young Jennet Device following the condemnation of her relatives and neighbours, the whole trial would have been rightfully exposed as a great miscarriage of justice, and those responsible would have suffered the consequences. If this had happened, Edmund Robinson and his father would not have gone on to exploit the law to bribe local women, and Jennet Device would not have died in a prison cell.

Given the interest that the 1612 Lancashire Witch Trials must have generated, especially following the publication of *The Wonderfull Discoverie*, it is more than a little strange that King James (a king famous for personally interrogating alleged witches and accusers) chose not to investigate further to establish whether the condemnation of so many people had been truly justified. But perhaps we might conclude that the King, on this occasion, had been too afraid to do so, for if it were discovered that young Jennet *had* lied and been groomed by JP Sir Roger Nowell, *Daemonologie* would have been revealed to be nothing more than a manual to help the corrupt get away with murder. And what's more, the absolute monarch and ultimate authority on witches would have been exposed as a fraud.

So, in this instance, the King probably considered that the potential risk to his position of authority was simply too high.

The Pendle Witches were executed in the name of justice for crimes they could not have possibly committed. The reality is that there is *no* evidence for the widespread practising of witchcraft in pre-modern Europe. The witch existed in the imaginations of men: inquisitors, witch-hunters, jurists, and theologians. In Continental Europe, medieval demonologists had forced women to confess to practising witchcraft by asking leading questions as they subjected them to horrific methods of torture. These dubious confessions were then deemed to be proof of the reality of witchcraft and made their way into demonological literature which actively sought to promote witch persecution. The demonologists encouraged communities to fear and persecute their female neighbours and relatives.

Although there is a general acknowledgement today that the European witch trials were the disgrace of the times – injustice on a colossal scale – the majority of the estimated 40,000 to 60,000 innocent people (mostly women) who were murdered on mass as witches during the European witch-craze have not been exonerated. This is a disgrace of our times. But there is some hope. On International Women's Day 2020, a campaign was launched for legal pardons, a government apology, and a national memorial for the thousands of people convicted of witchcraft and executed in Scotland between 1563 and 1736. Founded by QC Claire Mitchell, who recognized the miscarriage of justice in her own country, the petition received much support, and on International Women's Day 2022, the Scottish First Minister issued a formal posthumous apology to all of those accused, convicted, vilified, or executed under the Scottish Witchcraft Act of 1563, with an acknowledgement that the injustice was driven at least in part by misogyny. My hope is that this book will help the so-called Lancashire Witches and all of the men and women executed in Great Britain under the Witchcraft Acts to get justice in the form of a posthumous legal pardon, for this is what they greatly desire and deserve.

Those who do not see any need for pardons for British witches should be made aware that, due largely to ideas that were exported from Europe, witch persecution is still happening on a grand scale in various parts of the world today. Our failure to pardon these innocent people sends a message to the rest of the world that the British public condones the executions of alleged witches which are still being carried out in post-Colonial Africa, India, and Papua New Guinea. The reality is that women are still being accused of practising witchcraft and dying as a consequence. Over the past twenty years, an estimated 20,000 Tanzanians have been executed as witches, but this is just the tip of the iceberg. In fact, executions are so widespread that the United Nations recently passed a resolution calling on countries to deal with the problem of witchcraft accusations. Unbelievably, women's lives today are still adversely affected by antiquated, archaic, misogynistic laws and interpretations of Scripture. The witch endures.

After the trials, Roger Nowell, the judges, and the other JPs simply moved on with their lives, satisfied that it had been a job well done. More than 400 years later, the spirits of those wrongfully condemned in August 1612 are still suffering. The so-called Pendle Witches would like a memorial to all of them to be placed on Pendle Hill. It should simply read:

'To all of those innocent souls of the Pendle Witch Trials'.

WAYS YOU CAN HELP

If you have enjoyed learning the truth about the Lancashire Witch Trials, please scan the QR code below and leave a book review. Your support will help the so-called Lancashire Witches to be heard far and wide.

For the latest news regarding the Justice for Witches campaign—the campaign for a posthumous legal pardon for all of the men and women convicted and executed in Great Britain under the Witchcraft Acts between 1542 and 1736—and to add your support, visit:

www.charlottemeredith.co.uk/the-campaign

Notes

A Note on Referencing

The following conventions have been observed in setting out these endnotes to allow for easy traceability. Full publication details are given of each work cited in the notes to each chapter. When the sources involved are literary texts that exist in a number of editions and were originally published before 1950, unless stated otherwise, references are made to the relevant signatures, chapters, or sections of the original work, or to the work in its entirety rather than page numbers. In addition, spellings of titles have been copied from the original forms and have not been modernized or corrected.

Introduction

1. Thomas Hobbes, *Leviathan* (London, 1651), ch. 2.
2. See Thomas Potts, *The Wonderfull Discoverie of Witches in the Countie of Lancaster* (London, 1613).

The King, the Witch & the Bible

What the Hex Is a Witch Anyway?

1. See *Newes from Scotland: Declaring the Damnable life and death of Doctor Fian, a notable sorcerer, who was burned at Edenbrough in January last, 1591* (London, 1591).

2. Keith Thomas, *Religion and the Decline of Magic: Studies in Popular Beliefs in Sixteenth and Seventeenth-Century England* (4th edn, London, 1991), 27-28.
3. Thomas, *Religion*, 28.
4. Thomas, *Religion*, 31-40.
5. Ronald Hutton, *The Witch: A History of Fear, from Ancient Times to the Present* (2nd edn, New Haven, 2018), 148.
6. Wallace Notestein, *A History of Witchcraft in England from 1558 to 1718* (London, 1911), ch. 1.
7. Hutton, *The Witch*, 155-156.
8. The 1542 Witchcraft Act: *The Act against Conjurations, Witchcraft, Sorcery and Enchantments.*
9. Hutton, *The Witch*, 170-172.

The Wisest Fool in Christendom

1. Although the *Millenary Petition* (1603) is claimed to have been signed by 1000 Puritan ministers, this figure has not been proven.
2. See King James VI, *The Trve Lawe of free Monarchies: Or, The Reciprock and Mvtvall Dvtie Betwixt a free King, and his natural Subiectes* (Edinburgh, 1598).
3. Gordon Campbell, *Bible: The Story of the King James Version 1611-2011* (Oxford, 2010), 32-34.
4. The Holy Bible: The King James Version, Matthew 5:1, Matthew 15:14, Job 19:28, Matthew 5:13.
5. Campbell, *Bible*, 35.
6. King James VI, *Daemonologie, in forme of a Dialogve, divided into three Bookes* (Edinburgh, 1597).

Thou Shalt Not Suffer a Witch to Live

1. Gordon Campbell, *Bible: The Story of the King James Version 1611-2011* (Oxford, 2010), 10.
2. David Daniell, *The Bible in English: Its History and Influence* (London, 2003), 143.
3. For more information on the creation of the Wycliffe Bible see Daniell, *The Bible*, 66-95.
4. Daniell, *The Bible*, 176.

5. See Reginald Scot, *The Discoverie of Witchcraft* (London, 1584).
6. Ronald Hutton, *The Witch: A History of Fear, from Ancient Times to the Present* (2nd edn, New Haven, 2018), 54-59.
7. Hutton, *The Witch*, 59.
8. Hutton, *The Witch*, 153.
9. Hutton, *The Witch*, 60-61.
10. Scot, *Discoverie*, book 6, ch. 2.

The Witch-Hunters' Bible

1. The text by Regino of Prüm is the earliest known version of the *canon Episcopi* (c. AD 906). The English translation of the quote can be found in Norman Cohn, *Europe's Inner Demons: The Demonization of Christians in Medieval Christendom* (rev. edn, London, 1993), 167.
2. Ronald Hutton, *The Witch: A History of Fear, from Ancient Times to the Present* (2nd edn, New Haven, 2018), 145.
3. Cohn, *Inner Demons*, 1-15.
4. Cohn, *Inner Demons*, 114-115.
5. Hutton, *The Witch*, 171.
6. Hutton, *The Witch*, 171.
7. Hutton, *The Witch*, 173-174.
8. Hans Peter Broedel, *The Malleus Maleficarum and the Construction of Witchcraft: Theology and Popular Belief* (Manchester, 2003), 1-35.
9. Papal bull *Summis desiderantes affectibus* (1484)
10. Heinrich Kramer, *Malleus Maleficarum* (Speyer, 1486), part 1.
11. See Kramer, *Malleus*, part 2.

This Thou Knowest to Be True

The Witch & the Pedlar

1. Thomas Potts, *The Wonderfull Discoverie of Witches in the Countie of Lancaster* (London, 1613), sig. S.1.r.
2. Potts, *Wonderfull Discoverie*, sig. R.4.v.
3. Potts, *Wonderfull Discoverie*, sig. R.3.v.
4. Potts, *Wonderfull Discoverie*, sig. E.2.r.
5. Potts, *Wonderfull Discoverie*, sig. O.1.v.

6. Potts, *Wonderfull Discoverie*, sig. R.4.v.
7. Potts, *Wonderfull Discoverie*, sigs. R.3.v-R.4.r.
8. Potts, *Wonderfull Discoverie*, sig. S.1.r.
9. Potts, *Wonderfull Discoverie*, sig. R.4.v.
10. Potts, *Wonderfull Discoverie*, sig. R.4.v.
11. Potts, *Wonderfull Discoverie*, sig. R.4.r.
12. Potts, *Wonderfull Discoverie*, sig. R.4.v.
13. Potts, *Wonderfull Discoverie*, sig. R.4.r.
14. Potts, *Wonderfull Discoverie*, sig. S.1.r.
15. Potts, *Wonderfull Discoverie*, sig. S.1.r.
16. Potts, *Wonderfull Discoverie*, sig. S.1.v.
17. Stroke Association UK, 'Hallucinations and delusions', https://www.stroke.org.uk/effects-stroke/hallucinations-and-delusions, accessed 5 Oct. 2020.
18. Potts, *Wonderfull Discoverie*, sig. S.1.r.
19. Potts, *Wonderfull Discoverie*, sig. S.1,v.
20. Potts, *Wonderfull Discoverie*, sig. R.4.v.
21. Potts, *Wonderfull Discoverie*, sig. Y.2.r.

Hawkers, Pedlars, & Petty Chapmen

1. Margaret Spufford, *The Great Reclothing of Rural England: Petty Chapmen and their Wares in the Seventeenth Century* (London, 1984), 4.
2. Spufford, *Great Reclothing*, 33.
3. Spufford, *Great Reclothing*, 33.
4. Spufford, *Great Reclothing*, 12.
5. Spufford, *Great Reclothing*, 10.
6. Spufford, *Great Reclothing*, 8.
7. Spufford, *Great Reclothing*, 8.
8. Spufford, *Great Reclothing*, 8 n. 27.
9. Spufford, *Great Reclothing*, 8 n. 27.
10. Tyrone Marshall, 'Ribble Valley display lifts the lid on past of Pedlar's Trunk', *Lancashire Telegraph*, (9 Apr 2015), https://www.lancashiretelegraph.co.uk/news/12879956.ribble-valley-display-lifts-lid-past-pedlars-trunk/, accessed 7 May 2019.
11. Thomas Potts, *The Wonderfull Discoverie of Witches in the Countie of Lancaster* (London, 1613), sig. S.1.r.
12. Katherine Stewart, 'Shoemaking 1600-1850', Martel Fashion, https://www.martelnyc.com/seventeenth-century/shoemaking-1600-to-1850.html, accessed 3 Apr. 2019.

13. DSL: Dictionaries of the Scots Language, 'Elshin', https://www.dsl.ac.uk/entry/snd/elshin, accessed 20 May 2019.
14. Joseph Wright, *The English Dialect Dictionary* (Oxford, 1898-1905), vol. 2.
15. Spufford, *Great Reclothing*, 26.
16. Spufford, *Great Reclothing*, 26.
17. Spufford, *Great Reclothing*, 26.
18. Spufford, *Great Reclothing*, 23-31.
19. Spufford, *Great Reclothing*, 45.
20. Potts, *Wonderfull Discoverie*, sig. R.4.v.
21. Potts, *Wonderfull Discoverie*, sig. S.1.r.
22. Spufford, *Great Reclothing*, 69.
23. Spufford, *Great Reclothing*, 94.
24. Spufford, *Great Reclothing*, 69-83.
25. Spufford, *Great Reclothing*, 28.

On the Highway Called Colne Field

1. Thomas Potts, *The Wonderfull Discoverie of Witches in the Countie of Lancaster* (London, 1613), sig. R.4.v.
2. Potts, *Wonderfull Discoverie*, sig. R.3.v.
3. James Carr, *Annals of Colne: Annals and Stories of Colne and Neighbourhood* (Manchester, 1878), 136.
4. Carr, *Annals*, 32.
5. Carr, *Annals*, 73, 29.
6. Brian Earnshaw (ed.), *Colne Parish Church of St Bartholomew* (7th edn, n.p., n.d.), 7.
7. Pendle Council, *Bonnie Colne Welcomes You* (n.p., 2013), 16.
8. Carr, *Annals*, 23.
9. Gingerling Design, 'Fascinating Remnants of Greenfield Mill, Colne', Pendle Heritage Centre [web blog], https://www.pendleheritage.co.uk/2014/12/22/fascinating-remnants-of-greenfield-mill-colne/, accessed 7 Oct. 2020.
10. Carr, *Annals*, 143.
11. Carr, *Annals*, 143.
12. Carr, *Annals*, 143.
13. Carr, *Annals*, 137.
14. Carr, *Annals*, 138.
15. Carr, *Annals*, 136-137.
16. Carr, *Annals*, 137.
17. Carr, *Annals*, 137.

18. Joseph Robson Tanner, *Tudor Constitutional Documents, AD 1485–1603: With an Historical Commentary* (Cambridge, 1922), ch. 2.
19. Carr, *Annals*, 23.
20. Carr, *Annals*, 23.
21. Carr, *Annals*, 90.
22. Ordnance Survey, *Lancashire Sheet XLIX* (1895), https://maps.nls.uk/view/102343910, accessed 7 Feb. 2019.
23. Fred Bannister, *The Annals of Trawden Forest* (Colne, 1922), ch. 2.
24. Bannister, *Trawden Forest*, ch. 2.
25. Bannister, *Trawden Forest*, ch. 1.
26. William Farrer and John Brownbill (eds.), 'Townships: Colne', in *The Victoria History of the County of Lancaster* (London, 1911), vol. 6.
27. Bannister, *Trawden Forest*, ch. 1.
28. Colne Connected, *Three Villages Heritage Walk: Laneshaw Bridge, Trawden, Foulridge* (n.p. 2009).
29. Colne Town Council, 'Colne's Heritage Assets: An Assessment in Support of the Colne Neighbourhood Development Plan, October 2020', https://colnetowncouncil.org.uk/ctc/wp-content/uploads/2020/10/Colne-Local-Heritage-List-2020-10-26compressed.pdf, accessed 19 Jan. 2021, 49.
30. Colne Town Council, 'Colne's Heritage Assets: An Assessment in Support of the Colne Neighbourhood Development Plan, February 2022', https://colnetowncouncil.org.uk/ctc/wp-content/uploads/2022/08/Colne-Local-Heritage-List-2022-06-Final_compressed.pdf, accessed 10 Jan. 2023, 50.
31. Ben Johnson, 'Pub Signs of Britain', Historic UK, https://www.historic-uk.com/CultureUK/Pub-Signs-of-Britain/, accessed 15 May 2020.
32. Walter King, 'Regulation of Alehouses in Stuart Lancashire: An Example of Discretionary Administration of the Law', The Historic Society of Lancashire and Cheshire, https://www.hslc.org.uk/wp-content/uploads/2017/05/129-3-king.pdf, accessed 15 May 2020, 32.
33. King, 'Regulations', 33.
34. Colne Connected, *Three Villages.*

The Superstition Epidemic

Pigeon Slippers & Other Medicaments

1. Keith Thomas, *Religion and the Decline of Magic: Studies in Popular Beliefs in Sixteenth and Seventeenth-Century England* (4th edn, London, 1991), 10.
2. The 1421 petition is quoted in full in John H. Raach, 'English Medical Licensing in the Early Seventeenth Century', *The Yale Journal of Biology and Medicine,* 16/4 (1944), 268.
3. *Physicians and Surgeons Act, 1511.*
4. Raach, *Yale Journal*, 268-275.
5. Raach, *Yale Journal*, 276.
6. Raach, *Yale Journal*, 269.
7. *Physicians and Surgeons Act, 1511.*
8. Raach, *Yale Journal*, 268.
9. Raach, *Yale Journal*, 268.
10. Nicholas Culpeper, 'Original Epistle to the Reader', in *The Complete Herbal* (London, 1653).
11. Culpeper, *Herbal*, 'Epistle'.
12. Culpeper, *Herbal*, 'Epistle'.
13. William Harvey, *Exercitatio Anatomica de Motu Cordis et Sanguinis in Animalibus* (n.p. 1628).
14. Robert Ralley, and Lauren Kassell, 'Pigeon Slippers', The Recipes Project, [web blog], https://www.recipes.hypotheses.org/15085, accessed 20 Apr. 2020.
15. Thomas, *Religion*, 16.
16. Thomas, *Religion*, 17.
17. Thomas, *Religion*, 16-17.
18. Ralley and Kassell, 'Pigeon Slippers'.
19. Philippa Waring, *A Dictionary of Omens and Superstitions* (London, 1978), 62.
20. Joyce Froome, *Wicked Enchantments; A History of the Pendle Witches & their Magic* (Lancaster, 2010), 57-58.
21. Culpeper, *Herbal.*
22. Thomas, *Religion*, 640.
23. Raach, *Yale Journal*, 268.
24. Malcolm Stuart (ed.), *The Encyclopaedia of Herbs and Herbalism* (London, 1979), 21.
25. Rebecca LaRoche, 'History of 17th Century Herbal Medicine' [video],

YouTube (uploaded 12 Feb. 2013), https://youtu.be/EXV4t_0ZaSw, accessed 18 Apr. 2020.

26. Alun Withey, *Physick and the Family; Health, Medicine and Care in Wales, 1600-1750* (2nd edn, Manchester, 2013), 110.
27. Culpeper, *Herbal*, 'Ointments More Simple'.
28. Jean Walton, *Pendle Forest Folk* (n.p., n.d.), 27.
29. Walton, *Pendle*, 30.
30. Walton, *Pendle*, 30.
31. Walton, *Pendle*, 30.
32. Froome, *Wicked Enchantments*, 70.
33. Walton, *Pendle*, 31.

The Signature of All Things

1. Nicholas Culpeper, 'Original Epistle to the Reader', in *The Complete Herbal* (London, 1653).
2. Keith Thomas, *Religion and the Decline of Magic: Studies in Popular Beliefs in Sixteenth and Seventeenth-Century England* (4th edn, London, 1991), 265.
3. Giovanni Pico della Mirandola, *Oratio de homminis dignitate* (n.p., 1496).
4. William Perkins, *A Discourse of the Damned Art of Witchcraft: So Farre as it is revealed in the Scriptures, and manifest by true experience* (London, 1608), ch. 1.
5. Perkins, *A Discourse*, ch. 1.
6. Perkins, *A Discourse*, ch. 1.
7. Perkins, *A Discourse*, ch. 1.
8. Perkins, *A Discourse*, ch. 1.
9. Perkins, *A Discourse*, ch. 1.
10. Thomas, *Religion*, 265.
11. Jacob Boehme, *The Signature of All Things* (London, 1912), ch. 8. [Ger. orig., *De Signatura Rerum* (n.p., 1621)].
12. Culpepper, *Herbal*, 'Epistle'.
13. Thomas, *Religion*, 269.
14. Reginald Scot, *The Discoverie of Witchcraft* (London, 1584), book 12, ch. 13.
15. Scot, *Discoverie*, book 12, ch. 13.
16. Thomas Potts, *The Wonderfull Discoverie of Witches in the Countie of Lancaster* (London, 1613), sig. H.3.r.
17. Thomas, *Religion*, 38.
18. Gilbert White, *Natural History and Antiquities of Selbourne* (London,

1789), letter 28.
19. Samuel Pepys, 'Diary Entries from January 1665', The Diary of Samuel Pepys, https://www.pepysdiary.com/diary/1665/01/, accessed 24 Feb. 2020.

The Charms of Daft Wives

1. King James VI, *Daemonologie, in forme of a Dialogve, divided into three Bookes* (Edinburgh, 1597), book 1, ch. 4.
2. Thomas Potts, *The Wonderfull Discoverie of Witches in the Countie of Lancaster* (London, 1613), sig. E.2.v.-E.3.r.
3. Potts, *Wonderfull Discoverie*, sig. E.4.v.
4. Potts, *Wonderfull Discoverie*, sig. E.2.r.
5. Potts, *Wonderfull Discoverie*, sig. E.2.r.
6. Reginald Scot, *The Discoverie of Witchcraft* (London, 1584), book 12, ch. 14.
7. Scot, *Discoverie*, book 12, ch. 14.
8. Keith Thomas, *Religion and the Decline of Magic: Studies in Popular Beliefs in Sixteenth and Seventeenth-Century England* (4th edn, London, 1991), 211.
9. Thomas, *Religion*, 220.
10. Thomas, *Religion*, 211.
11. David Daniell, *The Bible in English: Its History and Influence* (London, 2003), 133.

Alizon Device

1. Thomas Potts, *The Wonderfull Discoverie of Witches in the Countie of Lancaster* (London, 1613), sig. C.1.v.
2. Potts, *Wonderfull Discoverie*, sig. K.1.r.
3. Potts, *Wonderfull Discoverie*, sig. K.1.v.
4. Keith Thomas, *Religion and the Decline of Magic: Studies in Popular Beliefs in Sixteenth and Seventeenth-Century England* (4th edn, London, 1991), 604.

The Wonderful Discovery of Witches

The Age of the Pamphleteer

1. Wallace Notestein, *A History of Witchcraft in England from 1558 to 1718*

(London, 1911), ch. 1.

2. Jonathan Lumby, *The Lancashire Witch-Craze: Jennet Preston and the Lancashire Witches, 1612* (2nd edn, Lancaster, 1999; repr. 2019), 61.
3. See note by Edward Bromley in Thomas Potts, *The Wonderfull Discoverie of Witches in the Countie of Lancaster* (London, 1613).
4. See note by James Altham and Edward Bromley, Potts, *Wonderfull Discoverie.*
5. Potts, *Wonderfull Discoverie*, 'The Epistle/Dedicatorie'.
6. See note by Edward Bromley, Potts, *Wonderfull Discoverie.*
7. Philip C. Almond, *The Lancashire Witches: A Chronicle of Sorcery and Death on Pendle Hill* (London, 2017), 7.
8. Potts, *Wonderfull Discoverie*, sig. X.4.r.
9. Potts, *Wonderfull Discoverie*, sig. X.3.r.
10. Almond, *Lancashire Witches*, 83.
11. Edward Arber, *A Transcript of the Registers of the Company of Stationers of London: 1554-1604* AD, (London, 1876), vol. 3, 228.
12. Notestein, *History of Witchcraft*, ch. 2.
13. See Potts, *Wonderfull Discoverie*, sig. X.4.v.
14. Potts, *Wonderfull Discoverie*, sig. B.1.v.
15. For the account of the Samlesbury Witch Trials, see Potts, *Wonderfull Discoverie*, sig. K.3.r.-N.3.r.
16. Potts, *Wonderfull Discoverie*, sig. B.1.v.
17. Alan Macfarlane, *Witchcraft in Tudor and Stuart England: A Regional and Comparative Study* (2nd edn, London, 1999), 25.
18. Potts, *Wonderfull Discoverie*, sig. B.1.r.
19. Potts, *Wonderfull Discoverie*, sig. B.1.r.
20. See note by James Altham and Edward Bromley, Potts, *Wonderfull Discoverie.*

Beyond the Border

1. John A. Clayton, *The Lancashire Witch Conspiracy: A History of Pendle Forest and the Pendle Witch Trials* (Barrowford, 2007), 149.
2. Thomas Potts, *The Wonderfull Discoverie of Witches in the Countie of Lancaster* (London, 1613), sig. X.4.v.-Y.1.r.
3. Potts, *Wonderfull Discoverie*, sig. X.4.v.
4. See Keith Thomas, *Religion and the Decline of Magic: Studies in Popular Beliefs in Sixteenth and Seventeenth-Century England* (4th edn, London, 1991).

5. Clayton, *Conspiracy*, 145-146.
6. Jonathan Lumby, *The Lancashire Witch-Craze: Jennet Preston and the Lancashire Witches, 1612* (2nd edn, Lancaster, 1999; repr. 2019), 70, 72.
7. Potts, *Wonderfull Discoverie*, sig. Y.2.v.
8. Potts, *Wonderfull Discoverie*, sig. Y.2.v.
9. Potts, *Wonderfull Discoverie*, sig. Y.2.v.
10. Potts, *Wonderfull Discoverie*, sig. Y.3.r.
11. Potts, *Wonderfull Discoverie*, sig. Y.2.v.
12. Potts, *Wonderfull Discoverie*, sig. X.4.v.
13. Potts, *Wonderfull Discoverie*, sig. Z.3.r.
14. Potts, *Wonderfull Discoverie*, sig. Y.3.r.
15. King James VI, *Daemonologie, in forme of a Dialogve, divided into three Bookes* (Edinburgh, 1597). Book 3, ch. 6.
16. Philip C. Almond, *The Lancashire Witches: A Chronicle of Sorcery and Death on Pendle Hill* (London, 2017), 102-103.
17. Potts, *Wonderfull Discoverie*, sig. Y.1.r.
18. Potts, *Wonderfull Discoverie*, sig. Y.1.r.
19. Potts, *Wonderfull Discoverie*, sig. X.4.v.

The Justice of the Peace

1. John A. Clayton, *The Lancashire Witch Conspiracy: A History of Pendle Forest and the Pendle Witch Trials* (Barrowford, 2007), 154.
2. Edgar Peel and Pat Southern, *The Trials of the Lancashire Witches* (3rd edn, Newton Abbot, 1985), 20.
3. Clayton, Conspiracy, 157.
4. James R. McVicker, 'The Seventeenth Century Justice of Peace in England', *Kentucky Law Journal*, 24/4/2 (1936), https://uknowledge.uky.edu/klj/vol24/iss4/2, accessed 13 Feb. 2021
5. McVicker, 'Justice', 24/4/2.
6. McVicker, 'Justice', 24/4/2.
7. McVicker, 'Justice', 24/4/2.
8. McVicker, 'Justice', 24/4/2.
9. McVicker, 'Justice', 24/4/2.
10. McVicker, 'Justice', 24/4/2.
11. McVicker, 'Justice', 24/4/2.
12. McVicker, 'Justice', 24/4/2.

Nowell's Ode to a Black Dog

1. The 1604 Witchcraft Act: *An Acte against Conjuration, Witchcrafte and dealing with evill and wicked Spirits.*
2. See 'AD 1127' in *The Anglo Saxon Chronicle: The Peterborough Manuscript.*
3. William de Blécourt, *De Praestigiis Daemonum,* book 2, ch. 5. The English translation of the quote can be found in George Mora (ed.), *Witches, Devils, and Doctors in the Renaissance* (Binghamton, NY, 1991), 113.
4. George More, *A true Discourse concerning the certaine possession and dispossession of seven persons in one familie in Lancashire, which also may serve as part of an Answere to a fayned and false Discoverie which speaketh very much evill, as well of this, as of the rest of those great and mightie workes of God which bee of the like excellent nature* (n.p. 1600), part 2.
5. Brian P. Levack (ed.), *The Witchcraft Sourcebook: Second Edition* (2nd edn, London, 2015), 303.
6. More, *A true Discourse*, part 1.
7. More, *A true Discourse*, part 1.
8. More, *A true Discourse*, part 1.
9. More, *A true Discourse*, part 1.
10. More, *A true Discourse*, part 1.
11. More, *A true Discourse*, part 1.
12. King James VI, *Daemonologie, in forme of a Dialogve, divided into three Bookes* (Edinburgh, 1597), book 1.
13. More, *A true Discourse*, part 1.
14. More, *A true Discourse*, part 1.
15. More, *A true Discourse*, part 1.
16. More, *A true Discourse*, part 1.

John Law

1. Thomas Potts, *The Wonderfull Discoverie of Witches in the Countie of Lancaster* (London, 1613), sig. S.2.r.

Familiars

1. Ronald Hutton, *The Witch: A History of Fear, from Ancient Times to the Present* (2nd edn, New Haven, 2018), 272.
2. Hutton, *The Witch*, 271.
3. Thomas Potts, *The Wonderfull Discoverie of Witches in the Countie of*

Lancaster (London, 1613), sig. B.1.v.
4. Potts, *Wonderfull Discoverie*, sig. D.2.r.
5. Potts, *Wonderfull Discoverie*, sig. F.4.r.
6. Potts, *Wonderfull Discoverie*, sig. E.1.r.-E.2.r.

Witches, Whores, & Simpletons

A Man's World

1. See James L Kugel, *How To Read The Bible: A Guide to Scripture, Then and Now* (New York, 2008).
2. Kugel, *Read The Bible*, 47-57.
3. Geoffrey Primm, *The Violent Abuse of Women in 17th & 18th Century Britain* (Yorkshire, 2019), p. ix.
4. Primm, *Violent Abuse*, 6-8.
5. Primm, *Violent Abuse*, 62.
6. Primm, *Violent Abuse*, 98-104.
7. Heinrich Kramer, 'Why Superstition is chiefly found in Women' in, *Malleus Maleficarum* (Speyer, 1486), part 1.
8. Kramer, *Malleus*, 'Why Superstition is chiefly found in Women', part 1.
9. Sylvia Federici, *Caliban and the Witch: Women, the Body and Primitive Accumulation* (Brooklyn, NY, 2004), 31.
10. Federici, *Caliban.*

Elizabeth Sowthernes

1. Thomas Potts, *The Wonderfull Discoverie of Witches in the Countie of Lancaster* (London, 1613), sig. B.1.v.
2. Potts, *Wonderfull Discoverie*, sig. B.1.v.
3. Potts, *Wonderfull Discoverie*, sig. C.1.v.
4. Potts, *Wonderfull Discoverie*, sig. C.1.v.
5. Potts, *Wonderfull Discoverie*, sig. B.3.r.
6. John A. Clayton, *The Lancashire Witch Conspiracy: A History of Pendle Forest and the Pendle Witch Trials* (Barrowford, 2007), 192.
7. Potts, *Wonderfull Discoverie*, sig. B.2.v.

Anne Whittle & Anne Redferne

1. Thomas Potts, *The Wonderfull Discoverie of Witches in the Countie of Lancaster* (London, 1613), sig. E.4.r.
2. Potts, *Wonderfull Discoverie*, sig. E.4.r.
3. Potts, *Wonderfull Discoverie*, sig. E.4.v.
4. Joyce Froome, *Wicked Enchantments; A History of the Pendle Witches & their Magic* (Lancaster, 2010), 47.
5. Potts, *Wonderfull Discoverie*, sig. E.2.r.
6. Potts, *Wonderfull Discoverie*, sig. E.2.r.
7. Potts, *Wonderfull Discoverie*, sig. E.2.r.-E.2.v.
8. Potts, *Wonderfull Discoverie*, sig. D.3.v.
9. Potts, *Wonderfull Discoverie*, sig. E.2.r.
10. Potts, *Wonderfull Discoverie*, sig. N.4.r.
11. Potts, *Wonderfull Discoverie*, sig. D.3.v.
12. Potts, *Wonderfull Discoverie*, sig. E.1.r.
13. Potts, *Wonderfull Discoverie*, sig. O.1.r.
14. Potts, *Wonderfull Discoverie*, sig. O.1.v.
15. Potts, *Wonderfull Discoverie*, sig. O.1.v.
16. Potts, *Wonderfull Discoverie*, sig. O.2.r.
17. Potts, *Wonderfull Discoverie*, sig. O.2.r.
18. Potts, *Wonderfull Discoverie*, sig. D.2.r.
19. Potts, *Wonderfull Discoverie*, sig. B.4.v.
20. Potts, *Wonderfull Discoverie*, sig. E.3.v.-E.4.r.

Elizabeth Device

1. Thomas Potts, *The Wonderfull Discoverie of Witches in the Countie of Lancaster* (London, 1613), sig. C.2.v.
2. Potts, *Wonderfull Discoverie*, sig. B.3.r.
3. Potts, *Wonderfull Discoverie*, sig. C.1.r.
4. James Carr, *Annals of Colne: Annals and Stories of Colne and Neighbourhood* (Manchester, 1878), 72.
5. Carr, *Annals*, 72-73.
6. Carr, *Annals*, 73.
7. Potts, *Wonderfull Discoverie*, sig. F.4.r.
8. Potts, *Wonderfull Discoverie*, sig. F.3.v.-F.4.v.
9. Potts, *Wonderfull Discoverie*, sig. B.3.v.
10. Potts, *Wonderfull Discoverie*, sig. G.1.r.

11. Potts, *Wonderfull Discoverie*, sig. F.2.r.

The Good Friday Meeting

1. Thomas Potts, *The Wonderfull Discoverie of Witches in the Countie of Lancaster* (London, 1613), sig. C.2.v.-C.3.v.

James Device

1. Thomas Potts, *The Wonderfull Discoverie of Witches in the Countie of Lancaster* (London, 1613), sig. H.3.r.
2. Potts, *Wonderfull Discoverie*, sig. H.1.v.-H.2.r.
3. Potts, *Wonderfull Discoverie*, sig. H.3.v.
4. Potts, *Wonderfull Discoverie*, sig. H.3.v.
5. Potts, *Wonderfull Discoverie*, sig. I.3.r.
6. Potts, *Wonderfull Discoverie*, sig. J.4.r.
7. Potts, *Wonderfull Discoverie*, sig. Y.4.r.
8. Potts, *Wonderfull Discoverie*, sig. I.2.v.
9. Potts, *Wonderfull Discoverie*, sig. P.3.v.
10. Potts, *Wonderfull Discoverie*, sig. I.2.v.
11. Potts, *Wonderfull Discoverie*, sig. I.2.v.-I.3.r.
12. Potts, *Wonderfull Discoverie*, sig. I.3.r.
13. Potts, *Wonderfull Discoverie*, sig. C.3.v.
14. Potts, *Wonderfull Discoverie*, sig, I.2.v.

Alice Nutter

1. King James VI, *Daemonologie, in forme of a Dialogve, divided into three Bookes* (Edinburgh, 1597), book 1, ch. 2.
2. King James VI, *Daemonologie*, book 1, ch. 2.
3. Thomas Potts, *The Wonderfull Discoverie of Witches in the Countie of Lancaster* (London, 1613), sig. O.3.v.
4. Potts, *Wonderfull Discoverie*, sig. O.3.v.
5. Potts, *Wonderfull Discoverie*, sig. O.3.v.
6. Potts, *Wonderfull Discoverie*, sig. O.3.v.
7. Potts, *Wonderfull Discoverie*, sig. O.4.r.
8. Potts, *Wonderfull Discoverie*, sig. O.4.r.
9. Potts, *Wonderfull Discoverie*, sig. O.4.v.

10. Joyce Froome, *Wicked Enchantments; A History of the Pendle Witches & their Magic* (Lancaster, 2010), 272.
11. Rachel Hasted, *The Pendle Witch-Trial 1612* (Lancashire, 1987), 7.
12. Dudley Julius Medley, *A Student's Manual of English Constitutional History* (6th edn, Oxford. 1925), 639-640.
13. John A. Clayton, *The Lancashire Witch Conspiracy: A History of Pendle Forest and the Pendle Witch Trials* (n.p., 2007), 240.
14. Clayton, *Conspiracy*, 238.
15. Gladys Whitaker, *Roughlee Hall: Fact and Fiction*, (Nelson, 1980), 24.

How to Hang a Witch

The Samlesbury Witches

1. King James VI, *Daemonologie, in forme of a Dialogve, divided into three Bookes* (Edinburgh, 1597), book 3, ch. 6.
2. King James VI, *Daemonologie*, book 3, ch. 6.
3. King James VI, *Daemonologie*, book 3, ch. 6.
4. Keith Thomas, *Religion and the Decline of Magic: Studies in Popular Beliefs in Sixteenth and Seventeenth-Century England* (4th edn, London, 1991), 519.
5. Michael Dalton, *The Countrey Justice*, (London, 1618).
6. Thomas Potts, *The Wonderfull Discoverie of Witches in the Countie of Lancaster* (London, 1613), sig. Z.1.r.
7. King James VI, *Daemonologie*, book 3, ch. 6.
8. James Sharpe, *The Bewitching of Anne Gunter: A Horrible and True Story of Deception, Witchcraft, Murder, and the King of England* (London, 2012).
9. Potts, *Wonderfull Discoverie*, sig. K.4.r.
10. Potts, *Wonderfull Discoverie*, sig. K.4.v.
11. Potts, *Wonderfull Discoverie*, sig. K.4.v.-L.1.r.
12. Potts, *Wonderfull Discoverie*, sig. L.1.r.
13. Potts, *Wonderfull Discoverie*, sig. L.1.r.-L.1.v.
14. Potts, *Wonderfull Discoverie*, sig. L.1.v.
15. Potts, *Wonderfull Discoverie*, sig. L.2.r.
16. Potts, *Wonderfull Discoverie*, sig. L.2.r.
17. Potts, *Wonderfull Discoverie*, sig. L.2.r.
18. Potts, *Wonderfull Discoverie*, sig. L.2.v.

19. Potts, *Wonderfull Discoverie*, sig. L.2.v.
20. Potts, *Wonderfull Discoverie*, sig. M.3.v.
21. Potts, *Wonderfull Discoverie*, sig. M.4.r.
22. Potts, *Wonderfull Discoverie*, sig. M.4.r.
23. Potts, *Wonderfull Discoverie*, sig. M.4.v.
24. Jonathan Lumby, *The Lancashire Witch-Craze: Jennet Preston and the Lancashire Witches, 1612* (2nd edn, Lancaster, 1999; repr. 2019), 136.
25. Potts, *Wonderfull Discoverie*, sig. M.2.r.
26. Potts, *Wonderfull Discoverie*, sig. M.2.v.

Katherine Hewit & Alice Gray

1. Thomas Potts, *The Wonderfull Discoverie of Witches in the Countie of Lancaster* (London, 1613), sig. P.3.v.
2. There are several examples throughout the text where the alias 'Mould-Heeles' is ascribed to Katherine Hewit and John Hewit. See 123-129 in particular.
3. Potts, *Wonderfull Discoverie*, sig. P.3.r.
4. Potts, *Wonderfull Discoverie*, sig. C.4.r.
5. See Potts, *Wonderfull Discoverie*, sig. O.4.r-Q.1.v.
6. Potts, *Wonderfull Discoverie*, sig. P.3.r.
7. King James VI, *Daemonologie, in forme of a Dialogve, divided into three Bookes* (Edinburgh, 1597), book 3, ch. 6.
8. John Skelton, 'The Tunning of Elenor Rumming', Poetry Foundation, https://www.poetryfoundation.org/poems/45172/the-tunning-of-elenor-rumming, accessed 2 Mar. 2019.

Sufficient Proofs of Witchcraft

1. King James VI, *Daemonologie, in forme of a Dialogve, divided into three Bookes* (Edinburgh, 1597), book 2, ch. 5.
2. Thomas Potts, *The Wonderfull Discoverie of Witches in the Countie of Lancaster* (London, 1613), sig. E.1.v.
3. Potts, *Wonderfull Discoverie*, sig. G.2.r.-G.2.v.
4. Potts, *Wonderfull Discoverie*, sig. H.3.v.
5. King James VI, *Daemonologie*, 'The Preface to the Reader'.
6. Potts, *Wonderfull Discoverie*, sig. C.1.v.
7. King James VI, *Daemonologie*, book 1, ch. 6.
8. Potts, *Wonderfull Discoverie*, sig. B.2.v.

John & Jane Bulcock, Margaret Pearson, & Isabel Robey

1. Thomas Potts, *The Wonderfull Discoverie of Witches in the Countie of Lancaster* (London, 1613), sig. Q.3.r.
2. Potts, *Wonderfull Discoverie*, sig. Q.4.r.
3. Potts, *Wonderfull Discoverie*, sig. Q.3.r.
4. Potts, *Wonderfull Discoverie*, see page entitled 'Faults escaped in the Printing'.
5. Potts, *Wonderfull Discoverie*, sig. S.4.r.
6. Potts, *Wonderfull Discoverie*, sig. S.3.v.
7. Potts, *Wonderfull Discoverie*, sig. T.1.r.
8. Potts, *Wonderfull Discoverie*, sig. S.4.v.
9. Potts, *Wonderfull Discoverie*, sig. W.4.r.
10. Potts, *Wonderfull Discoverie*, sig. T.3.r.
11. Potts, *Wonderfull Discoverie*, sig. U.4.v.
12. Potts, *Wonderfull Discoverie*, sig. T.3.r.
13. Potts, *Wonderfull Discoverie*, sig. T.3.v.
14. Potts, *Wonderfull Discoverie*, sig. T.3.v.
15. Potts, *Wonderfull Discoverie*, sig. T.3.v.
16. Potts, *Wonderfull Discoverie*, sig. U.4.v.
17. Rachel Hasted, *The Pendle Witch-Trial 1612* (Lancashire, 1987), 39-40.

The Search for Malkin Tower

1. BBC News, ' "Witch's cottage" unearthed near Pendle Hill, Lancashire' (8 Dec. 2011), https://www.bbc.co.uk/news/uk-england-lancashire-16066680.amp, accessed 8 Feb. 2019.
2. Sue M and Evangeline A, 'Malkin Tower: Rachel and Andrew Turner on their quest to find the witches' house', Pendlefolk, http://www.pendlefolk,com/malkin-tower-rachel-and-andrew-turner-on-their-quest-to-find-the-witches-house/, accessed, 7 Apr. 2020.
3. John A. Clayton, *The Lancashire Witch Conspiracy: A History of Pendle Forest and the Pendle Witch Trials* (Barrowford, 2007), 275.
4. John A. Clayton, 'Malkin Tower Farm', *Landscape Archaeology - Social History* (Barrowford, 2018), 32.
5. Ordnance Survey, *Lancashire Sheet XLVIII* (1848), https://maps.nls.uk/view/102343907, accessed 20 Feb. 2019.
6. The photo can be seen in Clayton, *Conspiracy*, 286.
7. Edgar Peel and Pat Southern, *The Trials of the Lancashire Witches* (3rd edn, Nelson, 1985), 157.

8. Clayton, *Landscape Archaeology*, 32.
9. Clayton, *Landscape Archaeology*, 32.
10. Marley Brown, 'Searching for the Witches' Tower', *Archaeology*, https://www.archaeology.org/issues/358-1911/features/8075-england-pendle-witch-hunt Archaeology.org, accessed 16 Jan. 2021.
11. Madeleine Connolly, 'An Analysis of Post-Medieval Ceramics from the Pendle Hill Witches Archaeological Excavation' [thesis], Oregon State University, https://ir.library.oregonstate.edu/concern/honors_college_theses/v405sg982, accessed 14 Jun. 2021, 49.
12. Clayton, *Conspiracy*, 269.
13. Peel and Southern, *Trials*, 155.
14. John A. Clayton, *The Pendle Witch Fourth Centenary Handbook: History and Archaeology, Fact and Fiction* (n.p., 2012), 165-172.
15. Clayton, *Centenary Handbook*, 162.
16. Clayton, *Conspiracy*, 270.
17. Stanley Graham, 'Sale of Damhead Farm and Property in Earby', One Guy From Barlick, https://www.oneguyfrombarlick.co.uk/viewtopic.php?t=7285, accessed 5 Jul. 2020.
18. Stanley Graham, 'The 1580 Whitemoor Map', One Guy From Barlick, https://www.oneguyfrombarlick.co.uk/viewtopic.php?t=14416, accessed, 25 Jul. 2020. Original map held by The National Archives, Kew, ref. MPC 1/91.
19. Clayton, *Conspiracy*, 273.
20. Alfred Watkins, *The Old Straight Track: The Classic Book on Ley Lines* (1974, London, repr. 2005), 110.
21. Clayton, *Conspiracy*, 268-269.
22. Clayton, *Conspiracy*, 270.
23. All of the definitions for italicized words in this chapter have been taken from Ernest A. Baker, (ed.), *New English Dictionary* (London, 1932).

Jennet Device

1. T.D. Whitaker, *An History of the Original Parish of Whalley and Honor of Clitheroe to Which is Subjoined An Account of the Parish of Cartmell* (Blackburn, 1800), vol. 1, ch. 4.
2. Whitaker, *Whalley*, vol. 1, ch. 4.
3. Nigel Cawthorne, *Witch Hunt: History of a Persecution* (London, 2003), 24.
4. Whitaker, *Whalley*, vol. 1, ch. 4.
5. Thomas Potts, *The Wonderfull Discoverie of Witches in the Countie of Lancaster* (London, 1613), sig. G.1.r.-G.1.v.

6. Potts, *Wonderfull Discoverie*, sig. G.1.r.-G.1.v.
7. Joyce Froome, *Wicked Enchantments; A History of the Pendle Witches & their Magic* (Lancaster, 2010), 308.
8. King James VI, *Daemonologie, in forme of a Dialogve, divided into three Bookes* (Edinburgh, 1597), book 3, ch. 6.
9. Potts, *Wonderfull Discoverie*, sig. G.3.v.
10. Potts, *Wonderfull Discoverie*, sig. P.2.r.
11. Potts, *Wonderfull Discoverie*, sig. R.1.r.
12. Potts, *Wonderfull Discoverie*, sig. R.1.r.
13. Potts, *Wonderfull Discoverie*, sig. P.2.r.
14. Potts, *Wonderfull Discoverie*, sig. P.2.v.

The Decline of Witchcraft Prosecutions

1. 1735 Witchcraft Act: *An Act to repeal the statute made in the first year of the reign of King James the First, intitutled, An Act against conjuration, witchcraft, and dealing with evil and wicked spirits,except so much thereof as repeals an Act of the fifth year of the reign of Queen Elizabeth, Against conjurations, inchantments and witchcrafts,and to repeal, an Act passed in the parliament of Scotland in the ninth parliament of Queen Mary, intituled, Anentis witchcrafts,and for punishing such persons as pretend to exercise or use any kind of witchcraft, sorcery, inchantment, or conjuration.*
2. 1735 Witchcraft Act.
3. Alan Macfarlane, *Witchcraft in Tudor and Stuart England: A Regional and Comparative Study* (2nd edn, London, 1999), 200.
4. For in-depth discussions regarding the decline of witch trials see Keith Thomas, *Religion and the Decline of Magic: Studies in Popular Beliefs in Sixteenth and Seventeenth-Century England* (1971) and Ronald Hutton, *The Witch: A History of Fear, from Ancient Times to the Present* (2017).
5. Wallace Notestein, *A History of Witchcraft in England from 1558 to 1718* (London, 1911), ch. 8.
6. See Malcolm Gaskill, *Witchfinders: A Seventeenth-Century English Tragedy* (London, 2005).
7. Nigel Cawthorne, *Witch Hunt: History of a Persecution* (London, 2003), 28.
8. John Gaule, *Select Cases of Conscience Touching Witches and Witchcraft* (London, 1645).
9. Elaine G. Breslaw (ed.), *Witches of the Atlantic World: An Historical Reader and Primary Sourcebook* (Manhattan, NYU, 2000), 40.
10. Hopkins, Matthew, *The Discovery of Witches: In Answer to Severall Queries,*

Lately Delivered to the Judges of Assize for the County of Norfolk (London, 1647).

11. Notestein, *History of Witchcraft*, ch. 8.
12. Gaskill, *Witchfinders*, 46.
13. Keith Thomas, *Religion and the Decline of Magic: Studies in Popular Beliefs in Sixteenth and Seventeenth-Century England* (4th edn, London, 1991), 771.

Select Bibliography

Almond, Philip C., *The Lancashire Witches: A Chronicle of Sorcery and Death on Pendle Hill* (London, 2017)

Bannister, Fred, *The Annals of Trawden Forest* (Colne, 1922)

Campbell, Gordon, *Bible: The Story of the King James Version 1611-2011* (Oxford, 2010)

Carr, James, *Annals of Colne: Annals and Stories of Colne and Neighbourhood* (Manchester, 1878)

Clayton, John A., 'Malkin Tower Farm' [pamphlet] *Landscape Archaeology - Social History* (Barrowford, 2018)

Clayton, John A., *The Lancashire Witch Conspiracy: A History of Pendle Forest and the Pendle Witch Trials* (Barrowford, 2007)

Clayton, John A., *The Pendle Witch Fourth Centenary Handbook: History and Archaeology, Fact and Fiction* (Barrowford, 2012)

Cohn, Norman, *Europe's Inner Demons: The Demonization of Christians in Medieval Christendom* (rev. edn, London, 1993)

Culpeper, Nicholas, *The Complete Herbal*, (London, 1653)

Daniell, David, *The Bible in English: Its History and Influence* (London, 2003)

Federici, Sylvia, *Caliban and the Witch: Women, the Body and Primitive Accumulation*, (Brooklyn, NY, 2004)

Froome, Joyce, *Wicked Enchantments; A History of the Pendle Witches & their Magic*, (Lancaster, 2010)

Gaskill, Malcolm, *Witchfinders: A Seventeenth-Century English Tragedy,* (London, 2005)

Hutton, Ronald, *The Witch: A History of Fear, from Ancient Times to the Present* (2nd edn, New Haven, 2018)

King James VI, *Daemonologie, in forme of a Dialogve, divided into three Bookes* (Edinburgh, 1597)

Kramer, Heinrich, *Malleus Maleficarum* (Speyer, 1486)

Kugel, James L., *How To Read The Bible: A Guide to Scripture, Then and Now* (New York, 2008)

Levack, Brian P. (ed.), *The Witchcraft Sourcebook: Second Edition* (2nd edn, London, 2015)

Lumby, Jonathan, *The Lancashire Witch-Craze: Jennet Preston and the Lancashire Witches, 1612* (2nd edn, Lancaster, 1999; repr. 2019)

Macfarlane, Alan, *Witchcraft in Tudor and Stuart England: A Regional and Comparative Study* (2nd edn, London, 1999)

McVicker, James R., 'The Seventeenth Century Justice of Peace in England', *Kentucky Law Journal*, 24/4/2 (1936)

More, George, *A true Discourse concerning the certaine possession and dispossession of seven persons in one familie in Lancashire, which also may serve as part of an Answere to a fayned and false Discoverie which speaketh very much evill, as well of this, as of the rest of those great and mightie workes of God which bee of the like excellent nature.* (1600)

Notestein, Wallace, *A History of Witchcraft in England from 1558 to 1718* (London, 1911)

Peel, Edgar and Southern, Pat, *The Trials of the Lancashire Witches* (3rd edn, Newton Abbot, 1985)

Perkins, William, *A Discourse of the Damned Art of Witchcraft: So Farre as it is revealed in the Scriptures, and manifest by true experience,* (London, 1608)

Potts, Thomas, *The Wonderfull Discoverie of Witches in the Countie of Lancaster* (London, 1613).

Primm, Geoffrey, *The Violent Abuse of Women in 17th & 18th Century Britain* (Yorkshire, 2019)

Raach, John H., 'English Medical Licensing in the Early Seventeenth Century', *The Yale Journal of Biology and Medicine,* 16/4 (1944)

Scot, Reginald, *The Discoverie of Witchcraft* (London, 1584)

Spufford, Margaret, *The Great Reclothing of Rural England: Petty Chapmen and their Wares in the Seventeenth Century* (London, 1984)

Thomas, Keith, *Religion and the Decline of Magic: Studies in Popular Beliefs in Sixteenth and Seventeenth-Century England* (4th edn, London, 1991)

Whitaker, Gladys, *Roughlee Hall: Fact and Fiction*, (Nelson, 1980)

Withey, Alun, *Physick and the Family; Health, Medicine and Care in Wales, 1600-1750* (2nd edn, Manchester, 2013)

Index

Printed in Great Britain
by Amazon

27282758R00179